THE VERBAL ICON

D1157619

THE VERBAL ICON

STUDIES IN THE MEANING OF POETRY

BY W. K. WIMSATT, JR., *and two preliminary essays written in collaboration with* MONROE C. BEARDSLEY

The University Press of Kentucky

Publication of this book is possible partly
by reason of a grant from the
Margaret Voorhies Haggin Trust
established in memory of her husband
James Ben Ali Haggin

For M. H. W. and E. L. B.

ACKNOWLEDGMENT

I OWE a great deal to numerous friends who have read my manuscript drafts, given me advice, discussed critical problems with me, and in various ways promoted the writing of these essays. Especially I acknowledge a debt to Monroe Beardsley, who joined me in writing two of the essays, and who for a period of several years engaged me in an almost unbroken conversation which is one of my finest memorial possessions. I owe a special debt also to my colleagues Cleanth Brooks, Maynard Mack, and René Wellek; to Philip Daghlian and Robert Daniel; and to my wife.

My colleague Theodore Greene had a good deal to do with prompting the observations that occur in the essay entitled "The Domain of Literary Criticism." He was my opponent in a joint presentation of papers at the Stanford Modern Language Meeting in 1949. His answer to me entitled "The Scope of Aesthetics" should be consulted in the *Journal of Aesthetics and Art Criticism,* VIII, June, 1950.

Eight of these essays, or drafts approaching them, were read before learned societies and clubs. Some were written specifically for the occasions. I am grateful to all the audiences and all the chairmen. Let me name the English Institute, the Modern Language Association of America, the American Society for Aesthetics, the Catholic Poetry Society of America, the Faculty Seminar in English at Indiana University, the Silliman College Workshop Talks, the Philosophy Club and the English Club at Yale.

The essays have appeared in the following places: "The Intentional Fallacy," "The Affective Fallacy," and "The Substantive Level" in the *Sewanee Review,* LIV, Summer, 1946; LVII, Winter, 1949; LIX, Autumn, 1951; "The Concrete Universal," "Verbal Style: Logical and Counterlogical," and "History and Criticism" in *PMLA,* LXII, March, 1947; LXV, March, 1950;

LXVI, February, 1951; "Poetry and Morals: A Relation Re-argued" and "Poetry and Christian Thinking" in *Thought*, XXIII, June, 1948, and XXVI, Summer, 1951; "Rhetoric and Poems: Alexander Pope" and "Explication as Criticism" in *English Institute Essays 1948* and *1951* (Columbia University Press, 1949 and 1952); "The Chicago Critics" in *Comparative Literature*, V, Winter, 1953; "The Structure of Romantic Nature Imagery" in *The Age of Johnson, Essays Presented to Chauncey Brewster Tinker* (Yale University Press, 1949); "Symbol and Metaphor" in the *Review of Metaphysics*, IV, December, 1950; "One Relation of Rhyme to Reason" in *Modern Language Quarterly*, V, September, 1944; "When is Variation 'Elegant'?" in *College English*, III, January, 1942; "The Domain of Criticism" in the *Journal of Aesthetics and Art Criticism*, VIII, June, 1950.

I wish to thank the editors of the magazines and the directors of the presses for their courtesy in extending permission for the republication of these materials.

The essays have all been revised, some of them extensively. "The Concrete Universal," "Poetry and Morals," "One Relation of Rhyme to Reason," and other essays to a less extent, have lost bibliographical footnotes, for which the reader having that kind of purpose is referred to the places of original publication.

W. K. W., JR.

Silliman College
Yale University
September 4, 1953

CONTENTS

A NOTE ON THE TITLE OF THIS BOOK: The term icon *is used today by semeiotic writers to refer to a verbal sign which* somehow *shares the properties of, or resembles, the objects which it denotes. The same term in its more usual meaning refers to a visual image and especially to one which is a religious symbol. The verbal image which most fully realizes its verbal capacities is that which is not merely a bright picture (in the usual modern meaning of the term* image) *but also an interpretation of reality in its metaphoric and symbolic dimensions. Thus:* The Verbal Icon.

INTRODUCTION

THE ESSAYS which compose this volume were written over a period of about eleven years, from 1941 to 1952. They arose out of several critical preoccupations and occasions, and largely without my planning that they should ever be put together to make a book. They represent, however, what I believe has been my consistent approach to the literary problem at various levels. In the sequence which I now give them, not that of their original publication, and after revisions aimed at the improvement of their relations to one another, I believe the essays approximate a rounded whole.

The volume begins with three negatives. First, two essays which my friend Monroe Beardsley and I wrote to expose as fallacies two very prevalent approaches to the critical object, that by way of its origins in the mind of its maker, and that by way of its results in the mind of its audience. And thirdly, my single-handed objections to a kind of neo-Aristotelianism expounded by a group of critics at Chicago, a critical approach which, as it happens, has some close relations with the "fallacies."

The next four essays attempt to face some of the more substantive responsibilities of the critic who, eschewing the psychologistic kinds of escape, is willing to defend literature as a form of knowledge. What kind of meaning does literature have? How far is this explained by certain concepts, especially the concepts of metaphor and symbol? And what is the relation of literary value to other values involved in verbal structures, especially to moral values?

The next five essays deal with various problems of verbal style, attempting to treat these to some extent by a logic of parallels and oppositions and in general to demonstrate that style is a level of meaning. The proportion of attention given to these matters reflects not any view of mine about the correct center of literary studies but simply one of my chief interests and most frequent lines of access to literary inquiry. The essay entitled "Rhetoric and Poems" includes an introductory section devoted to sorting out several of the main relations which literary scholars develop, often confusedly, between the literary theory and the literary practice of given historical periods.

The concluding group of four essays returns to broader bearings, the relation of literature to other arts and of literary criticism to general aesthetics, the relation of literary meaning (so far as it may be neutrally considered) to literary value and to more general concepts of value and disvalue, the relation of evaluative criticism to historical studies, and the relation of literature not only to morals, as in the fifth essay, but more broadly to the whole complex of the Christian religious tradition.

II

The theory of verbal meaning on which these essays are written might here and there be mistaken for, but is not actually, a form of monistic expressionism. I believe in the integration of literary meaning but at the same time in different kinds and levels of meaning. It is surely true that in a certain sense no two different words or different phrases ever mean fully the same. That is the literary sense. But there are other senses, the abstractive senses of science, philosophy, practical affairs, and religious dogma, in which different formulations can and do mean the same. The bungled phrase, the slipshod paragraph, the inept metaphor, the irrelevant excursion, the disproportionate development, the feeble conclusion, are indeed all failures of meaning, and the more poetically ambitious the verbal structure in which they occur, the deeper and more substantive the failure may be. In a writing of any complexity, either poetic or philosophic, a confusion of style is likely to be part of a confusion at a more substantive level. On the other hand, stylistic meanings in more prosaic and abstractive structures are almost always capable of being looked on merely as adjuncts to a literal or message meaning. The message can remain the same while changes in the other meanings occur. One improves the style or the organization of a paper written by a student or a friend, but without necessarily making any contribution to his message. The reason such a change may be an improvement, or may be the opposite, lies in the interdependence of levels of meaning. The reason is always a matter of meaning, though it may lie at highly formal and implicit levels. I have refined this distinction as far as I was able in the essay on "Verbal Style" and in particular have tried to show what may be meant by a level of *purely verbal* style.

The interpenetration of abstractly stated meaning and the more concrete, unspecified, and diffusive meaning of metaphors and dramatic structures is much more difficult to define. It involves the deep question of the relation between poetry and philosophy. All the essays in the second group and all those in the last touch on this relation in one way or another. I do not say that I have pushed the inquiry at all conclusively.

The volume is for the most part devoted not to the examination of whole works, but to the pursuit of critical themes. This is a mode which I justify as both interesting in itself to the literary theorist and, like the study of grammar, logic, and prosody, of possible interest to the practical critic. On the other hand, if any practical critic remembers any of my generalizations about figures of speech and the like, very likely he ought to drop them into the background when he is about his own business. Such fully evaluative expressions as I have here and there used (like the terms "virtue" and "fault" in the essay on "Verbal Style") are to be taken as provisional—applying perhaps to a great many instances—but never as fixed rules of thumb, or headings on a score sheet of evaluation. The kind of relations which I describe in the essays on style should be thought of as tendencies toward, or away from, coherent verbal expression, rather than as specific merits or demerits. My discussion of style is latitudinarian, moving out toward general issues of expression rather than in toward a canonical concept of poetry.

There are such things as general anatomy and general psychology, though we do not always employ them. In presenting a friend or in writing a character sketch, we do not say, "Observe he has a nose and breathes through it; he has a mind and thinks with it." Yet there may be treatises where such observations are in place. Some of the essays in this volume have been written on the assumption that the general anatomy of verbal powers is less widely understood than the most obvious anatomy of the human body.

III

In the first two chapters of his *Rhetoric*, Aristotle expounds a scheme for rhetorical studies which, with a certain reversal in emphasis, might serve very well as a paradigm of the complex verbal situation which is taken into account by the literary critic. Aristotle says there are four ways in which an orator can get at his audience: (1) by putting his own character in a good light, (2) by working on the emotions of the audience, (3) by using sound arguments, (4) by using apparently sound arguments. The last way would tend to involve verbal artifice. The first eleven chapters of the third book of the *Rhetoric* are devoted to matters coming broadly under the head of verbal style, the *how* rather than the *what*, as a rhetorical purpose is bound to conceive the distinction. Aristotle conceives verbal discourse as an act, complicated in itself, and having a personal context of two main dimensions, the speaker and the audience. But he looks on all the features of the verbal act in a pragmatic light—thinking how they will operate to produce an end, a vote by a jury or a senate. That is what rhetoric in the full classical sense means, a pragmatic art of discourse. But there is nothing in the nature of the verbal act to prevent us from looking at the same features not in a pragmatic, but in a dramatic, light, and if we do this we are looking at a given discourse as a literary work.[1]

Despite that aspect of poetic meaning which is commonly referred to as its "universality," a poem is not quite a statement which is viable indifferently between irrelevant persons. There are certain poems (poems of a lover to his mistress, for instance, or poems addressed to Death or to the wild West Wind) in which a particular dramatic listener has a great deal to do with determining a certain kind of style, a certain kind of structure, a certain kind of metaphor. Other poems we may conceive as poems for a sex, a caste, a party. *The Rape of the Lock* is addressed, immediately, to a more squeamish audience than *The Dunciad*. In what is called the "tone" of the poem, even the most universalized audience has to be taken into account. The actual reader of a poem is something like a reader over another reader's shoulder; he reads through the dramatic reader, the person to whom the full tone of the poem is addressed in the fictional situation.[2] This is the truth behind that often quoted statement by J. S. Mill that "Eloquence is *heard*, poetry is *over-heard*." The same dramatic principle applies, of course, and even more pointedly, to the speaker, or speakers, of a poem. The stage drama shows in a complicated way what holds also for the lyric and meditative monologue. The character of the

[1] I use the terms "literature" and "literary" throughout this book in a generic sense, and "poem," "poetry," and "poetic" in a more accented sense, relating to literature in its most intensive instances.

[2] Cp. Rebecca Parker, "Alexander Pope's Use of the Implied Dramatic Speaker," and Walker Gibson, "Authors, Speakers, Readers, and Mock Readers," in *College English*, XI (1949-1950), 137-40, 265-69.

speaker, his thoughts and responses, are reflected in style, structure, metaphor. The fact hardly calls for illustration here. Both
speaker and dramatic audience are assimilated into the implicit
structure of the poem's meaning. At the fully cognitive level
of appreciation we unite in our own minds both speaker and
audience. This principle, though it has to remain largely implicit in most rhetorical discussion, is actually that by which
the various levels of the poem's meaning are integrated. The
means-end situation of style and content becomes, in the dramatic focus, itself a terminal fact of structure.[3] The appreciation of this structure is that total experience or total knowledge
of which the critics speak.

One of the alternatives to the dramatic way of literary interpretation is that purely psychological way which is interested in both the speaker and the audience outside the poem
(as they are in real life), and which hence leads to the two
fallacies, the "intentional" and the "affective," with which this
book begins. In the third essay, I partly concur with the Chicago critics in thinking that these fallacies may develop as supposed escapes from more technical kinds of criticism, rules of
rhetoric and genre which have hardened into formalist fallacies.
I believe that the Chicago critics have correctly imputed such
a slantwise maneuver to the ancient critic Longinus and to the
general psychological drift of eighteenth century criticism, but
that in supposing this was the inevitable path of an escape
from the neoclassic genres and rules, they themselves have
fallen into similar confusions. Such is in part my argument in
the third essay. Here I would suggest a more general principle,
that the intentional and affective fallacies have frequently come
about through a critic's distaste for problems of technique, and
that a sound view of technique and its relation to that aspect
of poetry sometimes called "content" will come close to en-

---

[3] This is not merely a more complicated way of alluding to the "artistry"
which in some aesthetic theories even a murder or an embezzlement is said to
be capable of displaying. In the literary structure the "means" are limited and
characterized by the dignity of the "end."

suring avoidance of the psychological fallacies. For the explication of this view I risk the following table—conscious that
in reducing mental relations to spatial I may do less than full
justice to the former.

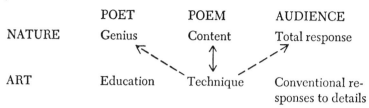

	POET	POEM	AUDIENCE
NATURE	Genius	Content	Total response
ART	Education	Technique	Conventional responses to details

The poem conceived as a thing in between the poet and the
audience is of course an abstraction. The poem is an act. The
only substantive entities are the poet and the audience. But
if we are to lay hold of the poetic act to comprehend and
evaluate it, and if it is to pass current as a critical object, it
must be hypostatized. The distinction between art and nature
is that posited in the classical tradition of criticism and never
fully denied in modern times except by forms of expressionistic
monism which in effect prohibit critical talk. In order to employ the distinction validly and usefully one need not commit
oneself to the notion that art and nature exist separately either
in poet, in poem, or in audience. The dotted arrow which
points diagonally to the left represents what I should call the
Longinian genetic fallacy of double distinction. The critic cries
out: "I am not interested in technique for itself; it is either
petty precision or exaggerated, even unnatural, figures of
speech. The only thing that can justify technique (or palliate
its outrages) is the lofty genius, the thoughts and passions of
the great poet." Thus the critic, in his hurry to escape from
art to nature, at the same time leaves the poem for the poet.
There is an ambiguous movement, and no true opposition. In
like manner, the dotted arrow pointing to the right represents
what I should call the Richardsian affective fallacy of double
distinction. The critic cries out: "Don't talk to me about technical features (rhyme or figures) or about parts of poems. They

are justified only as they help to elicit from the audience its total, unique response, which *is* the value of the poem." Again the helter-skelter ambiguity occurs.

In the above table various legitimate distinctions and various connections may be made by persons interested in various studies. Thus a person who was interested, like most of the ancient rhetoricians, in how to go about producing a good orator or poet might very well ponder whether the more important thing is that a candidate be born with genius or that he receive good training—or whether the second is needed at all if the first is present. The drawing up of such a table need not imply that each of the six areas located on it, or each of the possible connections and distinctions, can be managed with equal precision and emphasis. Causal connections, moving from left to right on the table, should perhaps always be double and quadruple. Both the poet's genius and his education contribute to both the content and the technique of his poem. The vertical relations are complementary oppositions. That in the center which I have indicated by the solid and two-pointed arrow (between content and technique) represents the axis and reciprocal motion of all cognitive literary criticism. Though this criticism may be pictured as reaching out to parenthesize the two dimensions of the dramatic speaker (not necessarily the poet) and the dramatic audience, still it moves in a vertical direction, from content to technique and back, constantly trying to see each in the light of the other and to explicate and assert their interdependence, and hence to see the poem as both expression and artifact—and the poet, if one will have him, as both sayer and maker.

1

He owns with toil he wrote the following scenes;
But, if they're naught, ne'er spare him for his pains:
Damn him the more; have no commiseration
For dullness on mature deliberation.

—WILLIAM CONGREVE, Prologue to
The Way of the World

c

THE INTENTIONAL FALLACY

THE CLAIM of the author's "intention" upon the critic's judgment has been challenged in a number of recent discussions, notably in the debate entitled *The Personal Heresy*, between Professors Lewis and Tillyard. But it seems doubtful if this claim and most of its romantic corollaries are as yet subject to any widespread questioning. The present writers, in a short article entitled "Intention" for a *Dictionary*[1] of literary criticism, raised the issue but were unable to pursue its implications at any length. We argued that the design or intention of the author is neither available nor desirable as a standard for judging the success of a work of literary art, and it seems to us that this is a principle which goes deep into some differences in the history of critical attitudes. It is a principle which accepted or rejected points to the polar opposites of classical "imitation" and romantic expression. It entails many specific truths about inspiration, authenticity, biography, literary history and scholarship, and about some trends of contemporary poetry, especially its allusiveness. There is hardly a problem of literary criticism in which the critic's approach will not be qualified by his view of "intention."

"Intention," as we shall use the term, corresponds to *what he intended* in a formula which more or less explicitly has had wide acceptance. "In order to judge the poet's performance, we must know *what he intended*." Intention is design or plan in the author's mind. Intention has obvious affinities for the author's attitude toward his work, the way he felt, what made him write.

We begin our discussion with a series of propositions summarized and abstracted to a degree where they seem to us axiomatic.

1. A poem does not come into existence by accident. The words of a poem, as Professor Stoll has remarked, come out of a head, not out of a hat. Yet to insist on the designing intellect as a *cause* of a poem is not to grant the design or intention as a *standard* by which the critic is to judge the worth of the poet's performance.

2. One must ask how a critic expects to get an answer to the question about intention. How is he to find out what the poet tried to do? If the poet succeeded in doing it, then the poem itself shows what he was trying to do. And if the poet did not succeed, then the poem is not adequate evidence, and the critic must go outside the poem—for evidence of an intention that did not become effective in the poem. "Only one *caveat* must be borne in mind," says an eminent intentionalist[2] in a moment when his theory repudiates itself; "the poet's aim must be judged at the moment of the creative act, that is to say, by the art of the poem itself."

3. Judging a poem is like judging a pudding or a machine. One demands that it work. It is only because an artifact works that we infer the intention of an artificer. "A poem should not mean but be." A poem can *be* only through its *meaning*—since its medium is words—yet it *is*, simply *is*, in the sense that we have no excuse for inquiring what part is intended or meant. Poetry is a feat of style by which a complex of meaning is handled all at once. Poetry succeeds because all or most of what is said or implied is relevant; what is irrevelant has been excluded, like lumps from pudding and "bugs" from machinery.

In this respect poetry differs from practical messages, which are successful if and only if we correctly infer the intention. They are more abstract than poetry.

4. The meaning of a poem may certainly be a personal one, in the sense that a poem expresses a personality or state of soul rather than a physical object like an apple. But even a short lyric poem is dramatic, the response of a speaker (no matter how abstractly conceived) to a situation (no matter how universalized). We ought to impute the thoughts and attitudes of the poem immediately to the dramatic *speaker*, and if to the author at all, only by an act of biographical inference.

5. There is a sense in which an author, by revision, may better achieve his original intention. But it is a very abstract sense. He intended to write a better work, or a better work of a certain kind, and now has done it. But it follows that his former concrete intention was not his intention. "He's the man we were in search of, that's true," says Hardy's rustic constable, "and yet he's not the man we were in search of. For the man we were in search of was not the man we wanted."

"Is not a critic," asks Professor Stoll, "a judge, who does not explore his own consciousness, but determines the author's meaning or intention, as if the poem were a will, a contract, or the constitution? The poem is not the critic's own." He has accurately diagnosed two forms of irresponsibility, one of which he prefers. Our view is yet different. The poem is not the critic's own and not the author's (it is detached from the author at birth and goes about the world beyond his power to intend about it or control it). The poem belongs to the public. It is embodied in language, the peculiar possession of the public, and it is about the human being, an object of public knowledge. What is said about the poem is subject to the same scrutiny as any statement in linguistics or in the general science of psychology.

A critic of our *Dictionary* article, Ananda K. Coomaraswamy, has argued[3] that there are two kinds of inquiry about a work of art: (1) whether the artist achieved his intentions; (2) whether the work of art "ought ever to have been undertaken at all" and so "whether it is worth preserving." Number (2), Coomaraswamy maintains, is not "criticism of any work of art *qua* work of art," but is rather moral criticism; number (1) is artistic criticism. But we maintain that (2) need not be moral criticism: that there is another way of deciding whether works of art are worth preserving and whether, in a sense, they "ought" to have been undertaken, and this is the way of objective criticism of works of art as such, the way which enables us to distinguish between a skillful murder and a skillful poem. A skillful murder is an example which Coomaraswamy uses, and in his system the difference between the murder and the poem is simply a "moral" one, not an "artistic" one, since each if carried out according to plan is "artistically" successful. We maintain that (2) is an inquiry of more worth than (1), and since (2) and not (1) is capable of distinguishing poetry from murder, the name "artistic criticism" is properly given to (2).

II

It is not so much a historical statement as a definition to say that the intentional fallacy is a romantic one. When a rhetorician of the first century A.D. writes: "Sublimity is the echo of a great soul," or when he tells us that "Homer enters into the sublime actions of his heroes" and "shares the full inspiration of the combat," we shall not be surprised to find this rhetorician considered as a distant harbinger of romanticism and greeted in the warmest terms by Saintsbury. One may wish to argue whether Longinus should be called romantic, but there can hardly be a doubt that in one important way he is.

Goethe's three questions for "constructive criticism" are "What did the author set out to do? Was his plan reasonable and sensible, and how far did he succeed in carrying it out?" If one leaves out the middle question, one has in effect the system of Croce—the culmination and crowning philosophic expression of romanticism. The beautiful is the successful intuition-expression, and the ugly is the unsuccessful; the intuition or private part of art is *the* aesthetic fact, and the medium or public part is not the subject of aesthetic at all.

The Madonna of Cimabue is still in the Church of Santa Maria Novella; but does she speak to the visitor of to-day as to the Florentines of the thirteenth century?

Historical interpretation labours . . . to reintegrate in us the psychological conditions which have changed in the course of history. It . . . enables us to see a work of art (a physical object) as its *author saw it* in the moment of production.[4]

The first italics are Croce's, the second ours. The upshot of Croce's system is an ambiguous emphasis on history. With such passages as a point of departure a critic may write a nice analysis of the meaning or "spirit" of a play by Shakespeare or Corneille—a process that involves close historical study but remains aesthetic criticism—or he may, with equal plausibility, produce an essay in sociology, biography, or other kinds of non-aesthetic history.

III

I went to the poets; tragic, dithyrambic, and all sorts. . . . I took them some of the most elaborate passages in their own writings, and asked what was the meaning of them. . . . Will you believe me? . . . there is hardly a person present who would not have talked better about their poetry than they did themselves. Then I knew that not by wisdom do poets write poetry, but by a sort of genius and inspiration.

That reiterated mistrust of the poets which we hear from Socrates may have been part of a rigorously ascetic view in which we hardly wish to participate, yet Plato's Socrates saw a truth about the poetic mind which the world no longer commonly sees—so much criticism, and that the most inspirational and most affectionately remembered, has proceeded from the poets themselves.

Certainly the poets have had something to say that the critic and professor could not say; their message has been more exciting: that poetry should come as naturally as leaves to a tree, that poetry is the lava of the imagination, or that it is emotion recollected in tranquillity. But it is necessary that we realize the character and authority of such testimony. There

is only a fine shade of difference between such expressions and
a kind of earnest advice that authors often give. Thus Edward
Young, Carlyle, Walter Pater:

I know two golden rules from *ethics,* which are no less golden in
Composition, than in life. 1. *Know thyself;* 2dly, *Reverence thyself.*

This is the grand secret for finding readers and retaining them:
let him who would move and convince others, be first moved and
convinced himself. Horace's rule, *Si vis me flere,* is applicable in a
wider sense than the literal one. To every poet, to every writer, we
might say: Be true, if you would be believed.

Truth! there can be no merit, no craft at all, without that. And
further, all beauty is in the long run only *fineness* of truth, or what
we call expression, the finer accommodation of speech to that vision
within.

And Housman's little handbook to the poetic mind yields
this illustration:

Having drunk a pint of beer at luncheon—beer is a sedative to the
brain, and my afternoons are the least intellectual portion of my
life—I would go out for a walk of two or three hours. As I went
along, thinking of nothing in particular, only looking at things
around me and following the progress of the seasons, there would
flow into my mind, with sudden and unaccountable emotion, sometimes a line or two of verse, sometimes a whole stanza at once.

This is the logical terminus of the series already quoted. Here
is a confession of how poems were written which would do as
a definition of poetry just as well as "emotion recollected in
tranquillity"—and which the young poet might equally well
take to heart as a practical rule. Drink a pint of beer, relax, go
walking, think on nothing in particular, look at things, surrender yourself to yourself, search for the truth in your own
soul, listen to the sound of your own inside voice, discover and
express the *vraie vérité.*

It is probably true that all this is excellent advice for poets.
The young imagination fired by Wordsworth and Carlyle is
probably closer to the verge of producing a poem than the mind

of the student who has been sobered by Aristotle or Richards. The art of inspiring poets, or at least of inciting something like poetry in young persons, has probably gone further in our day than ever before. Books of creative writing such as those issued from the Lincoln School are interesting evidence of what a child can do.[5] All this, however, would appear to belong to an art separate from criticism—to a psychological discipline, a system of self-development, a yoga, which the young poet perhaps does well to notice, but which is something different from the public art of evaluating poems.

Coleridge and Arnold were better critics than most poets have been, and if the critical tendency dried up the poetry in Arnold and perhaps in Coleridge, it is not inconsistent with our argument, which is that judgment of poems is different from the art of producing them. Coleridge has given us the classic "anodyne" story, and tells what he can about the genesis of a poem which he calls a "psychological curiosity," but his definitions of poetry and of the poetic quality "imagination" are to be found elsewhere and in quite other terms.

It would be convenient if the passwords of the intentional school, "sincerity," "fidelity," "spontaneity," "authenticity," "genuineness," "originality," could be equated with terms such as "integrity," "relevance," "unity," "function," "maturity," "subtlety," "adequacy," and other more precise terms of evaluation —in short, if "expression" always meant aesthetic achievement. But this is not so.

"Aesthetic" art, says Professor Curt Ducasse, an ingenious theorist of expression, is the conscious objectification of feelings, in which an intrinsic part is the critical moment. The artist corrects the objectification when it is not adequate. But this may mean that the earlier attempt was not successful in objectifying the self, or "it may also mean that it was a successful objectification of a self which, when it confronted us clearly, we disowned and repudiated in favor of another."[6] What is the standard by which we disown or accept the self? Professor Ducasse does not say. Whatever it may be, however, this standard is an element in the definition of art which will not reduce to terms of objectification. The evaluation of the work of art remains public; the work is measured against something outside the author.

IV

There is criticism of poetry and there is author psychology, which when applied to the present or future takes the form of inspirational promotion; but author psychology can be historical too, and then we have literary biography, a legitimate and attractive study in itself, one approach, as Professor Tillyard would argue, to personality, the poem being only a parallel approach. Certainly it need not be with a derogatory purpose that one points out personal studies, as distinct from poetic studies, in the realm of literary scholarship. Yet there is danger of confusing personal and poetic studies; and there is the fault of writing the personal as if it were poetic.

There is a difference between internal and external evidence for the meaning of a poem. And the paradox is only verbal and superficial that what is (1) internal is also public: it is discovered through the semantics and syntax of a poem, through our habitual knowledge of the language, through grammars, dictionaries, and all the literature which is the source of dictionaries, in general through all that makes a language and culture; while what is (2) external is private or idiosyncratic; not a part of the work as a linguistic fact: it consists of revelations (in journals, for example, or letters or reported conversations) about how or why the poet wrote the poem—to what lady, while sitting on what lawn, or at the death of what friend or brother. There is (3) an intermediate kind of evidence about the character of the author or about private or semiprivate meanings attached to words or topics by an author or by a coterie of which he is a member. The meaning of words is the history of words, and the biography of an author, his use of a word, and the associations which the word had for *him,* are part of the word's history and meaning.[7] But the three types of evidence, especially (2) and (3), shade into one another so subtly that it is not always easy to draw a line between examples, and hence arises the difficulty for criticism. The use of biographical evidence need not involve intentionalism, because while it may be evidence of what the author intended, it may also be evidence of the meaning of his words and the dramatic character of his utterance. On the other hand, it may not be all this. And a critic who is concerned with evidence of type (1) and moderately with that of type (3) will in the long run produce a different sort of comment from that of the critic who is concerned with (2) and with (3) where it shades into (2).

The whole glittering parade of Professor Lowes' *Road to Xanadu*, for instance, runs along the border between types (2) and (3) or boldly traverses the romantic region of (2). " 'Kubla Khan,' " says Professor Lowes, "is the fabric of a vision, but every image that rose up in its weaving had passed that way before. And it would seem that there is nothing haphazard or fortuitous in their return." This is not quite clear—not even when Professor Lowes explains that there were clusters of associations, like hooked atoms, which were drawn into complex relation with other clusters in the deep well of Coleridge's memory, and which then coalesced and issued forth as poems. If there was nothing "haphazard or fortuitous" in the way the images returned to the surface, that may mean (1) that Coleridge could not produce what he did not have, that he was limited in his creation by what he had read or otherwise experienced, or (2) that having received certain clusters of associations, he was bound to return them in just the way he did, and that the value of the poem may be described in terms of the experiences on which he had to draw. The latter pair of propositions (a sort of Hartleyan associationism which Coleridge himself repudiated in the *Biographia*) may not be assented to. There were certainly other combinations, other poems, worse or better, that might have been written by men who had read Bartram and Purchas and Bruce and Milton. And this will be true no matter how many times we are able to add to the brilliant complex of Coleridge's reading. In certain flourishes (such as the sentence we have quoted) and in chapter headings like "The Shaping Spirit," "The Magical Synthesis," "Imagination Creatrix," it may be that Professor Lowes pretends to say more about the actual poems than he does. There is a certain deceptive variation in these fancy chapter titles; one expects to pass on to a new stage in the argument, and one finds—more and more sources, more and more about "the streamy nature of association."[8]

"Wohin der Weg?" quotes Professor Lowes for the motto of his book. "Kein Weg! Ins Unbetretene." Precisely because the way is *unbetreten,* we should say, it leads away from the poem. Bartram's *Travels* contains a good deal of the history of certain words and of certain romantic Floridian conceptions that appear in "Kubla Khan." And a good deal of that history has passed and was then passing into the very stuff of our language. Perhaps a person who has read Bartram appreciates the poem more than one who has not. Or, by looking up the vocabulary of "Kubla Khan" in the *Oxford English Dictionary,* or by reading some of the other books there quoted, a person may know the poem better. But it would seem to pertain little to the poem to know that *Coleridge* had read Bartram. There is a gross body of life, of sensory and mental experience, which lies behind and in some sense causes every poem, but can never be and need not be known in the verbal and hence intellectual composition which is the poem. For all the objects of our manifold experience, for every unity, there is an action of the mind which cuts off roots, melts away context—or indeed we should never have objects or ideas or anything to talk about.

It is probable that there is nothing in Professor Lowes' vast book which could detract from anyone's appreciation of either *The Ancient Mariner* or "Kubla Khan." We next present a case where preoccupation with evidence of type (3) has gone so far as to distort a critic's view of a poem (yet a case not so obvious as those that abound in our critical journals).

In a well known poem by John Donne appears this quatrain:

> Moving of th' earth brings harmes and feares,
>   Men reckon what it did and meant,
> But trepidation of the spheares,
>   Though greater farre, is innocent.

A recent critic in an elaborate treatment of Donne's learning has written of this quatrain as follows:

He touches the emotional pulse of the situation by a skillful allusion to the new and the old astronomy. . . . Of the new astronomy, the "moving of the earth" is the most radical principle; of the old, the "trepidation of the spheres" is the motion of the greatest complexity. . . . The poet must exhort his love to quietness and calm upon his departure; and for this purpose the figure based upon the latter motion (trepidation), long absorbed into the traditional astronomy, fittingly suggests the tension of the moment without arousing the "harmes and feares" implicit in the figure of the moving earth.[9]

The argument is plausible and rests on a well substantiated thesis that Donne was deeply interested in the new astronomy and its repercussions in the theological realm. In various works Donne shows his familiarity with Kepler's *De Stella Nova*, with Galileo's *Siderius Nuncius*, with William Gilbert's *De Magnete*, and with Clavius' commentary on the *De Sphaera* of Sacrobosco. He refers to the new science in his Sermon at Paul's Cross and in a letter to Sir Henry Goodyer. In *The First Anniversary* he says the "new philosophy calls all in doubt." In the *Elegy on Prince Henry* he says that the "least moving of the center" makes "the world to shake."

It is difficult to answer argument like this, and impossible to answer it with evidence of like nature. There is no reason why Donne might not have written a stanza in which the two kinds of celestial motion stood for two sorts of emotion at parting. And if we become full of astronomical ideas and see Donne only against the background of the new science, we may believe that he did. But the text itself remains to be dealt with, the analyzable vehicle of a complicated metaphor. And one may observe: (1) that the movement of the earth according to the Copernican theory is a celestial motion, smooth and regular, and while it might cause religious or philosophic fears, it could not be associated with the crudity and earthiness of the kind of commotion which the speaker in the poem wishes to discourage; (2) that there is another moving of the earth, an earthquake, which has just these qualities and is to be associated with the tear-floods and sigh-tempests of the second stanza of the poem; (3) that "trepidation" is an appropriate opposite of earthquake, because each is a shaking or vibratory motion; and "trepidation of the spheres" is "greater far" than an earthquake, but not much greater (if two such motions can be compared as to greatness) than the annual motion of the earth; (4) that reckoning what it "did and meant" shows that the event has passed, like an earthquake, not like the incessant celestial movement of the earth. Perhaps a knowledge of Donne's interest in the new science may add another shade of meaning, an overtone to the stanza in question, though to say even this runs against the words. To make the geocentric and heliocentric antithesis the core of the metaphor is to disregard the English language, to prefer private evidence to public, external to internal.

V

If the distinction between kinds of evidence has implications for the historical critic, it has them no less for the contemporary poet and his critic. Or, since every rule for a poet is but another side of a judgment by a critic, and since the past is the realm of the scholar and critic, and the future and present that of the poet and the critical leaders of taste, we may say that the problems arising in literary scholarship from the intentional fallacy are matched by others which arise in the world of progressive experiment.

The question of "allusiveness," for example, as acutely posed by the poetry of Eliot, is certainly one where a false judgment is likely to involve the intentional fallacy. The frequency and depth of literary allusion in the poetry of Eliot and others has driven so many in pursuit of full meanings to the *Golden Bough* and the Elizabethan drama that it has become a kind of commonplace to suppose that we do not know what a poet means unless we have traced him in his reading—a supposition redolent with intentional implications. The stand taken by F. O. Matthiessen is a sound one and partially forestalls the difficulty.

If one reads these lines with an attentive ear and is sensitive to their sudden shifts in movement, the contrast between the actual Thames and the idealized vision of it during an age before it flowed through a megalopolis is sharply conveyed by that movement itself, whether or not one recognizes the refrain to be from Spenser.

Eliot's allusions work when we know them—and to a great extent even when we do not know them, through their suggestive power.

But sometimes we find allusions supported by notes, and it is a nice question whether the notes function more as guides to send us where we may be educated, or more as indications in themselves about the character of the allusions. "Nearly everything of importance . . . that is apposite to an appreciation of 'The Waste Land,' " writes Matthiessen of Miss Weston's book, "has been incorporated into the structure of the poem itself, or into Eliot's Notes." And with such an admission it may begin to appear that it would not much matter if Eliot invented his sources (as Sir Walter Scott invented chapter epigraphs from "old plays" and "anonymous" authors, or as Coleridge wrote marginal glosses for *The Ancient Mariner*). Allusions to Dante, Webster, Marvell, or Baudelaire doubtless gain something because these writers existed, but it is doubtful whether the same can be said for an allusion to an obscure Elizabethan:

> The sound of horns and motors, which shall bring
> Sweeney to Mrs. Porter in the spring.

"Cf. Day, *Parliament of Bees:*" says Eliot,

> When of a sudden, listening, you shall hear,
> A noise of horns and hunting, which shall bring
> Actaeon to Diana in the spring,
> Where all shall see her naked skin.

The irony is completed by the quotation itself; had Eliot, as is quite conceivable, composed these lines to furnish his own background, there would be no loss of validity. The conviction may grow as one reads Eliot's next note: "I do not know the origin of the ballad from which these lines are taken: it was reported to me from Sydney, Australia." The important word in this note—on Mrs. Porter and her daughter who washed their feet in soda water—is "ballad." And if one should feel from the lines themselves their "ballad" quality, there would be little need for the note. Ultimately, the inquiry must focus on the integrity of such notes as parts of the poem, for where they constitute special information about the meaning of phrases in the poem, they ought to be subject to the same scrutiny as any of the other words in which it is written. Matthiessen believes the notes were the price Eliot "had to pay in order to avoid what he would have considered muffling the energy of his poem by extended connecting links in the text itself." But it may be questioned whether the notes and the need for them are not equally muffling. F. W. Bateson has plausibly argued that Tennyson's "The Sailor Boy" would be better if half the stanzas were omitted, and the best versions of ballads like "Sir Patrick Spens" owe their power to the very audacity with which the minstrel has taken for granted the story upon which he comments. What then if a poet finds he cannot take so much for granted in a more recondite context and rather than write informatively, supplies notes? It can be said in favor of this plan that at least the notes do not pretend to be dramatic, as they would if written in verse. On the other hand, the notes may look like unassimilated material lying loose beside the poem, necessary for the meaning of the verbal symbol, but not integrated, so that the symbol stands incomplete.

We mean to suggest by the above analysis that whereas notes tend to seem to justify themselves as external indexes to the author's *intention*, yet they ought to be judged like any other parts of a composition (verbal arrangement special to a particular context), and when so judged their reality as parts of the poem, or their imaginative integration with the rest of the poem, may come into question. Mathiessen, for instance, sees that Eliot's titles for poems and his epigraphs are informative apparatus, like the notes. But while he is worried by some of the notes and thinks that Eliot "appears to be mocking himself for writing the note at the same time that he wants to convey something by it," Matthiessen believes that the "device" of epigraphs "is not at all open to the objection of not being sufficiently structural." "The *intention*," he says, "is to enable the poet to secure a condensed expression in the poem itself." "In each case the epigraph is *designed* to form an integral part of the effect of the poem." And Eliot himself, in his notes, has justified his poetic practice in terms of intention.

The Hanged Man, a member of the traditional pack, fits my purpose in two ways: because he is associated in my mind with the Hanged God of Frazer, and because I associate him with the hooded figure in the passage of the disciples to Emmaus in Part V. . . . The man with Three Staves (an authentic member of the Tarot pack) I associate, quite arbitrarily, with the Fisher King himself.

And perhaps he is to be taken more seriously here, when off guard in a note, than when in his Norton Lectures he comments on the difficulty of saying what a poem means and adds playfully that he thinks of prefixing to a second edition of *Ash Wednesday* some lines from *Don Juan:*

> I don't pretend that I quite understand
> My own meaning when I would be *very* fine;
> But the fact is that I have nothing planned
> Unless it were to be a moment merry.

If Eliot and other contemporary poets have any characteristic fault, it may be in *planning* too much.

Allusiveness in poetry is one of several critical issues by which we have illustrated the more abstract issue of intentionalism, but it may be for today the most important illustration. As a poetic practice allusiveness would appear to be in some recent poems an extreme corollary of the romantic intentionalist assumption, and as a critical issue it challenges and brings to light in a special way the basic premise of intentionalism. The following instance from the poetry of Eliot may serve to epitomize the practical implications of what we have been saying. In Eliot's "Love Song of J. Alfred Prufrock," toward the end, occurs the line: "I have heard the mermaids singing, each to each," and this bears a certain resemblance to a line in a Song

by John Donne, "Teach me to heare Mermaides singing," so
that for the reader acquainted to a certain degree with Donne's
poetry, the critical question arises: Is Eliot's line an allusion to
Donne's? Is Prufrock thinking about Donne? Is Eliot thinking
about Donne? We suggest that there are two radically different ways of looking for an answer to this question. There is
(1) the way of poetic analysis and exegesis, which inquires
whether it makes any sense if Eliot-Prufrock *is* thinking about
Donne. In an earlier part of the poem, when Prufrock asks,
"Would it have been worth while, . . . To have squeezed the
universe into a ball," his words take half their sadness and irony
from certain energetic and passionate lines of Marvel "To His
Coy Mistress." But the exegetical inquirer may wonder whether
mermaids considered as "strange sights" (to hear them is in
Donne's poem analogous to getting with child a mandrake root)
have much to do with Prufrock's mermaids, which seem to be
symbols of romance and dynamism, and which incidentally
have literary authentication, if they need it, in a line of a sonnet
by Gérard de Nerval. This method of inquiry may lead to the
conclusion that the given resemblance between Eliot and
Donne is without significance and is better not thought of, or
the method may have the disadvantage of providing no certain
conclusion. Nevertheless, we submit that this is the true and
objective way of criticism, as contrasted to what the very uncertainty of exegesis might tempt a second kind of critic to
undertake: (2) the way of biographical or genetic inquiry, in
which, taking advantage of the fact that Eliot is still alive, and
in the spirit of a man who would settle a bet, the critic writes
to Eliot and asks what he meant, or if he had Donne in mind.
We shall not here weigh the probabilities—whether Eliot would
answer that he meant nothing at all, had nothing at all in mind
—a sufficiently good answer to such a question—or in an un-
guarded moment might furnish a clear and, within its limit, ir-
refutable answer. Our point is that such an answer to such an
inquiry would have nothing to do with the poem "Prufrock";
it would not be a critical inquiry. Critical inquiries, unlike bets,
are not settled in this way. Critical inquiries are not settled by
consulting the oracle.

We might as well study the properties of wine by getting drunk.—EDUARD HANSLICK, The Beautiful in Music

THE AFFECTIVE
FALLACY

AS THE title of this essay invites comparison with that of our first, it may be relevant to assert at this point that we believe ourselves to be exploring two roads which have seemed to offer convenient detours around the acknowledged and usually feared obstacles to objective criticism, both of which, however, have actually led away from criticism and from poetry. The Intentional Fallacy is a confusion between the poem and its origins, a special case of what is known to philosophers as the Genetic Fallacy. It begins by trying to derive the standard of criticism from the psychological *causes* of the poem and ends in biography and relativism. The Affective Fallacy is a confusion between the poem and its *results* (what it *is* and what it *does*), a special case of epistemological skepticism, though usually advanced as if it had far stronger claims than the over-all forms of skepticism. It begins by trying to derive the standard of criticism from the psychological effects of the poem and ends in impressionism and relativism. The outcome of either Fallacy, the Intentional or the Affective, is that the poem itself, as an object of specifically critical judgment, tends to disappear.

In the present essay, we would discuss briefly the history and fruits of affective criticism, some of its correlatives in cognitive criticism, and hence certain cognitive characteristics of poetry which have made affective criticism plausible. We would observe also the premises of affective criticism, as they appear today, in certain philosophic and pseudophilosophic disciplines of wide influence. And first and mainly that of "semantics."

II

The separation of emotive from referential meaning was urged persuasively about twenty years ago in the earlier works of I. A. Richards. The types of meaning which were defined in his *Practical Criticism* and in the *Meaning of Meaning* of Ogden and Richards created, partly by suggestion, partly with the aid of direct statement, a clean "antithesis" between "symbolic and emotive use of language." In his *Practical Criticism* Richards spoke of "aesthetic" or "projectile" words—adjectives by which we project feelings at objects themselves altogether innocent of any qualities corresponding to these feelings. And in his succinct *Science and Poetry*, science is statement, poetry is pseudo statement which plays the important role of making us feel better about things than statements would.[1] After Richards —and under the influence too of Count Korzybski's non-Aristotelian *Science and Sanity*—came the semantic school of Chase, Hayakawa, Walpole, and Lee. Most recently C. L. Stevenson in his *Ethics and Language* has given an account which, as it is more careful and explicit than the others, may be taken as most clearly pleading their cause—and best revealing its weakness.

One of the most emphatic points in Stevenson's system is the distinction between what a word *means* and what it *suggests*. To make the distinction in a given case, one applies what the semeiotician calls a "linguistic rule" ("definition" in traditional terminology), the role of which is to stabilize responses to a word. The word "athlete" may be said to *mean* one interested in sports, among other things, but merely to suggest a tall young man. The linguistic rule is that "athletes are necessarily interested in sports, but may or may not be tall." All this is on the side of what may be called the *descriptive* (or *cognitive*) function of words. For a second and separate main function of words—that is, the *emotive*—there is no linguistic rule to stabilize responses and, therefore, in Stevenson's system, no parallel distinction between meaning and suggestion. Although the term "quasi-dependent emotive meaning" is recommended by Stevenson for a kind of emotive "meaning" which is "conditional to the cognitive *suggestiveness* of a sign," the main drift of his argument is that emotive "meaning" is something noncorrelative to and independent of descriptive (or cognitive) meaning. Thus, emotive "meaning" is said to survive sharp changes in descriptive meaning. And words with the same descriptive meaning are said to have quite different emotive "meanings." "License" and "liberty," for example, Stevenson believes to have in some contexts the same descriptive meaning, but opposite emotive "meanings." Finally, there are words which he believes to have no descriptive meaning, yet a decided emotive "meaning": these are expletives of various sorts.

But a certain further distinction, and an important one, which does not appear in Stevenson's system—nor in those of his forerunners—is invited by his persistent use of the word "meaning" for both cognitive and emotive language functions and by the absence from the emotive of his careful distinction between "meaning" and "suggestion." It is a fact worth insisting upon that the term "emotive meaning," as used by Stevenson, and the more cautious term "feeling," as used by Richards to refer to one of his four types of "meaning," do not refer to any such cognitive meaning as that conveyed by the name of an emotion —"anger" or "love." Rather, these key terms refer to the *expression* of emotive states which Stevenson and Richards believe to be effected by certain words—for instance "license," "liberty," "pleasant," "beautiful," "ugly"—and hence also to the emotive *response* which these words may evoke in a hearer. As the term "meaning" has been traditionally and usefully assigned to the cognitive, or descriptive, functions of language, it would have been well if these writers had employed, in such contexts, some less pre-empted term. "Import" might have been a happy choice. Such differentiation in vocabulary would have had the merit of reflecting a profound difference in linguistic function —all the difference between grounds of emotion and emotions themselves, between what is immediately meant by words and what is evoked by the meaning of words, or what more briefly might be said to be the "import" of the words themselves.

Without pausing to examine Stevenson's belief that expletives have no descriptive meaning, we are content to observe in passing that these words at any rate have only the vaguest emotive *import,* something raw, unarticulated, imprecise. "Oh!" (surprise and related feelings), "Ah!" (regret), "Ugh!" (distaste). It takes a more descriptive reference to specify the feeling. "In quiet she reposes. Ah! would that I did too." But a more central re-emphasis for Stevenson's position—and for that of his forerunners, including Richards—seems required by a fact scarcely mentioned in semantic writings: namely, that a large and obvious area of emotive *import* depends directly upon descriptive meaning (either with or without words of explicit valuation)—as when a person says and is believed: "General X ordered the execution of 50,000 civilian hostages," or "General X is guilty of the murder of 50,000 civilian hostages." And secondly, by the fact that a great deal of emotive *import* which does not depend thus directly on descriptive *meaning* does depend on descriptive *suggestion.* Here we have the "quasi-dependent emotive meaning" of Stevenson's system—a "meaning" to which surely he assigns too slight a role. This is the kind of emotive import, we should say, which appears when words change in descriptive *meaning* yet preserve a similar emotive "meaning"—when the Communists take over the term "democracy" and apply it to something else, preserving, however, the old descriptive *suggestion,* a government of, by, and for the people. It appears in pairs of words like "liberty" and "license," which even if they have the same descriptive meaning (as one may doubt), certainly carry different descriptive suggestions. Or one might cite the word series in Bentham's classic "Catalogue of Motives": "humanity, good-will, partiality," "frugality,

pecuniary interest, avarice." Or the other standard examples
of emotive insinuation: "Animals sweat, men perspire, women
glow." "I am firm, thou art obstinate, he is pigheaded." Or the
sentence, "There should be a revolution every twenty years,"
to which the experimenter in emotive responses attaches now
the name Karl Marx (and arouses suspicion), now that of
Thomas Jefferson (and provokes applause).

The principle applies conspicuously to the numerous examples offered by the school of Hayakawa, Walpole, and Lee.
In the interest of brevity, though in what may seem a quixotic
defiance of the warnings of this school against unindexed generalization—according to which semanticist (1) is not semanticist
(2) is not semanticist (3), and so forth—we call attention to
Irving Lee's *Language Habits in Human Affairs*, particularly
Chapters VII and VIII. According to Lee, every mistake that
anyone ever makes in acting, since in some direct or remote
sense it involves language or thought (which is related to language), may be ascribed to "bad language habits," a kind of
magic misuse of words. No distinctions are permitted. Basil
Rathbone, handed a scenario entitled *The Monster*, returns it
unread, but accepts it later under a different title. The Ephra-
imite says "Sibboleth" instead of "Shibboleth" and is slain. A
man says he is offended by four-letter words describing events
in a novel, but not by the events. Another man receives an
erroneously worded telegram which says that his son is dead.
The shock is fatal. One would have thought that with this
example Lee's simplifying prejudice might have broken down
—that a man who is misinformed that his son is dead may have
leave himself to drop dead without being thought a victim of
emotive incantation. Or that the title of a scenario is some
ground for the inference that it is a Grade-B horror movie;
that the use of phonetic principles in choosing a password is
reason rather than magic—as "lollapalooza" and "lullabye" were
used against infiltration tactics on Guadalcanal; that four-letter
words may suggest in events certain qualities which a reader
finds it distasteful to contemplate. None of these examples (except the utterly anomalous "Sibboleth") offers any evidence, in

short, that what a word *does* to a person is to be ascribed to anything except what it *means,* or if this connection is not apparent, at the most, by what it *suggests.*

A question about the relation of language to objects of emotion is a shadow and index of another question, about the status of emotions themselves. It is a consistent cultural phenomenon that within the same period as the *floruit* of semantics one kind of anthropology has delivered a parallel attack upon the relation of objects themselves to emotions, or more specifically, upon the constancy of their relations through the times and places of human societies. In the classic treatise of Westermarck on *Ethical Relativity* we learn, for example, that the custom of eliminating the aged and unproductive has been practiced among certain primitive tribes and nomadic races. Other customs, that of exposing babies, that of suicide, that of showing hospitality to strangers—or the contrary custom of eating them, the reception of the Cyclops rather than that of Alcinous —seem to have enjoyed in some cultures a degree of approval unknown or at least unusual in our own. But even Westermarck has noticed that difference of emotion "largely originates in different measures of knowledge, based on experience of the consequences of conduct, and in different beliefs." That is to say, the different emotions, even though they are responses to the same objects or actions, may yet be responses to different qualities or functions—to the edibility of Odysseus rather than to his comeliness or manliness. A converse of this is the fact that for different objects in different cultures there may be on cognitive grounds emotions of similar quality—for the cunning of Odysseus and for the strategy of Montgomery at El Alamein. Were it otherwise, indeed, there would be no way of understanding and describing alien emotions, no basis on which the science of the cultural relativist might proceed.

We shall not pretend to frame any formal discourse upon affective psychology, the laws of emotion. At this point, nevertheless, we venture to rehearse some generalities about objects, emotions, and words. Emotion, it is true, has a well known capacity to fortify opinion, to inflame cognition, and to grow upon itself in surprising proportions to grains of reason. We have

mob psychology, psychosis, and neurosis. We have "free-float-
ing anxiety" and all the vaguely understood and inchoate states
of apprehension, depression, or elation, the prevailing com-
plexions of melancholy or cheer. But it is well to remember
that these states are indeed inchoate or vague and by that fact
may even verge upon the unconscious.[2] We have, again, the
popular and self-vindicatory forms of confessing emotion. "He
makes me boil." "It burns me up." Or in the novels of Evelyn
Waugh a social event or a person is "sick-making." But these
locutions involve an extension of the strict operational meaning
of *make* or *effect*. A food or a poison causes pain or death, but
for an emotion we have a reason or an object, not merely an
efficient cause. If objects are ever connected by "emotional
congruity," as in the association psychology which J. S. Mill
inherited from the eighteenth century, this can mean only that
similar emotions attach to various objects because of similarity
in the objects or in their relations. What makes one angry is
something false, insulting, or unjust. What makes one afraid
is a cyclone, a mob, a holdup man. And in each case the emotion is somewhat different.

The tourist who said a waterfall was pretty provoked the silent disgust of Coleridge, while the other who said it was sublime won his approval. This, as C. S. Lewis so well observes,
was not the same as if the tourist had said, "I feel sick," and
Coleridge had thought, "No, I feel quite well."

The doctrine of emotive meaning propounded recently by
the semanticists has seemed to offer a scientific basis for one
kind of affective relativism in poetics—the personal. That is, if
a person can correctly say either "liberty" or "license" in a
given context independently of the cognitive quality of the
context, merely at will or from emotion, it follows that a reader
may likely feel either "hot" or "cold" and report either "bad" or
"good" on reading either "liberty" or "license"—either an ode
by Keats or a limerick. The sequence of licenses is endless.
Similarly, the doctrines of one school of anthropology have gone
far to fortify another kind of affective relativism, the cultural
or historical, the measurement of poetic value by the degree of
feeling felt by the readers of a given era. A different psycholo-

gical criticism, that by author's intention, as we noted in our first essay, is consistent both with piety for the poet and with antiquarian curiosity and has been heavily supported by the historical scholar and biographer. So affective criticism, though in its personal or impressionistic form it meets with strong dislike from scholars, yet in its theoretical or scientific form finds strong support from the same quarter. The historical scholar, if not much interested in his own personal responses or in those of his students, is intensely interested in whatever can be discovered about those of any member of Shakespeare's audience.

III

Plato's feeding and watering of the passions[3] was an early example of affective theory, and Aristotle's countertheory of catharsis was another (with modern intentionalistic analogues in theories of "relief" and "sublimation"). There was also the "transport" of the audience in the *Peri Hypsous* (matching the great soul of the poet), and this had echoes of passion or enthusiasm among eighteenth century Longinians. We have had more recently the infection theory of Tolstoy (with its intentionalistic analogue in the emotive expressionism of Veron), the *Einfühlung* or empathy of Lipps and related pleasure theories, either more or less tending to the "objectification" of Santayana: "Beauty is pleasure regarded as the quality of a thing." An affinity for these theories is seen in certain theories of the comic during the same era, the relaxation theory of Penjon, the laughter theory of Max Eastman. In their *Foundations of Aesthetics* Ogden, Richards, and Wood listed sixteen types of aesthetic theory, of which at least seven may be described as affective. Among these the theory of Synaesthesis (Beauty is what produces an equilibrium of appetencies) was the one they themselves espoused. This was developed at length by Richards in his *Principles of Literary Criticism*.

The theories just mentioned may be considered as belonging to one branch of affective criticism, and that the main one, the emotive—unless the theory of empathy, with its transport of the self into the object, belongs rather with a parallel and equally ancient affective theory, the imaginative. This is represented by the figure of vividness so often mentioned in the rhetorics—*efficacia, enargeia,* or the *phantasiai* in Chapter XV of *Peri Hypsous.* This if we mistake not is the imagination the "Pleasures" of which are celebrated by Addison in his series of *Spectators.* It is an imagination implicit in the theories of Leibniz and Baumgarten that beauty lies in clear but confused, or sensuous, ideas; in the statement of Warton in his *Essay on Pope* that the selection of "lively pictures . . . chiefly constitutes true poetry." In our time, as the emotive form of psychologistic or affective theory has found its most impressive champion in I. A. Richards, so the imaginative form has in Max Eastman, whose *Literary Mind* and *Enjoyment of Poetry* have much to say about vivid realizations or heightened consciousness.

The theory of intention or author psychology has been the intense conviction of poets themselves, Wordsworth, Keats, Housman, and since the romantic era, of young persons interested in poetry, the introspective amateurs and soul-cultivators. In a parallel way, affective theory has often been less a scientific view of literature than a prerogative—that of the soul adventuring among masterpieces, the contagious teacher, the poetic radiator—a magnetic rhapsode Ion, a Saintsbury, a Quiller-Couch, a William Lyon Phelps. Criticism on this theory has approximated the tone of the Buchmanite confession, the revival meeting. "To be quite frank," says Anatole France, "the critic ought to say: 'Gentlemen, I am going to speak about myself apropos of Shakespeare, apropos of Racine.' " The sincerity of the critic becomes an issue, as for the intentionalist the sincerity of the poet.

A "mysterious entity called the Grand Style" is celebrated by Saintsbury—something much like "the Longinian Sublime." "Whenever this perfection of expression acquires such force that it transmutes the subject and transports the hearer or reader, then and there the Grand Style exists, for so long, and in such degree, as the transmutation of the one and the transportation of the other lasts." This is the grand style, the emotive style, of nineteenth century affective criticism. A somewhat less resonant style which has been heard in our

columns of Saturday and Sunday reviewing and from our literary explorers is more closely connected with imagism and the
kind of vividness sponsored by Eastman. In the *Book-of-the-
Month Club News* Dorothy Canfield testifies to the power of a
novel: "To read this book is like living through an experience
rather than just reading about it." A poem, says Hans Zinsser,

means nothing to me unless it can carry me away with the gentle
or passionate pace of its emotion, over obstacles of reality into
meadows and covers of illusion. . . . The sole criterion for me is
whether it can sweep me with it into emotion or illusion of beauty,
terror, tranquility, or even disgust.[4]

It is but a short step to what we may call the physiological form
of affective criticism. Beauty, said Burke in the eighteenth
century, is something which "acts by relaxing the solids of the
whole system." More recently, on the side of personal testimony, we have the oft quoted goose-flesh experience in a letter
of Emily Dickinson, and the top of her head taken off. We have
the bristling of the skin while Housman was shaving, the "shiver
down the spine," the sensation in "the pit of the stomach."
And if poetry has been discerned by these tests, truth also.
"All scientists," said D. H. Lawrence to Aldous Huxley, "are
liars. . . . I don't care about evidence. Evidence doesn't mean
anything to me. I don't feel it *here*." And, reports Huxley, "he
pressed his two hands on his solar plexus."

An even more advanced grade of affective theory, that of
hallucination, would seem to have played some part in the neoclassic conviction about the unities of time and place, was given
a modified continuation of existence in phrases of Coleridge
about a "willing suspension of disbelief" and a "temporary half
faith," and may be found today in some textbooks. The hyp-
notic hypothesis of E. D. Snyder might doubtless be invoked in
its support. As this form of affective theory is the least theoretical in detail, has the least content, and makes the least claim
on critical intelligence, so it is in its most concrete instances not
a theory but a fiction or a fact—of no critical significance. In
the eighteenth century Fielding conveys a right view of the
hallucinative power of drama in his comic description of Part-

ridge seeing Garrick act the ghost scene in Hamlet. "O la! sir. . . . If I was frightened, I am not the only person. . . . You may call me coward if you will; but if that little man there upon the stage is not frightened, I never saw any man frightened in my life." Partridge is today found perhaps less often among the sophisticates at the theater than among the myriad audience of movie and radio. It is said, and no doubt reliably, that during World War II Stefan Schnabel played Nazi roles in radio dramas so convincingly that he received numerous letters of complaint, and in particular one from a lady who said that she had reported him to General MacArthur.[5]

IV

A distinction can be made between those who have testified what poetry does to themselves and those who have coolly investigated what it does to others. The most resolute researches of the latter have led them into the dreary and antiseptic laboratory, to testing with Fechner the effects of triangles and rectangles, to inquiring what kinds of colors are suggested by a line of Keats, or to measuring the motor discharges attendant upon reading it.[6] If animals could read poetry, the affective critic might make discoveries analogous to those of W. B. Cannon about *Bodily Changes in Pain, Hunger, Fear and Rage*— the increased liberation of sugar from the liver, the secretion of adrenin from the adrenal gland. The affective critic is today actually able, if he wishes, to measure the "psychogalvanic reflex" of persons subjected to a given moving picture. But, as Herbert J. Muller in his *Science and Criticism* points out: "Students have sincerely reported an 'emotion' at the mention of the word 'mother,' although a galvanometer indicated no bodily change whatever. They have also reported no emotion at the mention of 'prostitute,' although the galvanometer gave a definite kick." Thomas Mann and a friend came out of a movie weeping copiously—but Mann narrates the incident in support of his view that movies are not Art. "Art is a *cold* sphere."[7] The gap between various levels of physiological experience and the recognition of value remains wide, in the laboratory or out.

In a similar way, general affective theory at the literary level has, by the very implications of its program, produced little actual criticism. The author of the ancient *Peri Hypsous* is weakest at the points where he explains that passion and sublimity are the palliatives or excuses (*alexipharmaka*) of bold metaphors, and that passions which verge on transport are the lenitives or remedies (*panakeia*) of such audacities in speech as hyperbole. The literature of catharsis has dealt with the historical and theoretical question whether Aristotle meant a medical or a lustratory metaphor, whether the genitive which follows *katharsis* is of the thing purged or of the object purified. Even the early critical practice of I. A. Richards had little to do with his theory of synaesthesis. His *Practical Criticism* depended mainly on two important constructive principles of criticism which Richards has realized and insisted upon—(1) that rhythm (the vague, if direct, expression of emotion) and poetic form in general are intimately connected with and interpreted by other and more precise parts of poetic meaning, (2) that poetic meaning is inclusive or multiple and hence sophisticated. The latter quality of poetry may perhaps be the objective correlative of the affective state synaesthesis, but in applied criticism there would seem to be not much room for synaesthesis or for the touchy little attitudes of which it is composed.

The report of some readers, on the other hand, that a poem or story induces in them vivid images, intense feelings, or heightened consciousness, is neither anything which can be refuted nor anything which it is possible for the objective critic to take into account. The purely affective report is either too physiological or it is too vague. Feelings, as Hegel has conveniently put it, "remain purely subjective affections of myself, in which the concrete matter vanishes, as though narrowed into a circle of the utmost abstraction." And the only constant or predictable thing about the vivid images which more eidetic readers experience is precisely their vividness—as may be seen by requiring a class of average pupils to draw illustrations of a short story or by consulting the newest Christmas edition of a childhood classic which one knew with the illustrations of Howard Pyle or N. C. Wyeth. Vividness is not the thing in the work by which the work may be identified, but the result of a cognitive structure, which *is* the thing. "The story is good," as the student so often says in his papers, "because it leaves so much to the imagination." The opaque accumulation of physical detail in some realistic novels has been aptly dubbed by Middleton Murry "the pictorial fallacy."

Certain theorists, notably Richards, have anticipated some difficulties of affective criticism by saying that it is not intensity of emotion that characterizes poetry (murder, robbery, fornication, horse racing, war—perhaps even chess—take care of that better), but the subtle quality of patterned emotions which play at the subdued level of disposition or attitude. We have psychological theories of aesthetic distance, detachment, or disinterestedness. A criticism on these principles has already taken important steps toward objectivity. If Eastman's theory of imaginative vividness appears today chiefly in the excited puffs of the newspaper Book Sections, the campaign of the semanticists and the balanced emotions of Richards, instead of producing their own school of affective criticism, have contributed much to recent schools of cognitive analysis, of paradox, ambiguity, irony, and symbol. It is not always true that the emotive and cognitive forms of criticism will sound far different. If the affective critic (avoiding both the physiological and the abstractly psychological form of report) ventures to state with any precision what a line of poetry *does*—as "it fills us with a mixture of melancholy and reverence for antiquity"—either the statement will be patently abnormal or false, or it will be a description of what the meaning of the line *is*: "the spectacle of massive antiquity in ruins." Tennyson's "Tears, idle tears," as it deals with an emotion which the speaker at first seems not to understand, might be thought to be a specially emotive poem. "The last stanza," says Brooks in his recent analysis, "evokes an intense emotional response from the reader." But this statement is not really a part of Brooks' criticism of the poem—rather a witness of his fondness for it. "The second stanza"—Brooks might have said at an earlier point in his analysis—"gives us a momentary vivid realization of past happy

experiences, then makes us sad at their loss." But he says
actually: "The conjunction of the qualities of sadness and fresh-
ness is reinforced by the fact that the same basic symbol—the
light on the sails of a ship hull down—has been employed to
suggest both qualities." The distinction between these formulations may seem slight, and in the first example which we
furnished may be practically unimportant. Yet the difference
between translatable emotive formulas and more physiological
and psychologically vague ones—cognitively untranslatable—is
theoretically of the greatest importance. The distinction even
when it is a faint one is at the dividing point between paths
which lead to polar opposites in criticism, to classical objectivity and to romantic reader psychology.

The critic whose formulations lean to the emotive and the
critic whose formulations lean to the cognitive will in the long
run produce a vastly different sort of criticism.

The more specific the account of the emotion induced by a
poem, the more nearly it will be an account of the reasons for
emotion, the poem itself, and the more reliable it will be as an
account of what the poem is likely to induce in other—sufficiently informed—readers. It will in fact supply the kind of
information which will enable readers to respond to the poem.
It will talk not of tears, prickles, or other physiological symptoms, of feeling angry, joyful, hot, cold, or intense, or of
vaguer states of emotional disturbance, but of shades of distinction and relation between objects of emotion. It is precisely here that the discerning literary critic has his insuperable
advantage over the subject of the laboratory experiment and
over the tabulator of the subject's responses. The critic is not
a contributor to statistically countable reports about the poem,
but a teacher or explicator of meanings. His readers, if they
are alert, will not be content to take what he says as testimony,
but will scrutinize it as teaching.

V

Poetry, as Matthew Arnold believed, "attaches the emotion
to the idea; the idea *is* the fact." The objective critic, how-

ever, must admit that it is not easy to explain how this is done,
how poetry makes ideas thick and complicated enough to hold
on to emotions. In his essay on "Hamlet and His Problems"
T. S. Eliot finds Hamlet's state of emotion unsatisfactory because it lacks an "objective correlative," a "chain of events"
which are the "formula of that *particular* emotion." The emotion is "in *excess* of the facts as they appear." It is "inexpressi-
ble." Yet Hamlet's emotion must be expressible, we submit,
and actually expressed too (by something) in the play; otherwise Eliot would not know it is there—in excess of the facts.
That Hamlet himself or Shakespeare may be baffled by the
emotion is beside the point. The second chapter of Yvor
Winters' *Primitivism and Decadence* has gone much further
in clarifying a distinction adumbrated by Eliot. Without em-
bracing the extreme doctrine of Winters, that if a poem cannot
be paraphrased it is a poor poem, we may yet with profit re-
iterate his main thesis: that there is a difference between the
motive, as he calls it, or logic of an emotion, and the surface or
texture of a poem constructed to describe the emotion, and that
both are important to a poem. Winters has shown, we think,
how there can be in effect "fine poems" about nothing. There
is rational progression and there is "qualitative progression,"[8]
the latter, with several subtly related modes, a characteristic
of decadent poetry. Qualitative progression is the succession,
the dream float, of images, not substantiated by a plot. "Moister
than an oyster in its clammy cloister, I'm bluer than a wooer
who has slipped in a sewer," says Morris Bishop in a recent
comic poem:

> Chiller than a killer in a cinema thriller,
> Queerer than a leerer at his leer in a mirror,
> Madder than an adder with a stone in the bladder.
> If you want to know why, I cannot but reply:
>   It is really no affair of yours.[9]

The term "pseudo statement" was for Richards a patronizing
term by which he indicated the attractive nullity of poems. For
Winters, the kindred term "pseudo reference" is a name for the
more disguised kinds of qualitative progression and is a term

of reproach. It seems to us highly significant that for another psychological critic, Max Eastman, so important a part of poetry as metaphor is in effect too pseudo statement. The vivid realization of metaphor comes from its being in some way an obstruction to practical knowledge (like a torn coat sleeve to the act of dressing). Metaphor operates by being abnormal or inept, the wrong way of saying something. Without pressing the point, we should say that an uncomfortable resemblance to this doctrine appears in Ransom's logical structure and local texture of irrelevance.

What Winters has said seems basic. To venture both a slight elaboration of this and a return to the problem of emotive semantics surveyed in our first section: it is a well known but nonetheless important truth that there are two kinds of real objects which have emotive quality, the objects which are the reasons for human emotion, and those which by some kind of association suggest either the reasons or the resulting emotion: the thief, the enemy, or the insult that makes us angry, and the hornet that sounds and stings somewhat like ourselves when angry; the murderer or felon, and the crow that kills small birds and animals or feeds on carrion and is black like the night when crimes are committed by men. The arrangement by which these two kinds of emotive meaning are brought together in a juncture characteristic of poetry is, roughly speaking, the simile, the metaphor, and the various less clearly defined forms of association. We offer the following crude example as a kind of skeleton figure to which we believe all the issues can be attached.

     I. X feels as angry as a hornet.
     II. X whose lunch has been stolen feels as angry as a hornet.

No. I is, we take it, the qualitative poem, the vehicle of a metaphor, an objective correlative—for nothing. No. II adds the tenor of the metaphor, the motive for feeling angry, and hence makes the feeling itself more specific. The total statement has a more complex and testable structure. The element of aptitude, or ineptitude, is more susceptible of discussion. "Light thickens, and the crow makes wing to the rooky wood" might be a line from a poem about nothing, but initially owed much of its power, and we daresay still does, to the fact that it is spoken by a tormented murderer who, as night draws on, has sent his agents out to perform a further "deed of dreadful note."

These distinctions bear a close relation to the difference between historical statement which may be a reason for emotion because it is believed (Macbeth has killed the king) and fictitious or poetic statement, where a large component of suggestion (and hence metaphor) has usually appeared. The first of course seldom occurs pure, at least not for the public eye. The coroner or the intelligence officer may content himself with it. Not the chronicler, the bard, or the newspaperman. To these we owe more or less direct words of value and emotion (the murder, the atrocity, the wholesale butchery) and all the repertoire of suggestive meanings which here and there in history—with somewhat to start upon—a Caesar or a Macbeth—have created out of a mere case of factual reason for intense emotion a specified, figuratively fortified, and permanent object of less intense but far richer emotion. With a decline of heroes and of faith in external order, we have had during the last century a great flowering of poetry which has tried the utmost to do without any hero or action or fiction of these—the qualitative poetry of Winters' analysis. It is true that any hero and action when they become fictitious take the first step toward the simply qualitative, and all poetry, so far as separate from history, tends to be formula of emotion. The hero and action are taken as symbolic. A graded series from fact to quality might include: (1) the historic Macbeth, (2) Macbeth as Renaissance tragic protagonist, (3) a *Macbeth* written by Eliot, (4) a *Macbeth* written by Pound. As Winters has explained, "the prince is briefly introduced in the footnotes" of *The Waste Land;* "it is to be doubted that Mr. Pound could manage such an introduction." Yet in no one of these four stages has anything like a pure emotive poetry been produced. The semantic analysis which we have offered in our first section would say that even in the last stages a poetry of pure emotion is an illusion. What we have is a poetry where kings are only symbols or even a poetry of hornets and crows, rather than of human deeds. Yet a poetry about things. How these things are joined in patterns and with what names of emotion remains always the critical question. *"The Romance of the Rose* could not, without loss," observes C. S. Lewis, "be rewritten as *The Romance of the Onion."*

Poetry is characteristically a discourse about both emotions and objects, or about the emotive quality of objects. The emotions correlative to the objects of poetry become a part of the matter dealt with—not communicated to the reader like an infection or disease, not inflicted mechanically like a bullet or knife wound, not administered like a poison, not simply expressed as by expletives or grimaces or rhythms, but presented in their objects and contemplated as a pattern of knowledge. Poetry is a way of fixing emotions or making them more permanently perceptible when objects have undergone a functional change from culture to culture, or when as simple facts of history they have lost emotive value with loss of immediacy. Though the reasons for emotion in poetry may not be so simple as Ruskin's "noble grounds for the noble emotions," yet a great deal of constancy for poetic objects of emotion—if we will look for constancy—may be traced through the drift of human history. The murder of Duncan by Macbeth, whether as history of the eleventh century or chronicle of the sixteenth, has not tended to become the subject of a Christmas carol. In Shakespeare's play it is an act difficult to duplicate in all its immediate adjuncts of treachery, deliberation, and horror of conscience. Set in its galaxy of symbols—the hoarse raven, the thickening light, and the crow making wing, the babe plucked from the breast, the dagger in the air, the ghost, the bloody hands—this ancient murder has become an object of strongly fixed emotive value. The corpse of Polyneices, a far more ancient object and partially concealed from us by the difficulties of the Greek, shows a similar pertinacity in remaining among the understandable motives of higher duty. Funeral customs have changed, but not the intelligibility of the web of issues, religious, political, and private, woven about the corpse "unburied, unhonoured, all unhallowed." Again, certain objects partly obscured in one age wax into appreciation in another, and partly through the efforts of the poet. It is not true that they suddenly arrive out of nothing. The pathos of Shylock, for example, is not a creation of our time, though a smugly modern humanitarianism, because it has slogans, may suppose that this was not felt by Shakespeare or Southampton—and may not perceive its own debt to Shakespeare. "Poets," says Shelley, "are the unacknowledged legislators of the world." And it may be granted at least that poets have been leading expositors of the laws of feeling.[10]

To the relativist historian of literature falls the uncomfortable task of establishing as discrete cultural moments the past when the poem was written and first appreciated, and the present into which the poem with its clear and nicely interrelated meanings, its completeness, balance, and tension has survived. A structure of emotive objects so complex and so reliable as to have been taken for great poetry by any past age will never, it seems safe to say, so wane with the waning of human culture as not to be recoverable at least by a willing student. And on the same grounds a confidence seems indicated for the objective discrimination of all future poetic phenomena, though the premises or materials of which such poems will be constructed cannot be prescribed or foreseen. If the exegesis of some poems depends upon the understanding of obsolete or exotic customs, the poems themselves are the most precise emotive report on the customs. In the poet's finely contrived objects of emotion and in other works of art the historian finds his most reliable evidence about the emotions of antiquity—and the anthropologist, about those of contemporary primitivism. To appreciate courtly love we turn to Chrétien de Troyes and Marie de France. Certain attitudes of late fourteenth century England, toward knighthood, toward monasticism, toward the bourgeoisie, are nowhere more precisely illustrated than in the prologue to *The Canterbury Tales*. The field worker among the Zunis or the Navahos finds no informant so informative as the poet or the member of the tribe who can quote its myths.[11] In short, though cultures have changed and will change, poems remain and explain.

I challenge all the world, to show one good epic, elegiac or lyric poem . . .; one eclogue, pastoral, or anything like the ancients.—JONATHAN SMEDLEY, Gulliveriana

THE CHICAGO CRITICS

THE FALLACY OF
THE NEOCLASSIC SPECIES

BACK IN the mid 1930's Professor R. S. Crane of Chicago had a conversion, from straight, neutral history of literature and ideas to literary criticism. His essay, "History versus Criticism in the University Study of Literature," in the *English Journal*, October, 1935, was for its date a revolutionary document, a signal victory for criticism. It drew a line between history and criticism with convincing clarity, though perhaps so severely as to have helped raise some later needless embarrassment between academic critics and their colleagues.[1] Crane received the handsome compliments of a poet and critic, John Crowe Ransom, in his essay entitled "Criticism, Inc.," which appeared two years later in the *Virginia Quarterly Review*. "If criticism should get a hearing in the universities," said Ransom, "the credit would probably belong to Professor Ronald S. Crane . . . more than to any other man. He is the first of the great professors to have advocated it as a major policy for departments of English."

Yet Crane was in 1935 a pioneer advocate of criticism only with respect to his eminence inside an American university.

The critical study of literature had been violently incited during the 1920's and early 1930's in the works of I. A. Richards and at least strongly encouraged by other writers. The eruption of critical volumes and school texts by Tate, Ransom, Brooks and Warren, Winters, and others, which began in America almost immediately after Crane's essay, and the busy debate about university teaching of literature which went on in the quarterlies were events which had not come to a head overnight. With respect to the whole horizon of literary study, Crane's action of 1935 was not a novelty. Critics were already springing up here and there in force. It was a question of some strategic importance whether Crane would try to take command, as indeed Ransom seemed to invite.

In a set of three brief essays—two exercises in practical criticism by younger colleagues, Professors Norman Maclean and Elder Olson, and an introductory note by Crane himself, published in the Kansas City *University Review*, Winter, 1942 —the Chicago critics made, I believe, their first public revelation of how sweeping were to be not only their own neo-Aristotelian claims but their disapproval of the trend in criticism promoted by "such men as . . . Eliot . . . Richards . . . Brooks . . . Ransom, and . . . Tate." By the year 1944 the movement had attracted one outside ally in Professor Hoyt Trowbridge, who voiced his enthusiastic approval in an essay published in the *Sewanee Review*. Other expressions by the Chicago school followed during the 1940's, especially under Crane's editorship, in *Modern Philology*. Now, with the publication by the University of Chicago Press of the weighty *Critics and Criticism Ancient and Modern*,[2] containing fourteen previously published essays, six new ones, and an Introduction by Crane, the record is solidly and reiteratively established.

Five of the essays in this volume (222 pages, surely far too great a proportion of the book) are contributed by Professor Richard McKeon, a specialist in the history of philosophic systems, who looms massively and portentously behind the whole Chicago effort. Two things the Chicago literary critics apparently owe to him as mentor: a deep preoccupation with Aristotle's literary philosophy and a quasi-pluralistic theory regarding various historically recoverable critical systems.

McKeon's argument about the several systems and their basic assumptions follows a repeating pattern of take and put. The systems are represented mainly as parallels or analogues, using separate vocabularies for separate purposes and not translatable into one another except with great distortion. It is a matter of initial choice or assumption which system one picks. But this account frequently leads up to some sort of amendment or concession to the effect that, after all, the systems somehow do compete and can be compared and preferred to one another; there is some validity and truth if we can only get at it.[3] With the first of these emphases McKeon builds up a strong impression of pluralistic sophistication and hands-off tolerance, while with the second, linked to an insistent theme of Aristotelian "literal" and "scientific" criticism, he gains the advantage of seeming to know the secret of the one best way of constructing a poetics. Probably the stronger impression, at least quantitatively, is the pluralistic. The successive critics from Plato to Tolstoy and Richards are in a sense competitors, but somewhat like a tournament of tennis players playing each by himself in separate courts. The competition is by comparison of "forms" in analogical postures. The critics are shadow boxers in separate rings who can't lay a glove on one another.

Such basic assumptions are apparently not without their effects on McKeon's own way of thinking and his style of exposition, and to a lesser extent on that of his colleagues, especially Olson. Here I should like to enter a strong preliminary complaint against the frequent opaqueness of McKeon's writing, his absent-mindedness as it were, his neglect to make details of comparisons and antitheses go together, his lack of interest in criticizing the system which he is expounding. This is something I can only interpret as the expressive counterpart of the pluralistic approach to intellectual history, a handicap to vital discourse which might have appeared likely from the outset. From the instances in which his lengthy essays abound, I select just two, both of which have not only a broad doctrinal bearing on my dispute with the literary critics which is to follow, but also an exemplary relation to a literary principle which those critics strongly tend to deny, that style and thought are intimately dependent upon each other.

The perfection of style or diction in *both* rhetoric and poetic is achieved by choice of language at once *clear* and *appropriate,* without either meanness or undue elevation. The *difference* between poetry and prose is therefore to be found . . . in the fact that clarity is achieved easily in prose by the use of ordinary words, *whereas* meanness is avoided easily in poetry by the use of unfamiliar terms —such as strange words, metaphors, lengthened forms—which depart from the ordinary modes of speech. The center of interest in both poetic and rhetoric is *therefore* the metaphor, but for *opposite* reasons. Prose writers must pay specially careful attention to metaphor, because their other resources are scantier than those of poets, whereas for poets it is the most effective of the numerous poetic forms designed to give diction a nonprosaic character [p. 228].

The italics are mine. Why does it make a definitive *difference* between poetry and prose if you can achieve clarity in prose by ordinary words (*if* you can), and if you can avoid meanness in poetry by extraordinary words (*if* you can)? Waive the question of the truth of either of these statements. There is no real opposition—especially if we note that the norm of both poetry and "rhetoric" is language clear and appropriate. (The difference between my sister and my brother is that my sister has yellow hair, whereas my brother has blue eyes.) And why should the importance of metaphor follow (*therefore*) from the preceding muddled antithesis? And again, why is there anything *opposite,* and why isn't there something merely puzzling, in the supposition that metaphor, the most poetic resource of poetry, is the only poetic resource permitted to prose? My second example:

In addition to the task which the poet faces in the construction of his play he faces "problems" which take the form of objections to "errors" . . . he has committed. Since they are concerned with "errors," these problems are solved by inference from postulates or assumptions which the poet lays down concerning his art, such as would justify him in using as means to his end (which becomes at this stage the proper pleasure caused by his work) devices that may be subject to some defect relative to a science or to morals but irrelevant to the consideration of his art. One of these assumptions is that the standard of rightness in poetry differs from that of politics and other arts, for two kinds of error are possible in poetry; failures of art when the poet intended to describe a thing correctly, and technical errors, proper to some other art or science, which might be justified for the purposes of the poetic art [p. 516].

That is to say, if someone accuses the poet of being at fault through immorality or unreality, he may reply that it is one of his *assumptions* that a poet doesn't have to observe rules of morality or reality. The purposes and pleasures of poetry are just assumed to be different. Aristotle may be as bad as this here and there, but he is not often so flatly question-begging and does not often merely multiply words around so sheer an assumption. If this is his doctrine (I am far from sure it is), I fear both he and McKeon are going to have to yield both to the Platonic and to the modern critic who says: "What I want to know is why or how it is that a poet can get away with writing something immoral or unreal? Why is there any pleasure attached to this? Just to assume it doesn't advance my understanding at all. There seems to be a strange *fact* here concerning the relation of poetry and morals. This is one thing poetic theory has to *try* to explain. There is no other point in raising the question."

II

To come nearer now to the central combat aims of the Chicago team, especially as these are summarized in the Introduction by Crane—I imagine a stage on which stands a figure representing the contemporary critic, a composite, let us say, of Richards, Eliot, Empson, Brooks and Warren, and Tate. He is wearing the mask of his role in the drama to be enacted, a tolerably good, clean, bright critic's mask, though, let us say, it has some smudges on it (the psychologism of Richards, for in-

stance, the excessive ingenuities of Empson). Enter: Professor
Crane. He walks up to the critic and, taking a piece of burnt
cork from his pocket, proceeds to blacken the mask all over.
"There now," he says, "that is what you really look like." Professor Crane then removes the mask from the face of the critic
and, with a towel which he has brought along for the purpose,
attempts to wipe it off clean, leaving it, however, somewhat
more smudged than before and generally somewhat grey. Next
he writes across the forehead of the mask the word "Aristotle,"
the quotation marks being his own. He then puts the mask on
his own face. "There now again," he says. "This looks a lot better on me than it did on you. Of course I am well aware that
there is really no law that tells us what a critic's mask should be
like. You had as much right to your mask, white or black, as I
have to it in its present state. Still, it does look better on me
than it did on you."

Other modern critics are said by the Chicago critics to be
"dogmatic" and restrictive—the Chicago critics just the opposite. The history of criticism to which they contribute in Part
II is described as "the pluralistic philosophy of teaching by
example."

And perhaps the most general profit we can derive from it is the
habit of viewing critical principles as neither doctrinal absolutes nor
historically necessitated beliefs but instruments of inquiry and
analysis, to which a critic therefore need not commit himself dog-
matically, but only hypothetically [p. 11].

Crane announces that he and his colleagues "have viewed their
'Aristotelianism' as a strictly pragmatic and nonexclusive commitment." But it turns out—immediately and in the same sentence—that they look on the Aristotelian "hypotheses about
poetry and poetics" as "capable of being developed into a
comprehensive critical method, at once valid in itself and peculiarly adapted to the study of [certain] problems." And these
problems are

the problems that face us whenever we reflect on the undeniable
fact that what a poet does *distinctively as a poet* is not to express

himself or his age or to resolve psychological or moral difficulties or to communicate a vision of the world or to provide entertainment or to use words in such-and-such ways, and so on—though all these may be involved in what he does—but rather by means of his art, to build materials of language and experience into wholes of various kinds to which, as we experience them, we tend to attribute final rather than merely instrumental value [p. 13].[4]

In short, the section of Crane's Introduction which I have just been summarizing repeats the pattern of retracted pluralism which I have already described in McKeon's essays. But Crane is bolder and clearer. The only thing possibly hypothetical or pragmatic or in any sense tentative about his theory is that he has elected to theorize about poetry as poetry and not about something else. Given this choice and interest, he believes his theory valid and peculiarly adapted to discuss poetry as poetry—and he is no less "dogmatic" about this than any other critic who has a theory and believes in it. At another place in his Introduction he writes:

It follows from the pluralistic and instrumentalist view of criticism that we must accord to critics the right of free choice between different basic methods; this is as much a practical decision and hence immune to theoretical questioning, as is the decision (say) to study medicine rather than law [p. 9].

But this is scarcely a convincing parallel. If this is the case, why all the uproar? Why should Crane studying medicine quarrel with Brooks studying law? If Crane wanted to make a parallel, he should have said: "This is as much a practical decision . . . as is the decision to study Roman law rather than common law, or to study medicine out of Galen or out of Cecil's *Textbook of Medicine.*" And the second parallel would have revealed the legitimate implications of the pluralistic side of the Chicago philosophy better than the first. The "dogmatic" side of the Chicago theory is necessary if they are to have any theory at all, and I do not deny their right to it. Only it is a bit preposterous of Crane to keep professing at intervals that the "Aristotelian" method is not a "rival" but only a "needed supplement" to other current methods (p. 23) and that he and his friends are less "dogmatic" than Ransom or Wellek and Warren. Crane may believe his theory more flexible and more inclusive than theirs (p. 10); he may believe that he has a better theory. But this would not make his theory less "dogmatic" than anyone else's. And if the word "dogmatic" is taken as connoting not only commitment to a theory but a high degree of assurance and an intolerance of other theories, then Crane and his friends are especially dogmatic.

The Chicago critics profess (on the pages where they develop this side of their statement) to be taking only a pragmatic ride on a borrowed vehicle. I am apprehensive, therefore, that if I score a hit on them here or there, they are likely to smile and say it is only the vehicle I have hit. Nevertheless, their interpretation of Aristotle and of later critical theory is closely tied in with their own theory and their polemic against other modern critics. In the absence of a clear reason to the contrary in any instance, I shall treat their history as revealing and supporting the sense of their polemic.

This is the place, I believe, for a note on the high degree of respect shown by the Chicago writers for the wholeness and consistency of various separate systems of philosophy and methods of criticism. This follows from, or is needed in support of, McKeon's basic view of the systems as parallel, discrete, and aloof from one another, rather than successive, partial, and overlapping in an attempt upon common problems. Thus Olson is so confident about the method and consistency of Longinus that he deduces and fills in the "argument" of the lost portions of the treatise *Peri Hypsous*, amounting to more than a third of the whole. In the same spirit Professor William Keast, though confessing the weighty prima facie evidence to the contrary, undertakes to show a basic system of assumptions behind the varying critical pronouncements of Samuel Johnson.

It will be fair, and it will help the exposition, if I attempt a summary confession of my own critical principles. I am what Olson would call a "syncretist" (pp. 546–47), a person who tries to reconcile the good parts of various important theories and thus to make his own theory. I believe that there are three main poles of literary theory: (1) the mimetic or Aristotelian, which does justice to the world of things and real values and keeps our criticism from being merely idealistic; (2) the emotive (as seen, for instance, in Richards), which does justice to human response to values and keeps criticism from talking too much about either ethics or metaphysics; (3) the expressionistic and linguistic (par excellence, the Crocean), which does justice to man's knowledge as reflexive and creative and keeps criticism from talking about poetry as a literal recording of either things or responses. I believe that the second and the third of these poles are present in Aristotle along with the first, though the third, the expressionistic, is surely the weakest and least explicitly developed. I believe that these poles can be made the main points of reference for an indefinitely variable criticism of *all* poems. That is, there are no poems which are in some exclusively proper way "mimetic" and which hence should not be permitted a symbolic reading; and conversely, all "symbolic" poems, if they are real poems, are in some important sense "mimetic" and dramatic. Finally, I believe—in direct contradiction, as we shall see, of Chicago doctrine—that analogy and metaphor are not only in a broad sense the principle of all poetry but are also inevitable in practical criticism and will be present there in proportion as criticism moves beyond the historical report or the academic exercise.

III

One of McKeon's basic distinctions is that between (1) analogical, or dialectical, criticism—criticism which tries to connect poetry with anything else, with science, morals, philosophy, psychology, or linguistics (pp. 473, 530–43)—and (2) what he calls "literal" criticism, that which enables one to talk about poetry or some aspect of poetry and nothing else. There are several modes of literal criticism more or less incomplete and unscientific (the modes of Longinus, Horace, Richards, for instance), but there is also one which is full and scientific, one which actually defines poetry and its genres. This is the Aristotelian. And here comes a curious clause. The reason why

Aristotle's method has this great advantage is that it conceives a poem, or more precisely the mimetic form of poetry found in tragedy, as an object or thing, an "artificial thing," and moreover a thing determined in its unity and structure by a plot which is made up "of incidents, or more literally, of things" (p. 534). This, I say, is very curious. For if anything about poetry is clear at all it is that a poem is not really a thing, like a horse or a house, but only *analogically* so. The analogy I would maintain is a good one, highly instructive, and no doubt the only way by which criticism of a poem (rather than talk about its author and its audience or about its message) can be conducted. But at the same time, a poem is, if it is anything at all, a verbal discourse (a fact which Crane in his Introduction seems almost to doubt); hence it is a human act, physical and mental. The only "thing" is the poet speaking.[5] To treat this act of thought, feeling, and verbal expression not just in its psychological causes nor in its effects on hearers, nor yet in its abstract logical existence as communicable ideas merely, but precisely as a kind of solid "thing," an objectification of thought and feeling in verbal expression, is a requisite for critical thinking. This much one has to insist upon. But that is a long way from making a poem a literal nonverbal object. And it is a long way from making the criticism of the poem "literal" or "scientific" in any privileged sense. A modern critic might well ask what a "literal" theory as prescribed by McKeon can actually be if not a circularity. What can the predicate of a definition of poetry be if it does not contain terms drawn from the rest of human experience? A way of criticism which does not balk at so radical an analogy as that between poetic discourse and "thing" ought not to balk at other ways of trying to connect poetic discourse with the materials of life to which it refers.

It is a commonplace with the Chicago critics to assert that the critics they dislike deal only with "parts" of poems, not with the whole "objects." At the same time they assert that they themselves, the Chicago critics, are peculiarly devoted to the study of the concrete artistic whole (the Aristotelian *synolon*, p. 17). One would gather that Crane is somehow the inventor of modern holistic and organistic criticism, sole champion amid

a swarm of "Hellenistic-Roman-Romantic" connoisseurs of figures of speech and poetic diction. I think I may be excused
from the task of quoting passages from Richards, Brooks, or
Tate to demonstrate their concern for whole works of literary
art. Crane himself (p. 85) has quoted one such emphatic passage from Brooks.

It may be to the point, however, to attempt an explanation
of how the charge comes to be made. The reason, I venture to
say, is that the wholes contemplated by Crane and his friends
are, not only ideally but actually, those indicated by the main
and superficially inspectable shapes of works, those designated
by authors and publishers in their title pages—*Aureng-Zebe, a
Tragedy, Joan of Arc, an Epic Poem*—and by genre definitions
(a whole elegy, a whole didactic poem). Other critics, those
attacked by Crane, have shown a more marked tendency to
look on the larger architectural wholes as ideals to be recognized when encountered but also to be tested severely in their
parts. Faced with the frequent imperfection of such wholes,
these critics have been disposed to recognize the poetic whole
where they can find it, even though it is sometimes small and
nominally but a part of a larger whole which bears a clearer
external title. They have been not averse to finding good small
wholes inside good big wholes—for instance, speeches in Shakespearian plays. The holism of such modern critics as Eliot,
Richards, and Brooks (as, earlier, of Coleridge and the Germans) has been something not so much determined by size,
titles, and genre definitions as by the value principle of variety
in unity or the reconciliation of opposites; and hence it has been
something related quite practically to technical principles of
ambiguity, polysemy, paradox, and irony. Wholeness is not
just a form, but a form arising out of a certain kind of matter;
wholeness is a certain organization of meaning in words; it supposes a certain grade and intensity of meaning. Some clear contrasts to this philosophy emerge if we examine in detail the
performance of the Chicago critics. Thus, Olson rebukes Empson (p. 50) for not meaning it when he says that ambiguity
"must in each case arise from, and be justified by, the peculiar
requirements of the situation." But a few pages later (p. 73)

Olson announces that "language can be pleasing in itself, it has
an ornamental function in poetry as well." And to show that
this is no casual slip, in his later "Outline of Poetic Theory" he
expounds with Aristotelian aplomb: "Pleasure in poetry results
primarily from the imitation of the object and secondarily from
such embellishments as rhythm, ornamental language, and generally any such development of the parts as is naturally pleasing" (p. 556). "Masques, pageants, progresses, etc. are ornaments" (p. 563).

In the midst of an elaborate theory about poetic wholes and
a painstaking analysis of the "working or power" of the "plot"
of *Tom Jones,* Crane pauses to say that there are "qualities of
intelligence and moral sensibility" in the author "which are reflected in his conception and handling of the subject" but
which can be absent "no matter how excellent, in a formal
sense," the work may be (p. 623). "We clearly need other
terms and distinctions than those provided by a poetics of
forms if we are to talk discriminatingly about the general qualities of intelligence and feeling reflected in *Tom Jones*" (p. 646).
These pronouncements by Olson and Crane (whether correct
or incorrect) suggest that the writers have little conception of
the earnestness and thoroughness with which modern criticism
has embraced the doctrine of the "whole." None of the critics
attacked by the Chicago critics in this volume would come
even close to admitting the split between *form* on the one hand
and on the other *intelligence* and *feeling* which Crane so clearly
subscribes to. Nor would they, of course, have any part in
Olson's ornamentalism. It seems strange to me that Crane
should have raised the question of parts and whole against
those critics, and that he should hope to come out of an argument about it looking like a better holist than they.

IV

One of the central Chicago doctrines says that every poem
ought to be seen as belonging to a specific kind, species, or
genre of poems (tragic, comic, lyric, didactic) and ought to be

treated according to the "causes" which determine this specific kind. A poem should be treated as an instance not of poetry in general but of a specific kind of poetry. In some passages, as in Crane's Introduction (p. 15),[6] the Chicago critics deny that they mean to commit themselves to any antique rules of genre (the three unities, or the tragic protagonist of noble lineage), but these denials have very much the appearance of patches applied to a system which is basically different in texture. McKeon (p. 543) calls such an application of Aristotle a "perversion." It may well be a perversion of Aristotle, but it is one which is strongly invited by the Chicago reconstruction.

The attempt to criticize poetry by "species" goes along with the Chicago interest in objects or things. And so far as the Chicago philosophy is a reaction against positivism, process philosophy, and mere semantics (as it is clearly in Crane's essay on Richards[7] and near the beginning and end of McKeon's essay on the "Bases of Art and Criticism"), I am far from having any quarrel with it. But one does the philosophy of "things" no great service by attempting to revive anything like what has always been a "perversion" of that philosophy, the Hellenistic-Roman and neoclassic criticism by rules of genre. The place to defend things and species of things is in the areas where they are found, in the real world, especially the organic, not in that of verbal constructs. McKeon writes:

The differentiations of the scientific, practical, and artistic uses of language . . . do not depend . . . on classifying statements in fixed genera, as if they had natural forms, definitions, and species [p. 214].

The definitions of the virtues and of tragedy are not statements of the essences of "natural" things but rather of the formation of things which may be changed by human decision and choice [p. 219].

In the light of such statements it is difficult to see how either McKeon or his colleagues can really believe that poems are "things" or that they are divisible into clean-cut species.

It is true that as soon as we undertake to define or defend "poetry" or "poem" (as soon, that is, as we are convinced that there is any basic difference between types of discourse such as poetry, philosophy, or science), we are committed to some kind of "real" and "essential" inquiry. But, as in all our thinking, much depends on where we draw our main lines of discrimination and how many we draw. Literary critics in the Coleridgean tradition, if I understand them, have been Occamites with regard to literary entities and specific values. "Let not the categories be multiplied. We will defend the essential concept of poem, a work of verbal art, and insist that it applies always differently to an indefinite number of individual instances. The names of species (tragic, comic, lyric) will be neutral descriptive terms of great utility, but not different aesthetic essences and not points of reference for different sets of definable rules." The justice of this way of minimizing the essential lines cannot be deduced a priori. It must be seen if at all by experience. The cumulative experience of literary criticism does testify emphatically in favor of this way and against the neoclassic genres and the rules attached to them.

The rigidities of the Chicago system extend not only through the species and subspecies of literature but into certain accessory qualities which are no less definitely conceived as appearing overtly and uniformly through the main parts of a work or else simply as not appearing. The main one of these accessories with which the Chicago critics are preoccupied is "symbol." Toward the end of Olson's Socratic "Dialogue on Symbolism" occurs (pp. 589–93) a classification which I take the liberty of reducing to a table as follows:

MIMETIC POEM:
[Dramatic], narrative, lyric; the poet imitates whole actions; he aims at beauty, which results in pleasure.
 nonsymbolic (e.g., *The Odyssey*)
 symbolic (e.g., *Ulysses*)

DIDACTIC POEM:
The poet seeks to persuade us of some doctrine; the poem results in pleasure.
 nonsymbolic, e.g., allegory (e.g., Dante's *Commedia*)
 symbolic (e.g., Pound's *Cantos*)

SATIRE:
The poet seeks to convince us that something is ridiculous; [the poem results in pleasure].

ENTERTAINMENT:
The poet is concerned merely with giving pleasure; he furnishes only so much beauty or instruction as conduces to pleasure; subdivisions: comedy, sentiment, popular morality.

These are all the species and subspecies of poems. More precisely, didactic and mimetic are the only two serious or "real" species of poems. The two main emphases are on the difference between "mimetic" and "didactic" and on that between "symbolic" and "nonsymbolic." The point is that you can't go into a nonsymbolic poem with any bias of symbolism in your mind, and you can't go into either didactic or mimetic with any bias of the other. The parts and completeness of a mimetic poem depend upon an action. The parts and completeness of a didactic poem depend upon a doctrine. The prime example of a didactic poem is Dante's *Commedia,* and the didactic here assumes—the nonsymbolic form! It would be either wrong or unrewarding (Olson actually means this) to consider action or symbols in this poem!

The chief application of these distinctions is against modern critics—who "are likely to claim that all poetry is didactic, or something of the sort," and who are notoriously given to discovering symbols. Our volume furnishes us with two extended examples of the principle in action, the essay of Olson against R. P. Warren on *The Ancient Mariner* and that of Keast against Heilman on *Lear.* It appears to me that both Olson and Keast score some points. There is surely such a thing as extravagance in symbolic reading, and it will not be my aim here to adjudicate between the reviewers and the reviewed. What is wrong about the Chicago essays is the doctrinaire principle on which they are written. This comes out with sudden clarity at the end of Keast's. He announces that he will now present a final objection to Heilman's book, one that is "logically prior to all the others" and one which he has "reserved until now in order not to prejudice the discussion"—in other words, in order not to reveal that by prior commitment it was impossible for him to read Heilman's book.

Nothing in the text of the play, nothing in Shakespeare's habits as a dramatist, nothing in the circumstances of its composition and production, nothing in Elizabethan dramatic practice in general, nothing in the dramatic criticism of Shakespeare's day—nothing, in short, internal or external, suggests, or has been thought until recent years to suggest, that a literal reading of *King Lear* will fail to account for essential features of the play and that the tragedy must be interpreted, therefore, as an organized body of symbols [p. 136].

"Internal or external"—the arguments are different. If Keast thinks symbolism is irrevelant to a full appreciation of this play, that is a limitation of his reading which is without theoretical interest and which at any rate cannot be remedied here. Shakespeare's habits as a dramatist (that is, his other plays) are external to *Lear*, but Keast's reading of them is presumably subject to the same limitation as for *Lear*. And so for the rest of Elizabethan dramatic practice, though even if this were clearly and completely nonsymbolic, we might not have to conclude that Shakespeare had not improved on it. The remaining two external heads, the circumstances of composition and production and Elizabethan dramatic criticism, are things that might set up independently some sort of expectancy as to what would be found in a Shakespearian play. But that does not warrant any historical scholar in taking them as prescriptions for what he is going to find there, unless on the theory that writing for the Elizabethan theater precluded symbolism, or that (and here is the real intentionalistic crux) all critical insights stopped shortly after the time of Shakespeare and all sound theory had been developed by then. I am not at all sure that even this appeal to criticism will sustain Keast on his own terms. Some phrases of Sidney's general poetics begin to come to mind, about "images of virtues and vices" and the like. But if the criticism of Shakespeare has to be sanctioned by the casual and amateur echoes of Italian neoclassicism which prevailed among English critics of that day, what are we to say of the whole

history of Shakespearian criticism, not only Dryden and Coleridge but Maclean on *Lear* in this very volume?

V

One special notion entertained by the Chicago critics is that
the only alternative to a genre criticism is an escape into the
psychology of the author and reader. Thus they execute what
I shall call a double or slant antithesis, one which is not a true
or exclusive opposition. They say that, if criticism leaves the
species or kinds of poetry to search for the general definition of
poetry itself, then criticism leaves behind also the cognitive
object and passes into the realm of general psychology. They
seem to assume that there cannot be a general objective discussion of any topic. You have to divide it into its parts or species
in order to remain objective. If you try to pick up a pie whole,
it will melt into a plan for a pie or the taste of a pie. If you
cut it into slices, it will remain pie and *whole* pie. The argument might gain something in plausibility if we were able to
entertain that literal equation of poem with physical artifact
which has been criticized above. In the realm of artifacts, if
we were somehow constrained to talk only about "artifacts"
and never or little about "houses" and "hammers," the objects
of our discourse might conceivably tend (at least if we were
not on guard) to lose tangibility and become just qualities or,
by a further slip, just human aims and methods. But poems, as
we have said, are not physical artifacts; they are, to start with,
verbal acts. Their definition and defence have to be drawn
along a different line.

The kind of slant antithesis I have described is imputed by
the Chicago critics to two historical figures especially, Longinus
and Samuel Johnson, and to the whole eighteenth century with
its Longinian bias. Certain passages in the historical part of the
volume make the view much clearer than the argumentative
essays. Thus Keast:

[Johnson] is endeavoring to replace what he considers narrow principles with principles more commodious. And this endeavor regu-

larly leads him to forsake the view of art as manifesting itself in distinct species, a view presented in great detail in the treatises of his predecessors, for the ampler domain of nature. . . . Literary works, for Johnson, must be thought of not as specifically identifiable objects, instances of fixed classes of works, and embodying more or less perfectly an ideal form but as human acts to be judged *in relation to the agency of their production and appreciation* [p. 395; cp. pp. 401–406].[8]

And Maclean, in an essay which summarizes conveniently some of the main ideas of Olson's essay on Longinus:

[For Longinus] the totality of an individual poem (unless it be short) and the difference among kinds of poems are aesthetic considerations of little significance. Literary qualities that "transport" must, almost of necessity, occur in short and blinding passages and may occur in any literary genre (poetic, historical, philosophical, or rhetorical). In more modern language, Longinus is concerned not with poems or kinds of poems but with "poetry," or "pure poetry." . . . To Longinus . . . plot and character delineation were subsidiary interests. . . . The criticism of the last two centuries, as it has shifted over to a psychological basis, has likewise been marked by a subsidiary interest in plot and its needful agents [p. 413; cp. pp. 418, 421].

Maclean's essay is about the eighteenth century shift from the drama or narrative of action to the lyric of passion and image. This shift is seen by the Chicago critics partly as just a historical shift from a preference for one legitimate genre to a preference for another (lyric, we may remember, is one of Olson's subspecies of mimetic poems); but there is a tendency on the part of Maclean to see the shift as also a decline from the best or central genre to an inferior one, and furthermore as a shift, or an encouragement to a shift, out of poems and into the psychological sources of poems. The Chicago critics never come to the point of making the full mimesis of Aristotelian tragic theory a requirement for all poems, but there is a strong suggestion that such mimesis is the center of their poetics. And the Aristotelian *synolon,* or whole object, which *is* the avowed center of their poetics, is indeed best conceived as an external object when the poetic words refer to an action which can be so fully externalized as the Greek drama. At the romantic and lyrical end of the scale, the external action does tend to disappear; there remain the words, expressing emotions tied up with thoughts or with images.

And just here, it seems to me, the Chicago critics suffer one of their main failures of discrimination. They don't seem to distinguish between passion as objectified or embodied in poems—passion, that is, in its grounds and reasons as a public and negotiable "thing," the poem—and passion, along with intentions and other thoughts, as the psychological source of the poem, its inspiration, or "cause" in the efficient sense.[*] And it is quite important that one should do so. At different times in history it may have happened that a critic has been guilty of such a double shift as they describe, from specific poems to general psychology. I believe that Longinus actually executed some such maneuver. And I believe that Samuel Johnson's generalizing about works of literary art is accompanied by a strong inclination to psychologism. I admit too, and have maintained in print, that the romantic and lyric mind tends strongly to slip over into various genetic theories. But what then? Are we to say that all romantic and lyric poems are as weak as romantic inspirational and intentionalistic theory? And do we have to say that all generalizing about the "essence" of poem or even of poetry, rather than about that of tragedy or lyric, is bound to be psychological? As if there were no cognitive and objective generalities. The distinction I am trying to make clear is happily illustrated by a passage from a letter of Charles Lamb, quoted by Maclean as if it illustrated a kind of psychologism and geneticism which goes necessarily with an interest in lyric poetry. Lamb refused to accept Coleridge's corrections of his sonnets, because he thought a sonnet was too personal to be corrected by anybody but the author:

[*] The only one of the Aristotelian four "causes" which is still called a "cause" in ordinary speech. One source of obscurity in the Chicago writing is a resolute program of using "cause" indifferently and without explanation to mean *efficient* cause, *purpose, material,* and *form.*

I charge you, Col., spare my ewe lambs, and tho' a Gentleman may borrow six lines in an epic poem (I should make no objection to borrow 500 and without acknowledging) still in a Sonnet—a personal poem—I do not 'ask my friend the aiding verse.'

This is full romantic personalism and intentionalism. It is, as I have said, a likely enough attendant upon the lyric poetry of passion, but it is not a necessary attendant. Suppose Lamb had been willing to accept the changes Coleridge made in his sonnets—something by which the sonnets did not necessarily suffer. We should then have had romantic lyric poetry of passion *along with* an objective frame of mind about it.

My first point, then, concerning psychologism is that the Chicago critics are far too sweeping in their imputation of this vice to all modern critics in the Coleridgean tradition. My second point is that the Chicago critics themselves are more touched by it than they understand. It is quite clear that they want or believe they want to study the poem, not its origins or its results.[9] But two of the most important terms in the Chicago system are "pleasure" and "purpose." And if these terms have even in Aristotle some tendency away from poems toward genetic and affective psychology, they have it more decidedly for the Chicago critics.

To illustrate first their latent affectivism. A curious confusion appears in a device chosen by Crane against Brooks and by Olson against R. P. Warren. They say that Brooks and Warren have been unhappily influenced by a passage in Coleridge (*Biographia,* chap. XIV) which discusses "imagination" as a general power of the mind and "poetry" as a quality which may appear even in philosophy and theology. The influence has been unhappy because this kind of generalization refers only to faculties of the mind (poetic genius) rather than to poems. The passage in the same chapter of Coleridge to which an objective critic should rightly appeal is that in which Coleridge defines a "poem" as "that species of composition, which is opposed to works of science, by proposing for its *immediate* object pleasure, not truth." "It is at this point, with the introduction of ends," says Crane, "that Coleridge's criticism becomes specifically poetic" (p. 87). But pleasure, *not* truth! What becomes of the Aristotelian thing which was "more serious and more philosophic than history"? That particular statement by Coleridge, with its strong affective emphasis, does not actually go very well with his prevailing intentness upon the visionary dignity of the imagination. The imagination, even if it can appear in Plato and Jeremy Taylor, is after all the "synthetic and magical power" which constitutes poetic genius. I think the modern critics have done well to take the cognitive part of Coleridge's meaning and keep away from the affective lapses.°

As for the other kind of psychologism, the genetic, the case against the Chicago critics is simpler. They are always ready to appeal outside the poem to the intention of the poet. Their point of reference for the unity, the design, the end, of a poetic composition is so heavily schematized that it is almost bound to lie outside the composition itself—in the name or theory, for instance, of some poetic "species." We have already seen Keast's confession of the extent to which Elizabethan theory limits his own reading of *Lear*. Set beside this the following from Olson's "Dialogue":

And you would say that the parts and the whole are regulated by the moral doctrine and selected and shown in reference to it?
I would, since Dante himself says so [p. 590].

This intentionalistic principle can be seen clearly at work in a feature of the Chicago system which I have mentioned in my discussion of parts and whole. I mean the Chicago critics' extreme mistrust of the technique of verbal analysis which other modern critics have cultivated with such nicety. The Chicago critics are likely enough to assert that "the words are all we

° And I do not see why any modern critic should have to make a great deal of the statement, quoted of course by Crane, that no poem of any length either can or ought to be "all poetry." This makes "poetry" like a fluid or a dough, but with the embarrassing complication that a "poem" is a cake which is in part made of poetic dough, but not altogether. The relation between the mold (poetic form) and the dough (poetic material) is, as in the kitchen, quite superficial. This was what happened to Coleridge through juggling with genius, poem, and pleasure. Cp. the comment of Shawcross in *Biographia Literaria* (Oxford, 1907), II, 268.

have to go by, they alone disclose the poem to us" (Olson, p. 72; cp. p. 254), or that "there is no sharp line to separate the formula expressive of meaning from the meaning expressed in formula" (McKeon, p. 188; cp. pp. 192, 209, 212).[10] But they are likely at the same time to argue that one ought not to try to get into a play "from the outside in" (Keast, p. 121), as if there were any other way to get inside something. They will speak of "plot, the prime part of tragedy" as something "beautiful" in itself (Olson, p. 556). And having in mind clearly the poet himself rather than the poem or the reader, Olson will insist that the meaning "determines" and "governs" the words (p. 564) or is "presupposed" by them (p. 254). Both Crane and Olson argue repeatedly that the language is only the "means" of literary expression (as Aristotle said) or that it is the "matter" (as Scaliger put it).[11] Modern critics, in beginning with the language of poetry, neglect the larger things that loom behind and determine language, that is, plot, character, thought, and passions. When the Chicago critics say words are the "matter" of poetry, they mean that words are the matter of poetry in much the same way as wood is the material of a chair (p. 564) or steel the material of a saw (p. 62) or stone the material of a statue. The stone has the "form," borrowed from the external appearance of a man, imposed upon it. Presumably the words of a tragedy somehow have the form of the Oedipus story impressed upon them.

We might push this argument into a serious inquiry whether words really are the "matter" of a poem in the same way that stone is the material of a statue, and then we should have to discuss the peculiarly intimate relation between words and their meaning (convex and concave was Newman's fine image for it), and we should verge on the whole issue of expressionism, which the Chicago critics don't like. But I am stressing here the intentionalistic aspect. Olson and, echoing him recently, the Chicago sympathizer Hoyt Trowbridge say that if a critic begins with the words of a poem, it is just as if he were to say that "the shape and function of a saw are determined by the steel of which it is made."[12] But why wouldn't modern criticism of verbal meaning be more like saying that the goodness of a saw, its capacity to cut, is determined by the steel *fashioned in a certain shape?* I can't think of any modern critics who like to talk about just words and not their meanings and not the way the meanings are shaped together. The shaping of the words together is one main point of modern criticism. The Chicago argument depends on a mixup about form in the saw itself (in which the modern critic would surely be interested) and form (as intention) in the mind of the saw-maker (in which the modern critic might not be interested). The argument ought to talk about what makes the saw cut (that is, what the saw itself is); but the Chicago argument really talks about what made the saw become what it is, or rather about only part of that. For intention as intention didn't do the trick; intention had to be joined by skill. A man might intend a fine saw and make a botch of it.[13]

Both the intentionalism and the affectivism of the Chicago critical habit are protected from self-discovery and are capable of being projected upon other critics by virtue of an even more basic habit of mind which we have already discussed, the Chicago uncertainty whether their position is actually pluralistic or "dogmatic." This can be happily illustrated by two short quotations from Olson on successive pages:

Thus one aspect of art is its product; another, the instrumentality . . . which produced the product . . . another aspect is its production of a certain effect . . . upon those who are its spectators or auditors [p. 548].

Thus—to confine our illustrations to the various criticisms which deal with the product of art—we find criticisms differing as they center on either the subject matter of art or its medium or its productive cause or its end [p. 549].

That is to say, the productive cause of art and its end (its effect) are either not the same as the art product itself but separable topics (p. 548) or, on the contrary, they are aspects of the art taken precisely as art product (p. 549). And we will take them either way, as our own end happens to be either im-

puting noncritical psychologism to other modern critics or finding leeway for our own system. Neither the intentionalism nor
the affectivism of the Chicago critics ever, I believe, assumes
such rampant forms as Monroe Beardsley and I have been concerned to identify. The Chicago psychologism is rather a highly
theoretical dimension, a kind of reserve argument backing up
at a distance the abstractionism and apriorism of their concepts
of whole works and of labeled and firmly definable species of
works. Psychologism becomes in their thinking just the opposite of what they say it is, not the wholesale modern alternative
to classical genre criticism but an escape clause of genre criticism in its twentieth century Chicago version.

VI

The Chicago critics expect too much of their system, too
little (despite occasional protests to the contrary) of their own
capacity to read poems and respond to them. They are the
Scaligers, not the Aristotles, of modern criticism. Their program seems to me scarcely calculated to advance the cause
either of literary criticism or of a vital neo-Aristotelianism.
They have had little or nothing to say about the main issues
raised by what they call the "dialectical," rather than "literal,"
criticism of our time—the relations which poetry bears to religion, morals, philosophy, psychology, science, and language.
In short, they turn their backs on the whole modern critical
effort to scrutinize the relation of poetry to the rest of life.
They wish to construct a definition of poetry which will be
strictly self-contained—that is to say, circular.

Crane's Introduction complains that the Chicago critics have
before now been accused of such extreme and mutually inconsistent positions as, on the one hand, relativism and "aesthetic
atomism" and, on the other, "pseudo-Aristotelian formalism."
But something like these names will have to stand. The diversity of the charges results from the shiftiness of their tactics,
their pluralism devoted to removing the systems of other critics,
their dogmatism devoted to setting up their own instead. The

Chicago system grew out of two minds saturated with the history of ideas, Crane's and McKeon's, and the system remains, despite the "bold" reorientation toward criticism which Professor Wellek once kindly imputed to it, in one of its two main postures a historical one. It is difficult to know on which side of their general dialectic one ought to lay a concluding emphasis. But the union of their highly schematized dogmatism and their pluralism tempts me to let a Chicago critic write his own ending. Here are the final words of Olson's "Dialogue on Symbolism":

And he saw that there were many other approaches to the temple by ways not his and that these too offered a view, although a different view from his, and like it only in that they too were of reflections only. And, being a shadow, he was content; for the shadow must be content with the shadow of knowledge and rise as if full-fed from the shadow of food. Are you not also content?

I am content.

2

Nihil est autem esse, quam unum esse. Itaque in quantum quidque unitatem adipiscitur, in tantum est.—St. AUGUSTINE, De Moribus Manichaeorum, VI

THE CONCRETE UNIVERSAL

THE CENTRAL argument of this essay, concerning what I shall call the "concrete universal," proceeds from the observation that literary theorists have from early times to the present persisted in making statements which in their contexts seem to mean that a work of literary art is in some peculiar sense a very individual thing or a very universal thing or both. What that paradox can mean, or what important fact behind the paradox has been discerned by such various critics as Aristotle, Plotinus, Hegel, and Ransom, it will be the purpose of the essay to inquire, and by the inquiry to discuss not only a significant feature of metaphysical poetics from Aristotle to the present day but the relation between metaphysical poetics and more practical and specific rhetorical analysis. In the brief historical survey which forms one part of this essay it will not be my purpose to suggest that any of these writers meant exactly what I shall mean in later parts where I describe the structure of poetry. Yet throughout the essay I shall proceed on the theory not only that men have at different times used the same terms and have meant differently, but that they have sometimes used different terms and have meant the same or somewhat the same. In other words, I assume that there is continuity in the problems of criticism, and that à person who studies poetry today has a legitimate interest in what Plato said about poetry.

The view of common terms and their relations to classes of things from which I shall start is roughly that which one may read in the logic of J. S. Mill, a view which is not much different from the semantic view of today and for most purposes not much different from the Aristotelian and scholastic view. Mill speaks of the word and its denotation and connotation (the term, referent and reference, the sign, denotatum and designatum[1] of more recent terminologies). The denotation is the *it*, the individual thing or the aggregate of things to which the term may refer; the connotation is the *what*, the quality or classification inferred for the it, or implicitly predicated by the application of the term or the giving of the name.* One main difference between all modern positivistic, nominalistic, and semantic systems and the scholastic and classical systems is that the older ones stress the similarity of the individuals denoted by the common term and hence the real universality of meaning, while the modern systems stress the differences in the individuals, the constant flux even of each individual in time and space and its kinetic structure, and hence infer only an approximate or nominal universality of meaning and a convenience rather than a truth in the use of general terms. A further difference lies in the view of how the individual is related to the various connotations of terms which may be applied to it. That is, to the question: What is it? the older writers seem to hold there is but one (essentially right) answer, while the moderns accept as many answers as there are classes to which the individual may be assigned (an indefinite number). The older writers speak of a proper essence or whatness of the individual, a quality which in some cases at least is that designated by the class name most commonly applied to the

---

* The terms "denotation" and "connotation" are commonly and loosely used by literary critics to distinguish the dictionary meaning of a term (denotation) from the vaguer aura of suggestion (connotation). Both these are parts of the connotation in the logical sense.

individual: a bench is a bench, essentially a bench, accidentally a heavy wooden object or something covered with green paint. "When we say *what* it is," observes Aristotle, "we do not say 'white,' or 'hot,' or 'three cubits long,' but 'a man' or 'a god.'"[2] And this view is also a habit scarcely avoidable in our own daily thinking, especially when we think of living things or of artifacts, things made by us or our fellows for a purpose. What is it? Bench, we think, is an adequate answer. An assemblage of sticks painted green, we consider freakish.

II

Whether or not one believes in universals, one may see the persistence in literary criticism of a theory that poetry presents the concrete and the universal, or the individual and the universal, or an object which in a mysterious and special way is both highly general and highly particular. The doctrine is implicit in Aristotle's two statements that poetry imitates action and that poetry tends to express the universal. It is implicit again at the end of the classic period in the mystic doctrine of Plotinus, who in his later writing on beauty reverses the Platonic objection that art does not know the ultimate reality of the forms. Plotinus arrives at the view that the artist by a kind of bypass of the inferior natural productions of the world soul reaches straight to the forms that lie behind in the divine intelligence.[3] Another version of the classic theory, with affinities for Plotinus, lies in the scholastic phrase *resplendentia formae*.

Cicero's account of how Zeuxis painted an ideal Helen from the five most beautiful virgins of Crotona is a typical development of Aristotelian theory, in effect the familiar neoclassic theory found in Du Fresnoy's *Art of Painting*, in the writings of Johnson, especially in the tulip passage in *Rasselas*, and in the *Discourses* and *Idlers* of Reynolds. The business of the poet is not to number the streaks of the tulip; it is to give us not the individual, but the species. The same thing is stated in a more complicated way by Kant in telling how the imagination constructs the "aesthetical normal Idea":

It is the image for the whole race, which floats among all the variously different intuitions of individuals, which nature takes as archetype in her productions of the same species, but which seems not to be fully reached in any individual case.[4]

And Hegel's account is as follows:

The work of art is not only for the sensuous apprehension as sensuous object, but its position is of such a kind that as sensuous it is at the same time essentially addressed to the *mind*.[5]

In comparison with the show or semblance of immediate sensuous existence or of historical narrative, the artistic semblance has the advantage that in itself it points beyond self, and refers us away from itself to something spiritual which it is meant to bring before the mind's eye. . . . The hard rind of nature and the common world give the mind more trouble in breaking through to the idea than do the products of art.[6]

The excellence of Shakespeare, says Coleridge, consists in a "union and interpenetration of the universal and particular." In one terminology or another this idea of a concrete universal is found in most metaphysical aesthetic of the eighteenth and nineteenth centuries.

A modern literary critic, John Crowe Ransom, speaks of the argument of a poem (the universal) and a local texture or tissue of concrete irrelevance. Another literary critic, Allen Tate, manipulating the logical terms "extension" and "intension," has arrived at the concept of "tension" in poetry. "Extension," as logicians use the word, is the range of individuals denoted by a term (denotation); "intension" is the total of qualities connoted (connotation). In the ordinary or logical use of the terms, extension and intension are of inverse relationship—the wider the one, the shallower the other. A poem, says Tate, as I interpret him, is a verbal structure which in some peculiar way has both a wide extension and a deep intension.

Not all these theories of the concrete universal lay equal stress on the two sides of the paradox, and it seems indicative of the vitality of the theory and of the truth implicit in it that the two sides have been capable of exaggeration into antithetic schools and theories of poetry. For Du Fresnoy, Johnson, and Reynolds poetry and painting give the universal; the less said about the particulars the better. This is the neoclassic theory, the illustrations of which we seek in Pope's *Essay on Man* or in Johnson's *Ramblers,* where the ideas are moral and general and concerned with "nature," "one clear, unchanged, and universal light." The opposite theory had notable expression in England, a few years before Johnson wrote *Rasselas,* in Joseph Warton's *Essay on Pope:*

A minute and particular enumeration of circumstances judiciously selected, is what chiefly discriminates poetry from history, and renders the former, for that reason, a more close and faithful representation of nature than the latter.

And Blake's marginal criticism of Reynolds was: "THIS Man was Hired to Depress art." "To Generalize is to be an Idiot. To Particularize is the Alone Distinction of Merit. General Knowledges are those Knowledges that Idiots possess." "Sacrifice the Parts: What becomes of the whole?" The line from Warton's *Essay* to Croce's *Aesthetic* seems a straight and obvious one, from Thomson's specific descriptions of flowers to the individual act of intuition-expression which is art—its opposite and enemy being the concept or generality.[7] The two views of art (two that can be held by different theorists about the same works of art) may be startlingly contrasted in the following passages about fictitious character—one a well known statement by Johnson, the other by the philosopher of the *élan vital.*

[Shakespeare's] characters are not modified by the customs of particular places, unpractised by the rest of the world; by the peculiarities of studies or professions, which can operate but upon small numbers; or by the accidents of transient fashions or temporary opinions: they are the genuine progeny of common humanity, such as the world will always supply, and observation will always find. His persons act and speak by the influence of those general passions and principles by which all minds are agitated, and the whole system of life is continued in motion. In the writings of other poets a character is too often an individual; in those of Shakespeare it is commonly a species.

Hence it follows that art always aims at what is *individual*. What the artist fixes on his canvas is something he has seen at a certain spot, on a certain day, at a certain hour, with a colouring that will never be seen again. What the poet sings of is a certain mood which was his, and his alone, and which will never return. . . . Nothing could be more unique than the character of Hamlet. Though he may resemble other men in some respects, it is clearly not on that account that he interests us most.[8]

Other critics, notably the most ancient and the most modern, have tried to hold the extremes together. Neither of the extremes gives a good account of art and each leads out of art. The theory of particularity leads to individuality and originality (Edward Young was another eighteenth century Crocean), then to the idiosyncratic and the unintelligible and to the psychology of the author, which is not in the work of art and is not a standard for judgment. The theory of universality as it appears in Johnson and Reynolds leads to platitude and to a standard of material objectivity, the average tulip, the average human form, some sort of average.[9]

III

"Just representations of general nature," said Johnson, and it ought to be noted, though it perhaps rarely is, that two kinds of generality are involved, as indeed they are in the whole neoclassic theory of generality. There is the generality of logic or classification, of the more general as opposed to the more specific, "essential" generality, one might say. And there is the generality of literal truth to nature, "existential" generality. The assumption of neoclassic theory seems to be that these two must coincide. As a matter of fact they may and often do, but need not. Thus: "purple cow" is a more general (less specific) term and concept than "tan cow with a broken horn," yet the latter is more general or true to nature. We have, in short, realism or fantasy, and in either there may be various degrees of the specific or the general. We have *A Journal of the Plague Year* and *The Rambler*, *Gulliver's Travels* and *Rasselas*. The fact that there are a greater number of "vicissitudes" and "miscarriages" (favorite *Rambler* events) in human experience than plagues at London, that there are more tan cows than tan cows with broken horns, makes it true in a sense that a greater degree of essential generality involves a greater degree of existential. But in this sense the most generally reliable concept is simply that of "being."

The question is how a work of literature can be either more individual (unique) or more universal than other kinds of writing, or how it can combine the individual and the universal more than other kinds. Every description in words, so far as it is a direct description (The barn is red and square) is a generalization. That is the nature of words. There are no individuals conveyed in words but only more or less specific generalizations, so that Johnson is right, though we have to ask him what degree of verbal generality makes art, and whether "tulip" is a better or more important generality than "tulip with ten streaks," or whether "beauty" is not in fact a much more impressive generality than "tulip." On the other hand, one cannot deny that in some sense there are more tulips in poetry than pure abstracted beauty. So that Bergson is right too; only we shall have to ask him what degree of specificity in verbal description makes art. And he can never claim complete verbal specificity or individuality, even for Hamlet.

If he could, if a work of literary art could be looked on as an artifact or concrete physical work, the paradox for the student of universals would return from the opposite direction even more forcibly—as it does in fact for theorists of graphic art. If Reynolds' picture "The Age of Innocence" presents a species or universal, what species does it present? Not an Aristotelian essence—"man," or "humanity," nor even a more specific kind of being such as "womanhood." For then the picture would present the same universal as Reynolds' portrait of Mrs. Siddons as "The Tragic Muse," and all differences between "The Age of Innocence" and "The Tragic Muse" would be aesthetically irrelevant. Does the picture then present girlhood, or barefoot girlhood, or barefoot girlhood in a white dress against a gloomy background? All three are equally valid universals (despite the fact that makeshift phrases are required to express two of them), and all three are presented by the picture. Or is it the title which tells us what universal is presented, "The Age of Innocence," and without the title should we not know the universal? The question will be: What in the individual work of art demands that we attribute to it one universal rather than another?

We may answer that for poetry it is the generalizing power of words already mentioned, and go on to decide that what distinguishes poetry from scientific or logical discourse is a degree of irrelevant concreteness in descriptive details. This is in effect what Ransom says in his doctrine of argument and local irrelevance, but it seems doubtful if the doctrine is not a version of the theory of ornamental metaphor. The argument, says Ransom, is the prose or scientific meaning, what the poem has in common with other kinds of writing. The irrelevance is a texture of concreteness which does not contribute anything to the argument but is somehow enjoyable or valuable for its own sake, the vehicle of a metaphor which one boards heedless of where it runs, whether crosstown or downtown—just for the ride. So Ransom nurses and refines the argument, and on one page he makes the remark that the poet searches for "suitability" in his particular phrases, and by suitability Ransom means "the propriety which consists in their denoting the particularity which really belongs to the logical object."[10] But the difference between "propriety" and relevance in such a context is not easy to see. And relevance is logic. The fact is that all concrete illustration has about it something of the irrelevant. An apple falling from a tree illustrates gravity, but apple and tree are irrelevant to the pure theory of gravity. It may be that what happens in a poem is that the apple and the tree are somehow made more than usually relevant.

Such a theory, not that of Johnson and Reynolds, not that of Warton and Bergson, not quite that of Ransom, is what I would suggest—yet less as a novelty than as something already widely

implicit in recent poetical analyses and exegeses, in those of
Empson, for instance, Tate, Blackmur, or Brooks. If a work of
literature is not in a simple sense either more individual or
more universal than other kinds of writing, it may yet be such
an individual or such a complex of meaning that it has a special
relation to the world of universals. Some acute remarks on this
subject were made by Ruskin in a chapter of *Modern Painters*
neglected today perhaps because of its distasteful ingredient of
"noble emotion." Poetry, says Ruskin in criticizing Reynolds'
Idlers, is not distinguished from history by the omission of details, nor for that matter by the mere addition of details.
"There must be something either in the nature of the details
themselves, or the method of using them, which invests them
with poetical power." Their nature, one may add, as assumed
through their relation to one another, a relation which may also
be called the method of using them. The poetic character of
details consists not in what they say directly and explicitly (as
if roses and moonlight were poetic) but in what by their arrangement they *show* implicitly.

IV

"One," observes Ben Jonson, thinking of literature, "is considerable two waies: either, as it is only separate, and by it
self: or as being compos'd of many parts it beginnes to be one
as those parts grow or are wrought together."[11] A literary work
of art is a complex of detail (an artifact, if we may be allowed
that metaphor for what is only a verbal object), a composition
so complicated of human values that its interpretation is dic-
tated by the understanding of it, and so complicated as to seem
in the highest degree individual—a concrete universal. We are
accustomed to being told, for example, that what makes a
character in fiction or drama vital is a certain fullness or ro-
tundity: that the character has many sides. Thus E. M. Forster:

We may divide characters into flat and round. Flat characters were
called "humours" in the seventeenth century, and are sometimes
called types, and sometimes caricatures. In their purest form, they

are constructed round a single idea or quality: when there is more than one factor in them, we get the beginning of the curve towards the round. The really flat character can be expressed in one sentence such as "I never will desert Mr. Micawber."

It remains to be said, however, that the many traits of the round character (if indeed it is one character and not a hodgepodge) are harmonized or unified, and that if this is so, then all the traits are chosen by a principle, just as are the traits of the flat character. Yet it cannot be that the difference between the round and flat character is simply numerical; the difference cannot be merely that the presiding principle is illustrated by more examples in the round character. Something further must be supposed—a special interrelation in the traits of the round character. Bobadil is an example of the *miles gloriosus*, a flat humour. He swears by "The foot of Pharaoh," takes tobacco, borrows money from his landlady, is found lying on a bench fully dressed with a hangover, brags about his feats at the siege of Strigonium, beats Cob a poor water carrier, and so on. It is possible that he has numerically as many traits as Falstaff, one of the most vital of all characters. But one of the differences between Falstaff and Bobadil is that the things Falstaff says are funny; the things Bobadil says are not. Compared to Falstaff, Bobadil is unconscious, an opaque butt. There is the vitality of consciousness in Falstaff. And further there is the crowning complexity of self-consciousness. The fact that Morgann could devote a book to arguing that Falstaff is not a coward, that lately Professor Wilson has argued that at Gadshill Falstaff may exhibit " 'all the common symptoms of the malady' of cowardice" and at the same time persuade the audience that he has " 'never once lost his self-possession,' " the fact that one can conceive that Falstaff in the Gadshill running-away scene really knows that his assailants are the Prince and Poins—all this shows that in Falstaff there is a kind of interrelation among his attributes, his cowardice, his wit, his debauchery, his presumption, that makes them in a special way an organic harmony. He is a rounded character not only in the sense that he is gross (a fact which may have tempted critics to speak of a rounded character) or in the sense that he is a bigger bundle of attributes, stuffed more full, than Bobadil or Ralph Roister Doister; but in the sense that his attributes make a circuit and connection. A kind of awareness of self (a high and human characteristic), with a pleasure in the fact, is perhaps the central principle which instead of simplifying the attributes gives each one a special function in the whole, a double or reflex value. Falstaff or such a character of self-conscious "infinite variety"* as Cleopatra are concrete universals because they have no class names, only their own proper ones, yet are structures of such precise variety and centrality that each demands a special interpretation in the realm of human values.

Character is one type of concrete universal; there are other types, as many perhaps as the central terms of criticism; but most can be learned I believe by examination of metaphor—the structure most characteristic of concentrated poetry. The language of poets, said Shelley, "is vitally metaphorical: that is, it marks the before unapprehended relations of things and perpetuates their apprehension." Wordsworth spoke of the abstracting and modifying powers of the imagination. Aristotle said that the greatest thing was the use of metaphor, because it meant an eye for resemblances. Even the simplest form of metaphor or simile ("My love is like a red, red rose") presents us with a special and creative, in fact a concrete, kind of abstraction different from that of science. For behind a metaphor lies a resemblance between two classes, and hence a more general third class. This class is unnamed and most likely remains unnamed and is apprehended only through the metaphor. It is a new conception for which there is no other expression. Keats discovering Homer is like a traveler in the realms of gold, like an astronomer who discovers a planet, like Cortez gazing at the Pacific. The title of the sonnet, "On First Looking into Chapman's Homer," seems to furnish not so much the subject of the poem as a fourth member of a central meta-

---

* I do not mean that self-consciousness is the only principle of complexity in character, yet a considerable degree of it would appear to be a requisite for poetic interest.

phor, the real subject of the poem being an abstraction, a certain kind of thrill in discovering, for which there is no name and no other description, only the four members of the metaphor pointing, as to the center of their pattern. The point of the poem seems to lie outside both vehicle and tenor.

To take a more complicated instance, Wordsworth's "Solitary Reaper" has the same basic metaphorical structure, the girl alone reaping and singing, and the two bird images, the nightingale in Arabian sands and the cuckoo among the Hebrides, the three figures serving the parallel or metaphorical function of bringing out the abstraction of loneliness, remoteness, mysterious charm in the singing. But there is also a kind of third-dimensional significance, in the fact that one bird is far out in the northern sea, the other far off in southern sands, a fact which is not part of the comparison between the birds and the girl. By an implication cutting across the plane of logic of the metaphor, the girl and the two birds suggest extension in space, universality, and world communion—an effect supported by other details of the poem such as the overflowing of the vale profound, the mystery of the Erse song, the bearing of the song away in the witness' heart, the past and future themes which the girl may be singing. Thus a central abstraction is created, of communion, telepathy in solitude, the prophetic soul of the wide world dreaming on things to come—an abstraction which is the effect not wholly of the metaphor elaborated logically (in a metaphysical way) but of a working on two axes, by association rather than by logic, by a three-dimensional complexity of structure.

To take yet a third instance, metaphoric structure may appear where we are less likely to realize it explicitly—in poetic narratives, for example, elliptically concealed in the more obvious narrative outlines. "I can bring you," writes Max Eastman, "examples of diction that is metrical but not metaphoric —a great part of the popular ballads, for example—and you can hardly deny that they too are poetic." But the best story poems may be analyzed, I believe, as metaphors without expressed tenors, as symbols which speak for themselves. "La

Belle Dame Sans Merci," for example (if a literary ballad may
be taken), is about a knight, by profession a man of action, but
sensitive, like the lily and the rose, and about a faery lady with
wild, wild eyes. At a more abstract level, it is about the loss of
self in the mysterious lure of beauty—whether woman, poetry,
or poppy. It sings the irretrievable departure from practical
normality (the squirrel's granary is full), the wan isolation
after ecstasy. Each reader will experience the poem at his own
level of experience or at several. A good story poem is like
a stone thrown into a pond, into our minds, where ever widening concentric circles of meaning go out—and this because of
the structure of the story.

"A poem should not mean but be." It is an epigram worth
quoting in every essay on poetry. And the poet "nothing af-
firmeth, and therefore never lieth." "Sit quidvis," said Horace,
"simplex dumtaxat et unum." It seems almost the reverse of
the truth. "Complex dumtaxat et unum" would be better.
Every real poem is a complex poem, and only in virtue of its
complexity does it have artistic unity. A newspaper poem by
Edgar Guest° does not have this kind of unity, but only the
unity of an abstractly stated sentiment.

The principle is expressed by Aristotle when he says that
beauty is based on unity in variety, and by Coleridge when he
says that "The Beautiful, contemplated in its essentials, that is,
in *kind* and not in *degree,* is that in which the *many,* still seen
as many becomes one," and that a work of art is "rich in proportion to the variety of parts which it holds in unity."

° A reader whose judgment I esteem tells me that such a name appears in a
serious discussion of poetics anomalously and in bad taste. I have allowed it
to remain (in preference to some more dignified name of mediocrity) precisely
because I wish to insist on the existence of badness in poetry and so to establish
an antithetic point of reference for the discussion of goodness. Relativistic
argument often creates an illusion in its own favor by moving steadily in a
realm of great and nearly great art. See, for example, George Boas, *A Primer
for Critics* (Baltimore, 1937), where a cartoon by Daumier appears toward the
end as a startling approach to the vulgar. The purpose of my essay is not
judicial but theoretical, that is, not to exhibit original discoveries in taste, but
to show the relationship between examples acknowledged to lie in the realms
of the good and the bad.

V

It is usually easier to show how poetry works than to show why anyone should want it to work in a given way. Rhetorical analysis of poetry has always tended to separate from evaluation, technique from worth. The structure of poems as concrete and universal is the principle by which the critic can try to keep the two together. If it be granted that the "subject matter" of poetry is in a broad sense the moral realm, human actions as good or bad, with all their associated feelings, all the thought and imagination that goes with happiness and suffering (if poetry submits "the shews of things to the desires of the Mind"), then the rhetorical structure of the concrete universal, the complexity and unity of the poem, is also its maturity or sophistication or richness or depth, and hence its value. Complexity of form is sophistication of content. The unity and maturity of good poems are two sides of the same thing. The kind of unity which we look for and find in poetry is attained only through a degree of complexity in design which itself involves maturity and richness. For a visual diagram of the metaphysics of poetry one might write vertically the word complexity, a column, and give it a head with Janus faces, one looking in the rhetorical direction, unity, and the other in the axiological, maturity.

A final point to be made is that a criticism of structure and of value is an objective criticism. It rests on facts of human psychology (as that a man may love a woman so well as to give up empires), facts, which though psychological, yet are so well acknowledged as to lie in the realm of what may be called public psychology—a realm which one should distinguish from the private realm of the author's psychology and from the equally private realm of the individual reader's psychology (the vivid pictures which poetry or stories are supposed to create in the imagination, or the venerable action of catharsis —all that poetry is said to *do* rather than to *be*). Such a criticism, again, is objective and absolute, as distinguished from the relative criticism of idiom and period. I mean that this criticism will notice that Pope is different from Shakespeare, but will notice even more attentively that Shakespeare is different from Taylor the Water Poet and Pope different from Sir Richard Blackmore. Such a criticism will be interested to analyze the latter two differences and see what these differences have in common and what Shakespeare and Pope have in common, and it will not despair of describing that similarity (that formula or character of great poetry) even though the terms be abstract and difficult. Or, if we are told that there is no universal agreement about what is good—that Pope has not been steadily held in esteem, that Shakespeare has been considered a barbarian, the objective analyst of structures can at least say (and it seems much to say) that he is describing a class of poems, those which through a peculiar complexity possess unity and maturity and in a special way can be called both individual and universal. Among all recorded "poems," this class is of a relative rarity, and further this class will be found in an impressive way to coincide with those poems which have by some body of critics, some age of educated readers, been called great.

The function of the objective critic is by approximate descriptions of poems, or multiple restatements of their meaning, to aid other readers to come to an intuitive and full realization of poems themselves and hence to know good poems and distinguish them from bad ones. It is of course impossible to tell all about a poem in other words. Croce tells us, as we should expect him to, of the "impossibility of ever rendering in logical terms the full effect of any poetry or of other artistic work." "Criticism, nevertheless," he tells us, "performs its own office, which is to discern and to point out exactly where lies the poetical motive and to formulate the divisions which aid in distinguishing what is proper to every work."[12] The situation is something like this: In each poem there is something (an individual intuition—or a concept) which can never be expressed in other terms. It is like the square root of two or like pi, which cannot be expressed by rational numbers, but only as their *limit*. Criticism of poetry is like 1.414 . . . or 3.1416 . . ., not all it would be, yet all that can be had and very useful.

Il n'est point de serpent ni de monstre odieux
Qui, par l'art imité, ne puisse plaire aux yeux.
—BOILEAU, *L'Art Poétique*

POETRY
AND MORALS

A RELATION REARGUED

THE ANCIENT question whether poetry can appear independently of morals does not lack current answers, both affirmative and negative, and both earnestly argued. The separation of the beautiful and the good, urges one school, is a "fundamental self-deception which vitiates and depraves the very center" of the artist's character, "the fountains whence his energies as a human personality spring."[1] For this unified view of values I would at the outset confess my serious sympathy. It is difficult to dissent from it with thorough complacency. On the other hand the champions of the opposite view—most notably Professors Maritain and Adler—have assured us that "The artist is necessarily autonomous in his own sphere." It is in this direction that I myself would argue, yet I should sympathize with a critic of poetry who might argue that the *necessity* of this view is far from clear, that the solution is too smooth and triumphant. The same view has been advanced with great delicacy (if some wavering) by the distinguished poet and literary arbiter T. S. Eliot, yet it has suffered, I believe, on the whole from seeming to lack relevance to an art such as poetry, made of words and ideas, and notorious for imbroglios with

all sorts of moral interest. It will be the purpose of this essay
to inquire how in fact the doctrine of aesthetic autonomy *can*
apply to poetry. And first by noticing some related but distinct
issues, and then some alternative solutions to the proper issue.

Poetry, said Plato, in effect, is a kind of inspired ignorance;
it stands at two removes from the truth; it is furthermore at
fault in that it feeds and waters the passions. He drew a decided distinction between poetic quality and moral results.
"The greater the poetic charm . . . the less are they meet for
the ears of boys and men who are meant to be free." The conclusion was on the whole decidedly moral. Somewhere, in some
Utopian state, a truthful and moral poetry might occur. But
poetry as Plato had actually known it was intolerable. "And
so when we have anointed him with myrrh and set a garland
of wool upon his head, we shall send him away to another
city."

There, at the start of the tradition, we have at least three
main propositions (or bundles of related propositions) which
anyone entering upon a discussion of poetry and morals might
well distinguish and number for convenient reference.

Ia. Poetry has philosophic content—images and their interpretation—possibly true and moral, usually false and immoral.

Ib. The poetic value of poetry is not the same as or even
strictly determined by its truth or morality.

IIa. Poetry has moral power; that is, it produces moral effects
on those who hear it—possibly for good, mostly for evil.

IIb. The poetic value of poetry is not the same as or even
strictly determined by its moral effect.

III. Both philosophico-moral content and moral effect have
a claim on our allegiance which is prior to the claim of
poetic value.

It will be observed that the second pair of propositions, IIa
and IIb, concern what poetry *does*, its persuasory and contagious effect, but not as such what poetry *says* or is, poetry
objectively considered as a body of cognitive and analyzable
meaning. The first pair of propositions, Ia and Ib, consider

just this body of meaning. Ib, asserting the difference between
the poetic and the moral value of meaning, is the crucial
proposition which a certain school of moralists, Hamm among
them, would deny. Proposition III, the rule of arbitration between poetry and morals, follows from the concept of morals.
Yet the very meaning of this proposition, it is worth noting,
depends largely on Ib. If Ib is not true, III can relate only to
what poetry *does*. If poetry is not cognitively separable from
morals, if one makes no distinction between poetic meaning
and moral meaning, there can be no cognitive and intrinsic conflict: the poet in being moral is only following the rule of his
craft. Not III, of course, but the vindication of its premise in
Ib is the concern of the critic. Let the moralist assert that
poetry *should* be moral. The critic would ask whether poetry
need be moral in order to be poetry.

Moral critique of poetry has often forced proposition III into
close conjunction with the two affective propositions IIa and
IIb. From poetry, said Stephen Gosson, the English Plato of
1579, we advance to piping, "from pyping to playing, from play
to pleasure, from pleasure to slouth, from slouth to sleepe, from
sleepe to sinne, from sinne to death, from death to the Divel."
Such complaints, it should be said at the start, are not what
the theorist of poetry would discuss, nor any of the like moral
and political issues which arise from propositions IIa, IIb, and
III, the most frequent issues of conscience and censorship—the
chief concern of Adler in his *Art and Prudence*. Again, it should
be said that the issue for the theorist is not that of the author's
personal morals or philosophy. It may be true, as Hamm has
asserted, that "a literary work can never be indifferent morally
in its origins." It is certainly not true, as Adler has asserted,
that "intrinsic" criticism of art is that which "regards the work
in relation to the artist." We inquire now not about origins,
nor about effects, but about the work so far as it can be considered by itself as a body of meaning. Neither the qualities
of the author's mind nor the effects of a poem upon a reader's
mind should be confused with the moral quality of the meaning
expressed by the poem itself.

II

To take up the issue between poetry and morals at the cognitive level, it is to be observed that if Platonic proposition Ib, asserting the separability of poetry and morals, is not true, then one of two extremely unified and simplified views or claims will follow—or have followed at various times. Either (1) morals reaches over and claims poetry—not simply as superior to poetry but as defining poetry; or (2) poetry reaches over and claims to define morals. We have seen the second view in such romantic and postromantic statements as that of Shelley, "Poets are the unacknowledged legislators of the world," or in the system of Matthew Arnold, where poetry is a "criticism of life." "More and more mankind will discover that we have to turn to poetry to interpret life for us, to console us, to sustain us. Without poetry, our science will appear incomplete; and most of what now passes with us for religion and philosophy will be replaced by poetry." More recent psychological and anthropological theories of poetry have tended to continue in this direction. It is easy to see that a morality of this sort, determined by poetry, is not really a morality in the sense of a code, but a relative morality of almost indefinite diversity and flexibility—for such is poetry—and that hence what theorists of this school mean in the end is that they do not subscribe to a code. For these we may say that in the large sense the problem to be discussed in this essay does not exist, since there is no distinction between, and hence no need of explaining the relation between, poetry and morals.

Nor does the problem really exist for those of the other school, who deny Platonic proposition Ib for an opposite reason and make poetic value depend upon moral value: Sir Philip Sidney, for instance, when he answers Gosson with the argument that poetry is a "feigning notable images of virtues [and] vices,"[2] or Rymer and Dennis a century later, the school of "poetic justice," or the Earl of Roscommon in his couplet:

> Immodest words admit of no Defence,
> For want of Decency is want of Sense.

Among recent statements of the moral view the most extreme is perhaps that of Arthur Machen: "Literature is the expression, through the aesthetic medium of words, of the dogmas of the Catholic Church, and that which is out of harmony with these dogmas is not literature." More moderately the late Irving Babbitt and other neohumanists have said that poetry gives ethical insight.

If the Arnoldian view, as we have seen, leaves morals in a bad way, it should be equally clear that the rigorous moral view not only leaves little to the critic of poetry in his own right (a loss which might perhaps have to be overlooked) but also makes a vast invasion into the usually recognized canon of the world's poetry—so much of it is in one way or another immoral. One cannot really refute Plato. Or to put this more moderately and without the unhappy implication that a great part of the world's best literature is substantially evil, let us say that a moral code must be by its nature too rigid to accommodate, or at least too rigid to account for or specifically sanction, the widely heterogeneous concreteness of the world's recognized poetry. There is no religion or philosophy that will embrace Homer's heroes and gods, the fatalism of Greek tragedy, the atomism of Lucretius, the Heaven, Purgatory, and Hell of Dante, the Senecan Stoicism of Shakespeare, the occultism—what has seemed to many the diabolism—of Milton, the world soul of Wordsworth, the flowers of evil of Baudelaire. The choice between poetry and morals is not specifically a Christian one—though today in the Western world it may be felt most acutely by a serious Christian. It is the choice which appears for any moralist—for Plato banishing the poets from the city, for Tolstoy in his old age repudiating all of his own work except two of his simplest short stories, for the totalitarian Marxist—except that for the Marxist there is no nice problem. He simply rejects—almost everything.

III

This essay is an attempt to express the point of view of one who accepting a moral code would yet save poetic value—not as superior to moral value but as different from it. And it is not easy—in a full and thoughtful way—to affirm Platonic proposition Ib and escape between the relaxed simplification of the Arnoldian and the severe one of the moralist. A long tradition, beginning with Plato and with the separation by Aristotle of his *Poetics* from his *Ethics*, testifies to the utility of the distinction between poetry and morals. Today the moralist will often make the distinction quite casually:

> Just as an engineer may not construct and approve a bridge, the durability of which he doubts for the load he knows his clients will attempt to transport over it; and just as a chef may not serve food which he knows is even partially on the way to corruption and which might presently cause distress or worse to the consumer,—so also the poet or writer may not express anything, *however beautifully*, which both he and his critics have reason to believe will be subversive to thought or action on the part of him who reads it.[3]

Yet it is not easy, especially when the moralist phrases it, to see how this distinction can be seriously maintained. The bridge which was destined to fall might *look* well when inspected, but looks are surely not a profound test of a bridge. The bridge would simply be a bad bridge. The food might *taste* well before making the eater ill, and here is a more plausible resemblance to what is maintained about beautiful but dangerous poetry. The food answers one important (if specious) requirement of good food. But how can poetry, which concerns good and evil, which is an intellectual art and which exists and has quality only in being understood, be both beautiful and morally destructive? Here one must indeed agree with Hamm: "Language, unlike marble, pigments and musical sounds, is immediately and essentially expressive of ideas. . . . The literary artist expresses implicit moral judgments."[4] Few, if any, important poems are simply imagistic. The late Dr. Temple, Archbishop of Canterbury, in a lecture on literature found "Hardy's great masterpiece, 'Tess of the D'Urbervilles'" to be "among the worst books ever committed to paper." He was unable to yield "to the undoubted artistic power that is displayed by Hardy in that great artistic achievement." Upon which a writer in the *Times Literary Supplement* observed:

"The relationship of truth and beauty makes it impossible to accept that . . . a 'great masterpiece' can be numbered among the 'worst books ever committed to paper.' A masterpiece is not made by phrases, decorations and patterns; these qualities are imposed by the wisdom in their content." This, one might say, is a pronounced step in the Arnoldian direction. Yet the point of it cannot be overlooked. The problem has been made more acute in our day by schools of psychological criticism and of exhaustive rhetorical exegesis which have taught us to find the beauty of poems by sifting them to their minutest scruples of meaning. What Plato saw as the evil of poetry, the mixture of its emotions and the confusion of its advice, has become now, under such names as ironic "tension" and "synaesthesis," the richness of aesthetic value.

A hint at a solution was offered by Aristotle in his *Rhetoric* when he said that imitation is pleasant "even if the object imitated is not itself pleasant; for it is not the object itself which here gives delight—the spectator draws inferences ('That is a so-and-so') and thus learns something fresh." And the notion has been reiterated in diverse places—for example, in Plutarch's essay *How a Young Man Should Study Poetry,* in the *Summa Theologiae* of St. Thomas ("Imago dicitur esse pulchra, si perfecte repraesentat rem, quamvis turpem"), in Boileau's *Art Poétique,* in a *Spectator* on Imagination by Joseph Addison ("The Description of a Dunghill is pleasing . . . if the Image be represented to our Minds by suitable Expressions"). Today the same notion is invoked to justify the historical study of literature: the scholar, says Professor H. N. Fairchild, "can admire a fine statement of a detestable fallacy in the spirit of a surgeon who speaks of a 'beautiful tumour.'" A refined version of the theory is thus defined by Maritain:

The artist takes for stuff and substance of his work whatever is most profound, most exalted and most vile, the moral life of man, the heart of man "hollow and full of filth"—and the rarest passions and the life of the spirit itself, nay, the Gospel and sanctity, everything; but with it all an absolute prohibition, upon pain of committing a sacrilege against art, against pursuing any other end than the pure delight, order, richness, tranquillity and rapture, which the soul ought to savour in the work. This is no longer art *on nothing* as in the theory of gratuitousness in its first form; but art *for nothing*, for nothing but art's sake.

Maritain does not subscribe to this view, but in another place he himself has said: "Art . . . comes into the midst of our hierarchies like a moon prince whom etiquette has not foreseen, and who embarrasses all the masters of ceremonies. . . . It can be mad and remain art." This is all very well. It should be obvious from what has been said so far that the argument of this essay tends rather in this direction than in the opposite. Yet such an explanation certainly runs the risk of leaving the poem in a posture of serious embarrassment. If poetry can say what is vile and full of filth as well as what is exalted and sacred—if it can even be mad—then it would seem to make no difference what poetry says. The theory must be another version of imitation for the sake of imitation—of art as sheer form —a theory of external rhetoric.

IV

The main thesis of Plato's *Phaedrus* is that an ideal rhetoric or art of using words would by dialectic and a certain inspiration rise to the level of philosophy—that is, would deal with truth. Actual rhetoric, that of the sophists, what was known to Socrates, was not an art—had no contact with the truth—for it could be put to purposes of deception. This view of rhetoric and implicitly of poetry followed from the Socratic ethic, where virtue was wisdom. If to know was to do, then that which did wrong (rhetoric) did not know. The ethic of Aristotle was, on the other hand, a step away from the ethic of sheer wisdom, and accordingly Aristotle is able, both in his *Poetics* and in his *Rhetoric*, to say more than Plato in favor of verbal art as it was actually practiced. Rhetoric is a power which, like all other powers except virtue itself, can be misused. The misuse lies not in the art but in the moral purpose. Book III, chapters 1-13, of Aristotle's *Rhetoric*, on the devices of verbal style, is the natural complement of this basic view.

An idea of verbal rhetoric as distinct from the pith and worth of what is meant by words is thus from the start intrinsic to the theory of separable poetic and moral values which we have sketched so far and which we are struggling to improve. And something indeed may be said on the score of merely verbal rhetoric, and should be said here, though with the distinct reservation that such rhetoric must be far from enough to permit any important or profound distinction between poetic and moral values. It is possible to name certain formal levels of expression which, though intimately bound up with and deriving their value only from their relation to the stated meaning, are yet not parts of this meaning in the sense that they always add to it or in their absence subtract from it. Under this head come the various forms of syntactic and phonetic support of statement (the *parisosis* and *paromoeosis* of Aristotle), to some extent the intimations of what is called prose rhythm, and, for certain kinds of writing and within limits, even correctness of diction—much, in short, though not all, of what is commonly thought of as "style." This might include the kind of values one may see in the prose of Edgar Allan Poe, where, though the message is often meretricious and merely lurid, yet a kind of cogent swing or rhythm of logic is felt. It might include what critics have alluded to as more music than sense in many lines of a decadent poet like Swinburne or Dowson. But if the nonmoral value of poetry lay only here, it would be a trivial thing, worth the contempt of Socrates. "The style is excellent," says Pope, alluding to the judgment of a certain kind of critics; "The sense they humbly take upon content."

It is at deeper levels of meaning that more important distinctions must be sought. And if we understand the depth, subtlety, and indirectness of the total and many-dimensional meaning which modern criticism rightly discerns as the poetic object, we shall not despair of distinctions.

We may first of all make short work of a case often described with approval by the moralist, where evil is represented *as* evil —in the novels, for example, of Graham Greene (if so simple a statement does them justice, or if so simple a case ever really occurs). Here, of course, there is no moral evil, and no problem. The effects of the presentation may be unhappy for this or that reader (a moral, not an artistic, issue), but the meaning itself, the interpretation, is moral. Whatever literary quality is present, it has its moral basis. If the theory of gratuitousness means vileness of this sort, the theory is really no different from that of the moral critic. The moral judgment fits the matter or the situation. If the theory is to be different from a moral theory, vileness must be vileness represented as attractive, vileness with an apology, or vileness recommended. In short, the poem must be vile.

There are two main ways in which a poem may approach vileness—that is, in which it may be ethically defective: (1) by asserting an unacceptable philosophy; (2) by approving, commending, or inviting an immoral choice or passion. It is perhaps easier to see that the first way will rarely of itself be incompatible with some wisdom and with some or even a great deal of poetic value. One may agree with T. S. Eliot that poetry does not characteristically state philosophies. "In truth," says Eliot, "neither Shakespeare nor Dante did any real thinking—that was not their job." Poetry does not think, but presents the feelings connected with thinking, or thoughts as the grounds of feeling. It is perhaps true that, as Professor Norman Foerster says, Wordsworth's "Tintern Abbey" expresses a degree of "unwisdom." But then this unwisdom—the fusion of teleological naturalism, associationism, and pantheism which pervades the poem and without which indeed the poem would not be—is unwise simply in that it is not enough, it comes short of being an acceptable philosophy. Indeed we know this deficiency not so much through the poem itself as through our knowledge of its philosophic antecedents in Hartley or in Cudworth. As a philosophy it is better than no philosophy, or better, say, than dialectical materialism—because it contains much larger elements of truth. As an idea in a poem, a semimetaphoric notion of a spirit pervading a landscape, it need be no more of a philosophy than one chooses to make it. It is one way of being inspired by a landscape, one approach, we may easily say, toward

God. Poems, on the whole, as dramatic and specific utterances, here and now, tend to escape the defect of philosophic incompleteness. The philosophy need only be adequate to the situation in hand—or reach beyond that by symbolic extension.

A harder case is the second of the two named above, that of a poem which embodies a clear approval of an evil choice and its evil emotion. An answer to the question how we are to find poetic value in such a poem may be suggested in the statement that on the assumption of a Socratic ethic we might have more difficulty in doing so. On the Christian grounds of an ethic of will, we may find the distinction easier. The fact indeed that it seems to us possible to distinguish this class, the simply immoral, from the other, the philosophically wrong, marks the great difference between an ethic where the virtuous man is he who resists temptation and that where the virtuous man is he who is never tempted. But once admit temptation, and much is open to us—a wide realm of motives which may be profoundly moving and sympathetic though falling short of the morally acceptable. We have a question of how much good can be the cause of sin. Here I would be strictly Thomistic and would accept Maritain and Adler for a certain distance as my guides. The human sinner, so we are instructed in the classic explanation, does not choose evil *qua* evil—a contradiction, since *bonum* is defined as *terminus appetitus*. He chooses a lower good or one inappropriate to the moment—*quod non est vel nunc vel hoc modo bonum*. But of lower and inappropriate goods there are many levels, lower and higher, and in the gamut of human goods which in some situations the virtuous man foregoes, there is room for an indefinite range of complexity, richness, and sympathy.[5]

As a ground on which to explore this principle I choose the *Antony and Cleopatra* of Shakespeare. "The tragedy of *Antony and Cleopatra*," says Benedetto Croce, "is composed of the violent sense of pleasure, in its power to bind and to dominate, coupled with a shudder at its abject effects of dissolution and of death."[6] If this is so, then of course there is no problem. *Antony and Cleopatra* is simply one of the easy cases, already

alluded to, in which evil is represented as evil: the implications
are basically moral. Again, there is the explanation of the
theologically minded critic S. L. Bethell, according to which
Antony and Cleopatra celebrates "affections rooted deep in
the sensual nature," intuitive, spontaneous, and positive, with
all their "moral and aesthetic corollaries." The antitype is
Caesar, the cold politician whose heart is set entirely on the
passing world. In the tragic denouement the "element of self-
giving inherent in the sensual nature" is "purged of selfish fear"
and "revealed in its eternal significance."[7] It is not my purpose
to deny the availability of such views to the interpretation of
Antony and Cleopatra or in general of other poems which present similar moral problems. The solution of Bethell may, in
fact, appear to differ only by a twist of emphasis from what I
myself propose. The difference is that I seek a formulation
which will enable us to say frankly that a poem is a great poem,
yet immoral.

What is celebrated in *Antony and Cleopatra* is the passionate
surrender of an illicit love, the victory of this love over practical, political, and moral concerns, and the final superiority
of the suicide lovers over circumstance. That is a crudely one-
sided statement which makes the play as plainly immoral as it
can be made. There is of course far more—the complex, wan-
ton, and subtle wiles of the voluptuary queen, her infinite
variety which age cannot wither nor custom stale, the grizzled
and generous manhood and the military bravery of Antony—
the whole opulent and burnished panorama of empire and its
corruptions. Such intricacies and depths surely at least add to
the interest of immorality and—without making it any more
moral—yet make it more understandable, more than a mere
barren vileness, a filthy negation. It is to be noted that the
reasons on the side of morality are so far as possible undercut,
diminished, or removed from the play. The politics from which
Antony secedes are not a noble Roman republicanism, the
ideals of a Brutus or a Cato, but the treacheries and back-stab-
bing of a drunken party on a pirate's barge. The victimized

Octavia is a pallid and remote figure, never (as in Dryden's version) made to appear as a rival motive to the Egyptian seductions.[8] The suicides which provide the catastrophe have at least the subjective palliation that they are within the Stoic code which is the standard of the whole scene.[9]

> Give me my robe, put on my crown; I have
> Immortal longings in me; now no more
> The juice of Egypt's grape shall moist this lip.
> Yare, yare, good Iras; quick. Methinks I hear
> Antony call; I see him rouse himself
> To praise my noble act; I hear him mock
> The luck of Caesar, which the gods give men
> To excuse their after wrath: husband, I come:
> Now to that name my courage prove my title!
> I am fire and air; my other elements
> I give to baser life.

There is no escaping the fact that the poetic splendor of this play, and in particular of its concluding scenes, is something which exists in closest juncture with the acts of suicide and with the whole glorified story of passion. The poetic values are strictly dependent—if not upon the immorality as such— yet upon the immoral acts. Even though, or rather because, the play pleads for certain evil choices, it presents these choices in all their mature interest and capacity to arouse human sympathy. The motives are wrong, but they are not base, silly, or degenerate. They are not lacking in the positive being of deep and complex human desire. It is not possible to despise Antony and Cleopatra. If one will employ the classic concept of "imitation," the play imitates or presents the reasons for sin, a mature and richly human state of sin. Imitation, on this understanding, is not prior to and exclusive of interpretation, but follows it. The interpretation and judgment are taken as presented objects. This is the meaning of the defense repeated in every generation by the poet. "I moot," says Chaucer, "reherce Hir tales alle. . . . Or elles falsen som of my mateere." "Art," says William Butler Yeats, "is a revelation, and not a criticism."

V

Poetic value, though different from moral value, cannot thereby be considered as something autonomously remote from the rest of human experience. In the total of any concrete human situation—even that of the anchorite in his cell—there are multiple values inviting recognition or choice. The moral value in any given situation, what is right, is abstract; it is known by rule and conscience. By necessity it excludes. Neither a right nor a wrong choice, however, excludes the awareness of many values, some interrelated and supporting, some rival, some sacrificed by a choice, some in some situations held in ironic balance or entering into unresolved tensions. Poetry, by its concreteness and dramatic presentation of value situations, whether it inclines to a right answer or to a wrong answer—by the very fullness and hence imaginative power of its presentation—has the meaning and being which makes it poetry. This is the poetic value. It is a rhetorical value only inasmuch as the nuances of rhetoric, the symbolic complexities of a rhetorical unity, are the counterparts of the psychological complexities which make the meaning of a poem. Rhetoric, except in the most superficial sense, does not exist unless in a meaning of a certain stature.

It would seem to follow from what has just been said that there could be virtuous choices and right philosophy—or at least verbal descriptions of these—which would be too simple, severe, and abstracted from living reality to have poetic interest. Certainly there can be verbal presentations of evil which are too simply negative or too naively mistaken to have this interest.

As the husband is, the wife is: thou art mated with a clown,
And the grossness of his nature shall have weight to drag thee down.

He will hold thee, when his passion shall have spent its novel force,
Something better than his dog, a little dearer than his horse.

The young man in *Locksley Hall* who muses thus is not only a bad young man but a callow one. There is a shallow simplicity about this poem that is expressed even in its rhythm. No irony or other tension advises us that we are not to share the young man's experience to the full and approve it. This kind of evil, one may suppose, is not what the theory of gratuitousness means. One will be hard pressed here to explain the "pure delight, order, riches, tranquillity and rapture, which the soul ought to savour."

The areas which are to be defined by such a conception of poetic badness will be at higher levels of course much disputed. It is with no thought of expressing an opinion about the poetry of Shelley that I cite here another of Eliot's delicate adjustments to the balance between poetry and doctrine. In his essay on Shakespeare and Seneca he believed it was not the job of the poet to think. Yet in his Harvard lectures on *The Use of Poetry and the Use of Criticism* he finds himself, for something like a philosophic reason, unable to accept the poetry of Shelley. For there are some beliefs which are acceptable (in these obviously a poetry can be grounded), others again which if not acceptable yet correspond so well to some large area of human experience that we may call them "tenable" (the Stoicism of Seneca, for instance, or the atomism of Lucretius)—but again others which are neither acceptable nor tenable. The poetry of Shelley, one would gather, is inextricably wound up in beliefs of the third class.

One of the faults which Plato found with poetry was that in imitating the actions and feelings of men, poetry discovered the lack of unity in their lives, the strife and inconsistency. Recent schools of criticism, as we have said, have likewise noted the importance to poetry of the elements of variety and strife in human living and have seen the poem as a report made under tension or an ironically suspended judgment rather than a commitment to solutions. And this view would seem to put the poem clearly in the realm of the amoral or premoral. But again, recent criticism has noted with approval the Coleridgean doctrine of a resolution or *reconciliation* of opposites, a doctrine which may not read so well with the ironic. To the present writer it would seem that though poetry is inclusive, it is also exclusive in the sense that a poem has a presiding idea, attitude, and coherence and thus at least a tendency to an assertion. As certain critics of a theological leaning have recently been saying, poetry, though it is not dogma and cannot take the place of dogma, yet finds in a frame of beliefs its "ultimate character" and "latent presuppositions."[10] If it is possible, as it has been the main burden of this essay to insist, that a poem, even a great poem, may fall short of being moral—or to put it another way, if it is true that starting with the fixity of dogma we cannot hope to define the content of poems—it is yet true that poems as empirically discovered and tested do tend, within their limits and given the peculiar *données* or presuppositions of each, to point toward the higher integration of dogma. The Christian critic, if he cares to insist to the full at all moments on his Christianity as well as on his critical discernment, may without doing violence to the latter follow the direction recently pointed out to the poet: "Christian dogma will aid the artist not by giving him a privileged and special subject-matter but rather by defining for him a perspective from which 'full light' can be had on all subject matters."[11] Perhaps it follows that in this light the greatest poems for the Christian will never be that kind, the great though immoral, which it has been our labor to describe. *Antony and Cleopatra* will not be so great as *King Lear*. The testimony of the critical tradition would seem to confirm this. The greatest poetry will be morally right, even though perhaps obscurely so, in groping confusions of will and knowledge—as *Oedipus the King* foreshadows *Lear*. All this is but the consistent capstone which completes but does not contradict a system of values in which poetic is distinguished from moral and both are understood in relation to the master ideas of evil as negation or not-being, a gap in order, and of good as positive, or being—in the natural order the designed complexity of what is most truly one or most has being.

The puddle is filled with preternatural faces.
—WILLIAM HAZLITT, On Mr. Wordsworth's
Excursion

THE STRUCTURE OF
ROMANTIC NATURE
IMAGERY

STUDENTS OF romantic nature poetry have had a great deal to tell us about the philosophic components of this poetry: the specific blend of deistic theology, Newtonian physics, and pantheistic naturalism which pervades the Wordsworthian landscape in the period of "Tintern Abbey," the theism which sounds in the "Eolian Harp" of Coleridge, the conflict between French atheism and Platonic idealism which even in "Prometheus Unbound" Shelley was not able to resolve. We have been instructed in some of the more purely scientific coloring of the poetry—the images derived from geology, astronomy, and magnetism, and the coruscant green mystery which the electricians contributed to such phenomena as Shelley's Spirit of Earth. We have considered also the "sensibility" of romantic readers, distinct, according to one persuasive interpretation, from that of neoclassic readers. What was exciting to the age of Pope, "Puffs, Powders, Patches, Bibles, Billet-doux" (even about these the age might be loath to admit its excitement), was not, we are told, what was so manifestly exciting to the age of Wordsworth. "High mountains are a feeling, but the hum of cities torture." Lastly, recent critical history has reinvited attention to the romantic theory of imagination, and especially to the version of that theory which Coleridge derived from the German metaphysicians, the view of poetic imagination as the *esemplastic* power which reshapes our primary awareness of the world into symbolic avenues to the theological.[1]

We have, in short, a *subject*—simply considered, the nature of birds and trees and streams—a *metaphysics* of an animating principle, a special *sensibility*, and a *theory* of poetic imagination—the value of the last a matter of debate. Romantic poetry itself has recently suffered some disfavor among advanced critics. One interesting question, however, seems still to want discussion; that is, whether romantic poetry (or more specifically romantic nature poetry) exhibits any imaginative *structure* which may be considered a special counterpart of the subject, the philosophy, the sensibility, and the theory—and hence perhaps an explanation of the last. Something like an answer to such a question is what I would sketch.

For the purpose of providing an antithetic point of departure, I quote here a part of one of the best known and most toughly reasonable of all metaphysical images:

> If they be two, they are two so
>   As stiff twin compasses are two,
> Thy soul the fixed foot, makes no show
>   To move, but doth, if th' other do.

It will be relevant if we remark that this similitude, rather far-fetched as some might think, is yet unmistakable to interpretation because quite overtly stated, but again is not, by being stated, precisely defined or limited in its poetic value. The kind of similarity and the kind of disparity that ordinarily obtain between a drawing compass and a pair of parting lovers are things to be attentively considered in reading this image. And the disparity between living lovers and stiff metal is not least important to the tone of precision, restraint, and conviction which it is the triumph of the poem to convey. Though the

similitude is cast in the form of statement, its mood is actually
a kind of subimperative. In the next age the tension of such
a severe disparity was relaxed, yet the overtness and crispness
of statement remained, and a wit of its own sort.

> 'Tis with our judgments as our watches, none
> Go just alike, yet each believes his own.

We may take this as typical, I believe, of the metaphoric structure in which Pope achieves perfection and which survives a
few years later in the couplets of Samuel Johnson or the more
agile Churchill. The difference between our judgments and
our watches, if noted at all, may be a pleasant epistemological
joke for a person who questions the existence of a judgment
which is taken out like a watch and consulted by another judgment.

But the "sensibility," as we know, had begun to shift even in
the age of Pope. Examples of a new sensibility, and of a different structure, having something to do with Miltonic verse
and a "physico-theological nomenclature," are to be found in
Thomson's *Seasons*. Both a new sensibility and a new structure
appear in the "hamlets brown and dim-discovered spires" of
Collins' early example of the full romantic dream. In several
poets of the mid century, in the Wartons, in Grainger, or in
Cunningham, one may feel, or rather see stated, a new sensibility, but at the same time one may lament an absence of poetic
quality—that is, of a poetic structure adequate to embody or
objectify the new feeling. It is as if these harbingers of another
era had felt but had not felt strongly enough to work upon the
objects of their feelings a pattern of meaning which would
speak for itself—and which would hence endure as a poetic
monument.

As a central exhibit I shall take two sonnets, that of William
Lisle Bowles "To the River Itchin" (1789)[2] and for contrast
that of Coleridge "To the River Otter" (1796)—written in con-
fessed imitation of Bowles.[3] Coleridge owed his first poetic inspiration to Bowles (the "father" of English romantic poetry)
and continued to express unlimited admiration for him as late

as 1796. That is, they shared the same sensibility—as for that matter did Wordsworth and Southey, who too were deeply impressed by the sonnets of Bowles. As a schoolboy Coleridge read eagerly in Bowles' second edition of 1789* (among other sonnets not much superior):

> Itchin, when I behold thy banks again,
> Thy crumbling margin, and thy silver breast,
> On which the self-same tints still seem to rest,
> Why feels my heart the shiv'ring sense of pain?
> Is it—that many a summer's day has past
> Since, in life's morn, I carol'd on thy side?
> Is it—that oft, since then, my heart has sigh'd,
> As Youth, and Hope's delusive gleams, flew fast?
> Is it—that those, who circled on thy shore,
> Companions of my youth, now meet no more?
> Whate'er the cause, upon thy banks I bend
> Sorrowing, yet feel such solace at my heart,
> As at the meeting of some long-lost friend,
> From whom, in happier hours, we wept to part.

Here is an emotive expression which once appealed to the sensibility of its author and of his more cultivated contemporaries, but which has with the lapse of time gone flat. The speaker was happy as a boy by the banks of the river. Age has brought disillusion and the dispersal of his friends. So a return to the river, in reminding him of the past, brings both sorrow and consolation. The facts are stated in four rhetorical questions and a concluding declaration. There is also something about how the river looks and how its looks might contribute to his feelings—in the metaphoric suggestion of the "crumbling" margin and in the almost illusory tints on the surface of the stream which surprisingly have outlasted the "delusive gleams" of his own hopes. Yet the total impression is one of simple association (by contiguity in time) simply asserted—what might be described in the theory of Hume or Hartley or what Hazlitt talks about in his essay "On the Love of the Country." "It is because

---

* "I made, within less than a year and a half, more than forty transcriptions, as the best presents I could offer." *Biographia Literaria*, chap. I.

natural objects have been associated with the sports of our childhood, . . . with our feelings in solitude . . . that we love them as we do ourselves."

Coleridge himself in his "Lines Written at Elbingerode in 1799" was to speak of a "spot with which the heart associates Holy remembrances of child or friend." His enthusiasm for Hartley in this period is well known. But later, in the *Biographia Literaria* and in the third of his essays on "Genial Criticism," he was to repudiate explicitly the Hartleyan and mechanistic way of shifting back burdens of meaning. And already, in 1796, Coleridge as poet was concerned with the more complex ontological grounds of association (the various levels of sameness, of correspondence and analogy), where mental activity transcends mere "associative response"—where it is in fact the unifying activity known both to later eighteenth century associationists and to romantic poets as "imagination." The "sweet and indissoluble union between the intellectual and the material world" of which Coleridge speaks in the introduction to his pamphlet anthology of sonnets in 1796 must be applied by us in one sense to the sonnets of Bowles, but in another to the best romantic poetry and even to Coleridge's imitation of Bowles. There is an important difference between the kinds of unity. In a letter to Sotheby of 1802 Coleridge was to say more emphatically: "The poet's heart and intellect should be *combined*, intimately combined and unified with the great appearances of nature, and not merely held in solution and loose mixture with them."* In the same paragraph he says of Bowles' later poetry: "Bowles has indeed the *sensibility* of a poet, but he has not the *passion* of a great poet . . . he has no native passion because he is not a thinker."

The sententious melancholy of Bowles' sonnets and the asserted connection between this mood and the appearances of

---

* Coleridge has in mind such loose resemblances as need to be stated "in the shape of formal similes." *Letters* (Boston, 1895), I, 404. Cp. Bowles, *Sonnets* (2d ed., Bath, 1789), Sonnet V, "To the River Wenbeck," "I listen to the wind, And think I hear meek sorrow's plaint"; Sonnet VI, "To the River Tweed," "The murmurs of thy wand'ring wave below Seem to his ear the pity of a friend."

nature are enough to explain the hold of the sonnets upon Coleridge. Doubtless the metaphoric coloring, faint but nonetheless real, which we have remarked in Bowles' descriptive details had also something to do with it. What is of great importance to note is that Coleridge's own sonnet "To the River Otter" (while not a completely successful poem) shows a remarkable intensification of such color.

> Dear native Brook! wild Streamlet of the West!
> How many various-fated years have past,
> What happy and what mournful hours, since last
> I skimmed the smooth thin stone along thy breast,
> Numbering its light leaps! yet so deep imprest
> Sink the sweet scenes of childhood, that mine eyes
> I never shut amid the sunny ray,
> But straight with all their tints thy waters rise,
> Thy crossing plank, thy marge with willows grey,
> And bedded sand that veined with various dyes
> Gleamed through thy bright transparence! On my way,
> Visions of Childhood! oft have ye beguiled
> Lone manhood's cares, yet waking fondest sighs:
> Ah! that once more I were a careless Child!

Almost the same statement as that of Bowles' sonnet—the sweet scenes of childhood by the river have only to be remembered to bring both beguilement and melancholy. One notices immediately, however, that the speaker has kept his eye more closely on the object. There are more details. The picture is more vivid, a fact which according to one school of poetics would in itself make the sonnet superior. But a more analytic theory will find it worth remarking also that certain ideas, latent or involved in the description, have much to do with its vividness. As a child, careless and free, wild like the streamlet, the speaker amused himself with one of the most carefree motions of youth—skimming smooth thin stones which leapt lightly on the breast of the water. One might have thought such experiences would sink no deeper in the child's breast than the stones in the water —"yet so deep imprest"—the very antithesis (though it refers overtly only to the many hours which have intervened) defines imaginatively the depth of the impressions. When he closes his eyes, they *rise* again (the word *rise* may be taken as a trope which hints the whole unstated similitude); they rise like the tinted waters of the stream; they gleam up through the depths of memory—the "various-fated years"—like the "various dyes" which vein the sand of the river bed. In short, there is a rich ground of meaning in Coleridge's sonnet beyond what is overtly stated. The descriptive details of his sonnet gleam brightly because (consciously or unconsciously—it would be fruitless to inquire how deliberately he wrote these meanings into his lines) he has invested them with significance. Here is a special perception, "invention" if one prefers, "imagination," or even "wit." It can be explored and tested by the wit of the reader. In this way it differs from the mere flat announcement of a Hartleian association, which is not open to challenge and hence not susceptible of confirmation. If this romantic wit differs from that of the metaphysicals, it differs for one thing in making less use of the central overt statement of similitude which is so important in all rhetoric stemming from Aristotle and the Renaissance. The metaphor in fact is scarcely noticed by the main statement of the poem.* Both tenor and vehicle, furthermore, are wrought in a parallel process out of the same material. The river landscape is both the occasion of reminiscence and the source of the metaphors by which reminiscence is described.[4] A poem of this structure is a signal instance of that kind of fallacy (or strategy) by which death in poetry occurs so often in winter or at night, and sweethearts meet in the spring countryside. The tenor of such a similitude is likely to be subjective—reminiscence or sorrow or beguilement—not an object distinct from the vehicle, as lovers or their souls are distinct from twin compasses. Hence the emphasis of Bowles, Coleridge, and all other romantics on spontaneous feelings and sincerity. Hence the recurrent themes of One Being and Eolian Influence and Wordsworth's "ennobling interchange of action

---

* See the more overt connections in the poem "Recollection" (*Watchman*, no. V, April 2, 1796) from which lines 2-11 of this sonnet were taken. "Where blameless Pleasures dimpled Quiet's cheek, As water-lilies *ripple* thy slow stream!" "Ah! fair tho' faint those forms of memory seem, Like Heaven's bright bow on thy smooth evening stream."

from within and from without." In such a structure again the element of tension in disparity is not so important as for metaphysical wit. The interest derives not from our being aware of disparity where likeness is firmly insisted on, but in an opposite activity of discerning the design which is latent in the multiform sensuous picture.

Let us notice for a moment the "crossing plank" of Coleridge's sonnet, a minor symbol in the poem, a sign of shadowy presences, the lads who had once been there. The technique of this symbol is the same as that which Keats was to employ in a far more brilliant romantic instance, the second stanza of his "Ode to Autumn," where the very seasonal spirit is conjured into reality out of such haunted spots—in which a gesture lingers—the half-reaped furrow, the oozing cider press, the brook where the gleaners have crossed with laden heads.* To return to our metaphysics—of an animate, plastic Nature, not transcending but immanent in and breathing through all things—and to discount for the moment such differences as may relate to Wordsworth's naturalism, Coleridge's theology, Shelley's Platonism, or Blake's visions: we may observe that the common feat of the romantic nature poets was to read meanings into the landscape. The meaning might be such as we have seen in Coleridge's sonnet, but it might more characteristically be more profound, concerning the spirit or soul of things—"the one life within us and abroad." And that meaning especially was summoned out of the very surface of nature itself. It was embodied imaginatively and without the explicit religious or philosophic statements which one will find in classical or Christian instances—for example in Pope's "Essay on Man":

> Here then we rest: "The Universal Cause
> Acts to one end, but acts by various laws,"

or in the teleological divines, More, Cudworth, Bentley, and others of the seventeenth and eighteenth centuries, or in Paley during the same era as the romantics. The romantic poets want to have it and not have it too—a spirit which the poet himself

---

* Compare the "wooden bridge" in Arnold's Keatsian "Scholar Gipsy."

as superidealist creates by his own higher reason or esemplastic imagination. Here one may recall Ruskin's chapter of *Modern Painters* on the difference between the Greek gods of rivers and trees and the vaguer suffusions of the romantic vista—"the curious web of hesitating sentiment, pathetic fallacy, and wandering fancy, which form a great part of our modern view of nature." Wordsworth's "Prelude," from the cliff that "upreared its head" in the night above Ullswater to the "blue chasm" that was the "soul" of the moonlit cloudscape beneath his feet on Snowdon, is the archpoet's testament, both theory and demonstration of this way of reading nature. His "Tintern Abbey" is another classic instance, a whole pantheistic poem woven of the landscape, where God is not once mentioned. After the "soft inland murmur," the "one green hue," the "wreaths of smoke . . . as . . . Of vagrant dwellers in the houseless woods" (always something just out of sight or beyond definition), it is an easy leap to the "still, sad music of humanity," and

> a sense sublime
> Of something far more deeply interfused,
> Whose dwelling is the light of setting suns.

This poem, written as Wordsworth revisited the banks of a familiar stream, the "Sylvan Wye," is the full realization of a poem for which Coleridge and Bowles had drawn slight sketches. In Shelley's "Hymn to Intellectual Beauty" the "awful shadow" of the "unseen Power" is substantiated of "moonbeam" showers of light behind the "piny mountain," of "mist o'er mountains driven." On the Lake of Geneva in the summer of 1816 Byron, with Shelley the evangelist of Wordsworth at his side, spoke of "a living fragrance from the shore," a "floating whisper on the hill." We remark in each of these examples a dramatization of the spiritual through the use of the faint, the shifting, the least tangible and most mysterious parts of nature —a poetic counterpart of the several theories of spirit as subtile matter current in the eighteenth century, Newton's "electric and elastic" active principle, Hartley's "infinitesimal elementary body." The application of this philosophy to poetry by way of

direct statement had been made as early as 1735 in Henry
Brooke's "Universal Beauty," where an "elastick Flue of fluctu-
ating Air" pervades the universe as "animating Soul." In the
high romantic period the most scientific version to appear in
poetry was the now well recognized imagery which Shelley
drew from the electricians.

In such a view of spirituality the landscape itself is kept in
focus as a literal object of attention. Without it Wordsworth
and Byron in the examples just cited would not get a start. And
one effect of such a use of natural imagery—an effect implicit
in the very philosophy of a World Spirit—is a tendency in the
landscape imagery to a curious split. If we have not only the
landscape but the spirit which either informs or visits it, and if
both of these must be rendered for the sensible imagination, a
certain parceling of the landscape may be the result. The most
curious illustrations which I know are in two of Blake's early
quartet of poems to the seasons. Thus, "To Spring":

> O THOU with dewy locks, who lookest down
> Thro' the clear windows of the morning, turn
> Thine angel eyes upon our western isle,
> Which in full choir hails thy approach, O Spring!
>
> The hills tell each other, and the list'ning
> Vallies hear; all our longing eyes are turned
> Up to thy bright pavillions; issue forth,
> And let thy holy feet visit our clime.
>
> Come o'er the eastern hills, and let our winds
> Kiss thy perfumed garments; let us taste
> Thy morn and evening breath; scatter thy pearls
> Upon our love-sick land that mourns for thee.

And "To Summer":

> O THOU, who passest thro' our vallies in
> Thy strength, curb thy fierce steeds, allay the heat
> That flames from their large nostrils! thou, O Summer,
> Oft pitched'st here thy golden tent, and oft
> Beneath our oaks hast slept, while we beheld
> With joy thy ruddy limbs and flourishing hair.

> Beneath our thickest shades we oft have heard
> Thy voice, when noon upon his fervid car
> Rode o'er the deep of heaven; beside our springs
> Sit down, and in our mossy vallies, on
> Some bank beside a river clear, throw thy
> Silk draperies off, and rush into the stream.

Blake's starting point, it is true, is the opposite of Wordsworth's or Byron's, not the landscape but a spirit personified or allegorized. Nevertheless, this spirit as it approaches the "western isle" takes on certain distinctly terrestrial hues. Spring, an oriental bridegroom, lives behind the "clear windows of the morning" and is invited to issue from "bright pavillions," doubtless the sky at dawn. He has "perfumed garments" which when kissed by the winds will smell much like the flowers and leaves of the season. At the same time, his *own* morn and evening breaths are most convincing in their likeness to morning and evening breezes. The pearls scattered by the hand of Spring are, we must suppose, no other than the flowers and buds which literally appear in the landscape at this season. They function as landscape details and simultaneously as properties of the bridegroom and—we note here a further complication—as properties of the land taken as lovesick maiden. We have in fact a double personification conjured from one nature, one landscape, in a wedding which approximates fusion. Even more curious is the case of King Summer, a divided tyrant and victim, who first appears as the source and spirit of heat, his steeds with flaming nostrils, his limbs ruddy, his tent golden, but who arrives in our valleys only to sleep in the shade of the oaks and be invited to rush into the river for a swim. These early romantic poems are examples of the Biblical, classical, and Renaissance tradition of allegory as it approaches the romantic condition of landscape naturalism—as Spring and Summer descend into the landscape and are fused with it. Shelley's Alastor is a spirit of this kind, making the "wild his home," a spectral "Spirit of wind," expiring "Like some frail exhalation; which the dawn Robes in its golden beams." Byron's Childe Harold desired that he himself might become a "portion" of that around him, of the tempest and the night. "Be thou, Spirit fierce," said Shelley to the West Wind, "My spirit! Be thou me."

An English student of the arts in the Jacobean era, Henry Peacham, wrote a book on painting in which he gave allegorical prescriptions for representing the months, quoted under the names of months by Dr. Johnson in his *Dictionary:*

April is represented by a young man in green, with a garland of myrtle and hawthorn buds; in one hand primroses and violets, in the other the sign Taurus.

July I would have drawn in a jacket of light yellow, eating cherries, with his face and bosom sunburnt.*

But that would have been the end of it. April would not have been painted into a puzzle picture where hawthorn buds and primroses were arranged to shadow forth the form of a person.[5] There were probably deep enough reasons why the latter nineteenth century went so far in the development of so trivial a thing as the actual landscape puzzle picture.

In his Preface of 1815 Wordsworth spoke of the *abstracting* and *"modifying* powers of the imagination." He gave as example a passage from his own poem, "Resolution and Independence," where an old leech gatherer is likened to a stone which in turn is likened to a sea beast crawled forth to sun itself. The poems which we have just considered, those of Coleridge, Wordsworth, and Blake especially, with their blurring of literal and figurative, might also be taken, I believe, as excellent examples. In another of his best poems Wordsworth produced an image which shows so strange yet artistic a warping, or modification, of vehicle by tenor that, though not strictly a nature image, it may be quoted here with close relevance. In the ode "Intimations of Immortality":

> Hence, in a season of calm weather,
> Though inland far we be,
> Our souls have sight of that immortal sea

---

* With these prescriptions compare the allegorical panels of seasons and months in Spenser's *Cantos of Mutabilitie,* VII, xxviii ff.

> Which brought us hither;
> Can in a moment travel thither—
> And see the children sport upon the shore,
> And hear the mighty waters rolling evermore.

Or, as one might drably paraphrase, our souls in a calm mood look back to the infinity from which they came, as persons inland on clear days can look back to the sea by which they have voyaged to the land. The tenor concerns souls and age and time. The vehicle concerns travelers and space. The question for the analyst of structure is: Why are the children found on the seashore? In what way do they add to the solemnity or mystery of the sea? Or do they at all? The answer is that they are not strictly parts of the traveler-space vehicle, but of the soul-age-time tenor, attracted over, from tenor to vehicle. The travelers looking back in both space and time see themselves as children on the shore, as if just born like Venus from the foam. This is a sleight of words, an imposition of image upon image, by the *modifying* power of imagination.

Poetic structure is always a fusion of ideas with material, a statement in which the solidity of symbol and the sensory verbal qualities are somehow not washed out by the abstraction. For this effect the iconic or directly imitative powers of language are important—and of these the well known onomatopoeia or imitation of sound is only one, and one of the simplest. The "stiff twin compasses" of Donne have a kind of iconicity in the very stiffness and odd emphasis of the metrical situation. Neoclassic iconicity is on the whole of a highly ordered, formal, or intellectual sort, that of the "figures of speech" such as antithesis, isocolon, homoeoteleuton, or chiasmus. But romantic nature poetry tends to achieve iconicity by a more direct sensory imitation of something headlong and impassioned, less ordered, nearer perhaps to the subrational. Thus: in Shelley's "Ode to the West Wind" the shifts in imagery of the second stanza, the pell-mell raggedness and confusion of loose clouds, decaying leaves, angels and Maenads with hair uplifted, the dirge, the dome, the vapors, and the enjambment from tercet to tercet combine to give an impression beyond statement of the very wildness, the breath and power which is the vehicle of the poem's radical metaphor. If we think of a scale of structures having at one end logic, the completely reasoned and abstracted, and at the other some form of madness or surrealism, matter or impression unformed and undisciplined (the imitation of disorder by the idiom of disorder), we may see metaphysical and neoclassical poetry as near the extreme of logic (though by no means reduced to that status) and romantic poetry as a step toward the directness of sensory presentation (though by no means sunk into subrationality). As a structure which favors implication rather than overt statement, the romantic is far closer than the metaphysical to symbolist poetry and the varieties of postsymbolist most in vogue today. Both types of structure, the metaphysical and the romantic, are valid. Each has gorgeously enriched the history of English poetry.

The knowledge imposes a pattern and falsifies,
For the pattern is new in every moment.
                        —East Coker

It seems, as one becomes older,
That the past has another pattern, and ceases
        to be a mere sequence—
Or even development.
                        —The Dry Salvages

SYMBOL AND
METAPHOR

MARTIN FOSS' *Symbol and Metaphor in Human Experience*[1] is a somewhat romantic hyperdevelopment of the distinction between the literal and the metaphoric which is today a normal preoccupation with philosophers of literature and of symbolic form. *Symbol*, it may be well to explain at once, does not in Foss' usage enjoy its usual literary and honorific alliance with *metaphor*, but, carrying rather a logical connotation, means what for Foss is the opposite of metaphor, the conceptual. This much understood, one may go on to say that the main difference between Foss and other writers on the same theme lies in the thoroughness and ingenuity with which he has worked out his central distinction and in the intensity of his evaluations, the fullness of worth which he has assigned to metaphor, and the corresponding meagerness which is left for the concept. Or, to put the matter more briefly, metaphor for Foss is not only a problem of language but the throbbing heart of all knowledge and reality. The first rule for reading Foss is that *symbol*, in all contexts and relations, be taken as what is limited, reduced, and false, and that *metaphor*, on the other hand, be taken as what is ideally directed and true.

Foss employs a kind of Tacitean metaphysical eloquence which is at all moments decorous and close to his business, but which has its difficulties for the reader. Let me attempt a drastic summary, or symbolic reduction, of his adeptly metaphorical exposition. The use of the copula *is*, implicit in the appositive series, will do some violence to the complexity of the argument, but since causes and parts are frowned on by the same argument, the simpler arrangement (if its possibilities of metaphoric interpretation are kept in mind) cannot be altogether out of keeping. In logical and grammatical terms, we have on two sides of a profound ledger: "symbolic reduction," the divisive subject and predicate, and "metaphoric process," the underlying and unifying energy of the proposition. The negations of dialectic operate to show the insufficiency of symbolic concepts and are the "door to philosophic truth." And in ontological terms, we have on the one hand number, time, space, cause and effect, coincidence and contingency; and on the other the different, the naught, the apeiron, the potential, the tension of process (and of doubt), freedom and necessity in metaphoric lawful unity. There are two closely similar extremes of reduction between which one locates the transcendent philosophy of metaphor: that of sensationalism, the philosophy of the brute and atomic, and that of rationalism, the philosophy of expedient action. And in more or less theological terms, we have on the one hand the environment and its complement the ego, purposive and possessive; on the other, World, the I (a free potential) and the Thou (its realization), prayer, sin and grace in the metaphorical unity of consciousness, the widening power of personality in intercession or metaphorical representation. On the one hand, birth and death, past and future, and a present extending *ad libitum* into either; on the other, the eternal present of the integrated process stretching over past and future, expressed in its purest form in art. And so in aesthetic terms: on the one hand catharsis, a rationalized mixture of the ego's pleasure and pain, asceticism and hedonism, play; on the other, drama—especially tragedy, which is par excellence action—eudaemonia, purification, artistic distance, stylization, imagination, conscience, love. On the one hand,

comedy in the sense of farce, environment symbolically reduced, actions and persons according to type, the mechanism
of means and ends, rules, rituals, tricks, chance, the caricature
of symbolic fixation—producing laughter; on the other hand,
true and great comedy, the attempt to understand life in all its
contradictions, producing the smile.

If for the sake of getting on we may omit certain parallel
oppositions under the heads of music, fine arts, law, and ethics
—and indeed almost unlimited niceties of extension under the
heads already named—we may say in short that we have a
monism of the expressive process. "Existence reveals the metaphorical truth that Being is Becoming. . . . This paradoxical
unity of Becoming and Being, of movement and rest is the
Heraclitean Logos, and it is Life" (p. 67).

The passage just quoted I should take to be the central
statement of the book. If the foregoing synopsis seems too
dense a galaxy of bright terms, I plead justification from the
highly compressed yet synthetically ambitious character of
Foss' argument. One can only admire the consistency with
which he explores the fields of human experience and his agility
and thoroughness in lining up all the details his own way. At
the same time I suspect that almost any critical reader—and not
merely so invincible a realist and dualist as I confess myself to
be—will be caught wondering what criteria could be invoked
to test the numerous equations of the system. The voracity of
the polar concepts, their capacity to assimilate into order the
wild raggle-taggle of our usual pluralistic thought, is something
indeed frightening.

Perhaps the key to Foss' method and the point where it will
be scrutinized most closely by the logician is the ingenuity with
which, taking as a start two recognizable opposites, metaphoric
process and symbolic fixation, he manages to shuffle so great a
multitude of intermediates or disparates in one or the other direction, or to confer on certain of these intermediates a kind of
two-directional or "hybrid" character. Aristotelian "entelechy"
and modern "force," for instance, are symbolic reductions which
seem to receive a friendly pat for a certain striving in the right
direction. The "universal" is a fixation with a tendency of ex-

pansion. "Reflection" too is a good conceptual beginning of transcendence. "We reflect and compare in order to enter by free reflection, comparison, and simultaneity of coincidence, into a sphere of necessity" (p. 51). Comedy, as we have seen, is in its most characteristic farcical forms on the bad side; but then there is "truly great comedy," which is not funny, but humorous, and tries to understand life in its contradictions. Measure arises from the mechanical and orgiastic element of beat, but measure mediates toward the transcendence of rhythm. A certain group of hierarchical abstract terms, for example, "personality," "stylization," "expression," "process," "transcendence," tend to assume rather indeterminate relations to one another—any one revealing another, for instance, or being its essence.

Let me add to these querulous hints an expression of radical discomfiture at Foss' systematic depression of the concept. It is true that Foss is again and again at pains to assert a qualified tolerance in that direction. It is clear that in some sense symbolic reductions are needed in his system—of course for the negations of dialectic (What else could dialectic negate?)—and even too for the creative drive of the metaphoric process.

Force cannot even be conceived without resistance, nor substance without matter, nor the metaphorical process without the symbolic reductions which have to be exact, fixed, detached in order to be transcended and overcome in the process which carries them beyond. (p. 42)

If he [the philosopher] . . . does not at all consider the symbolic order, he becomes vague and loses the ground under his feet. (p. 43)

It is wrong to seek this life by eliminating all symbols and by plunging into the darkness of nothingness as some mystics have tried to do. The simple is not the exclusion of the complex, it is the overcoming of complexity. (p. 62)

We need a system of symbols, . . . this system is a ground on which we stand and has therefore to be regarded as a highly valuable treasure, but . . . its true meaning lies beyond its own fixation. (p. 102)

Science without philosophy would stagnate and hypostatize its symbolic reduction and limitation, and philosophy without the symbolic structure of fixed and finite answers would lose the incentive to ever newly formulate its problems. (p. 105)

Or, as one might say, trying to construct an image or metaphor for all this: our concepts or symbols seem to be small platforms of fixation from which we send out continual streams into the sea of process, into which in turn our platforms themselves are continually swallowed. But I have a trouble with this imagery. Whence come the streams when the platforms are dissolved, whence any new platforms, or whence the originals? In symbolic reduction what is reduced? Or change the metaphor: say that Foss' philosophy is a celebration of the bonfire to the ultimate negation of the fuel. The peacock flames of imagination leap up and up forever, the driftwood logs fall back and vanish. But I would shift the area of magic in this image by positing a fuel that is perpetually renewed— and perpetually the same. The fun is no doubt in the flames, the inexhaustibly varied metaphoric process. But the source is something that remains and produces. Beyond the limitless realm of metaphoric relationship and sustaining it, beyond Becoming and dynamically manifest in Becoming—Beings. (The plural denotes the concrete.) And of these, for sanity, at least three: myself as a limited being, the external world (or merely environment as Foss would insist), and God. It is largely because this is so that we can read Homer in 1950. The opposite view enters the boundless gas. It abandons, or at least relaxes, what has been the perennial philosophic struggle, to salvage from the indefinite both epistemology and ontology by the assertion of Being.

At the literary and linguistic level, Foss has numerous companions in the school of symbol and myth which derives triumphantly today from the anthropology of the Golden Bough and from the semantics of symbolic form established by Cassirer. This is not to say that these are in every respect close companions. For example, as Foss makes the primitive fixation of ritual a reduction from myth, he is bidding for contempt from the confident school of ritual origins[2] (where the myth of American Independence might be derived from firecrackers on the Fourth of July).

Yet the theorist of literature is likely to say on the whole that Foss is right. That is, his philosophy of metaphor (so far as it will permit us to take metaphor as a way of expression and knowing rather than a process of being) is a literary philosophy, and it is as such, that is, as something different from a philosophy of science, religion, or ethics, that I should choose to canvass it. Foss gives eloquent utterance to the notion of poetry as organic imagination which prevails today in the postsymbolist world of letters. Imagination, let us agree approximately with Foss, is "intensive reality," "the discovery of the infinite metaphorical present in the fragmentary symbols of transitional things and events." Words—especially words in poems—exhibit "ambiguous radiation," "manifold refraction." Art is neither merely subjective, nor merely objective. Expressiveness asks for stylization and surpasses mere imitation of natural proportions. A work of art is recognized by the necessity of its inner form—the uniqueness of its rhythm. These views are nearly normal today, though perhaps not always uttered in a way which testifies to so profound a realization as here.

The limitations of this view as it is entertained by Foss are entailed by his more fundamental monism of the metaphoric process, though paradoxically they may be manifest only as the argument approaches a judgment upon particular works of art or schools. On Foss' premises, not only does Aristotle's causal account of tragedy become inarticulate when it encounters the irregularity of the *peripeteia*, but the modern tragedy of subject (the blurring of fantasy and environment) is rated as decidedly an improvement over the Greek contest with external fate. It is not clear what Foss actually thinks of the irony and reversal in the career of Oedipus. But one may suppose these cannot make much sense to an expansive philosophy in which the "ethics of service" leaves no room for the ethics of acceptance, and in which, despite vaguely recurrent allusions to "sin" and "grace," the concept of *hamartia* can have little place, and that of *hubris* certainly none. The same order of deficiency,

I should say, appears in the attitude toward comedy, a Berg-
sonian seriousness which amounts nearly to disapproval. The
smile is tolerated, not laughter; humor, not wit. Laughter is
thought to leave emptiness, indifference, fatigue.

"Concepts clearly and explicitly expressed are thereby con-
demned to death. The question then becomes how long they
can be kept alive in the death-house." This note is found among
the recently published posthumous papers of a distinguished
American poet.[3] Both definition and analysis are of course excluded from true literary study by the system of Foss—in a
manner already axiomatic with poets and quite familiar to
philologists in the aesthetic of Croce. Nevertheless, I shall conclude this discussion by turning to the key term *metaphor* itself—in its more limited grammatical and rhetorical sense—and
inquiring whether in fact a semantic beginning can be made in
this direction without some quite special invocation of symbolic
fixity.

One of the best features of Foss' book is that, in emphasis at
least, it is antiprimitivistic. It is true we find such Crocean
statements as that words do not (like building stones) come
first, but language itself, the living and complete communication. Reflection, we are told, transforms living words into fixed
objects, mechanical atoms, which must be drawn by a new
force of unification back into the vortex of living process. But
the view of time held in this philosophy prevents this meaning
from being emphatically chronological, and an alignment of
concept with ritual and orgy leads naturally to the view that
primitive man has a strong tendency to abstraction, that only
classical maturity restores the metaphoric unity thus lost. The
whole question about metaphor seems to me, however, to have
been already much obscured by other writers on symbolic form
in their primitivistic speculations upon the birth of language.
To call a man a pig, or his sweetheart a flower, is not, says Foss,
to utter a metaphor—it is an exaggerated, one-sided statement,
a symbolic reduction to a *tertium comparationis*. Perhaps so,
though I doubt it is so in all contexts. The point I would now
make is that the alternative to such simplified metaphor, as expounded by the writers on symbolic form and perhaps implicitly

by Foss, assumes the shape of something which has been called
"prelogical" thought and which I believe might as well be
called "solid" or "opaque" thought. It is a kind most conveniently imputed either to young children or to prehistoric
men, because no documents can be adduced which really illustrate it—if indeed it can be conceived. We must "imagine,"
says Owen Barfield, a time when *spiritus* or *pneuma* "meant
neither *breath* nor *wind,* nor *spirit,* nor yet all three of these
things, but when they simply had *their own old peculiar meaning.*"[4] And the following reverie of Herder *Ueber den Ursprung
der Sprache* is quoted by Cassirer:

A certain savage sees a tree, with its majestic crown; the crown
rustles! That is stirring godhead! The savage falls prostrate and
worships! Behold the history of sensuous Man . . . and the easiest
transition to abstract thought![5]

The tree is not compared to a king, but mistaken for one. Or
is the idea of king, or tree-king, actually born at this moment?
Did real kings later wear crowns because they looked like tree-
tops? Or had the savage previously seen a real king with a
crown? If the latter is the case, one must suppose that the
stage of culture is rather late for the mistake to be made.

These questions—to which answers are scarcely available—
are not the same as an inquiry into the status of metaphor or
simile as we actually find it in literary documents—early and
late. Here what is most striking is a kind of imaginative thick-
ness which subsists not in confusion but in distinction—whether
explicitly in the *qualis-talis* of the classical epic simile or implicitly in the highly figurative nature images of modern romantic poetry—the charged landscapes of a Collins or a Wordsworth. In these latter there is always a statable, if not stated,
element of difference (between the tree and the god, the "setting suns" and the "presence"), and in this difference, tension,
without which indeed there would be no poetry.

It is understandable and excusable that in so densely written
a synthesis as that of Foss few quotable examples of "true"
metaphor should appear. I am not sure how much can be made

of the two examples from German which are adduced—*Klang-farbe, Farbton*—tone-color or timbre, color-tone or tint. But Foss' way of describing these hyphen metaphors is worth notice.

Two symbols are here brought together, not in a comparison by which the one, as unfamiliar, shall be clarified in its relation to the other as the familiar one. On the contrary, two highly familiar words are brought together in order to question their familiarity and in order to arrive at a problematic insight of a still unknown unity. (p. 59)

So far as this refers to the main locus of interest in the metaphor, we may wish to say that the statement might be much better illustrated from a wide range of twentieth century poetry than from the relatively prosaic examples adduced. It would seem actually that the function of *-farbe* is mainly to explain a certain quality of *Klang,* and conversely for *Farb* and *-ton.* Yet the general implication is correct—that in understanding imaginative metaphor we are often required to consider not how B (vehicle) explains A (tenor), but what meanings are generated when A and B are confronted or seen each in the light of the other. The emphasis may be on likeness or on the opposite, a kind of antithesis or repugnance (as in a recent French instance, *Cheval de Beurre*)—but in any case a copresence of likeness and difference is necessary for the indefinite radiations of meaning, the solidity and concreteness, for which metaphor is prized.[*]

"The dissimilarity," observes Foss, is so strong that psychoanalysis has been "inclined to interpret the 'sick simile' as an attempt to hide, dissemble, disguise the truth, or to shock the audience by the violence and inadequacy of the analogy" (p. 53). But this difference lies not between a concept and the vastness of merely possible negations, the apeiron, but between

[*] Foss' remarks on the proverb "Among blind men the one-eyed is king" seem to me excellent. They carry further than he would admit for the whole discussion of metaphor. "The true significance of the proverb goes far beyond the blind, the one-eyed, and the king: It points to a wisdom in regard to which the terms of comparison are only unimportant cases of reference" (p. 56).

two formulated and namable concepts, and it is their distinct-
ness from each other which keeps the metaphor alive. "Every
language," says Foss, "is full of 'dead metaphors.'" But how
else shall we define the dead metaphor except as a collapsed
metaphor, one in which A and B have come together so completely that only one is left holding the field? When the distinct or definably separate characters of A and B have been
merged, then it is that the "tension" of which Foss likes to
speak has been relaxed, the "problem"—another of his chiefly
honored conceptions—has been if not solved (no worse fate
could be named), at least dismissed.

The theorist of poetry tends more and more today to make
metaphor the irreducible element of his definition of poetry,
but in attempting to define metaphor itself he tends furthermore to shoot off into an endlessly interesting series of metaphors. Let me draw to a conclusion by calling attention to one
of the most precise attempts to define metaphor which I know,
that of W. B. Stanford in his *Greek Metaphor: Studies in Theory
and Practice* (Oxford, 1936). Metaphor, he says, is

the process and result of using a term (X) normally signifying an
object or concept (A) in such a context that it must refer to another
object or concept (B) which is distinct enough in characteristics
from A to ensure that in the composite idea formed by the synthesis
of the concepts A and B and now symbolized in the word X, the
factors A and B retain their conceptual independence even while
they merge in the unity symbolized by X. (p. 101)

And this process, result, or situation is one upon which Stanford
confers the happily conceived metaphoric name *stereoscope of
ideas*. A poem itself, I shall venture to add, is the *context* of
Stanford's description. It is a structure of verbal meaning which
keeps a metaphor alive, that is, which holds the focal terms A
and B in such a way that they remain distinct and illuminate
each other, instead of collapsing into literalness. (That this
structure itself will participate in the color of the metaphor
may be asserted, but need not here be specially elaborated.) It
is just when metaphors are carelessly repeated out of context
that they most readily become simplified, literal, and cliché.

Metaphor then may be a roundabout way of exhibiting concepts, but it does seem to do so, and to be a function of concepts. It is easy to underestimate the role of the conceptual or definite in poetry, and along with it all that may have suffered from time to time, in a loosely derogatory way, the names of "convention," "pattern," or "rule." "Stylization" is a term which ordinarily has conceptual affinities but which Foss appropriates to his own cause and uses along with "metaphor" in far too pronounced an antithesis to the technicalities. In poetry it is with the established techniques that the poet works, and if his "expressiveness," as Foss would say, transcends these, it is not as if they were left behind. The Petrarchan conceits, to take a fairly simple and well understood instance, remain and operate as conceits in the fun which they provide for Sidney, Spenser, or Donne. If they lost their conceited (that is, conceptual) character, they would have no poetic power.

In the second chapter of Croce's *Aesthetic* occurs an analogy which may well be used to summarize the difference between the "metaphoric" or boundless view of poetry, and the conceptual or classically definite.

He who conceives a tragedy puts into a crucible a great quantity, so to say, of impressions: expressions themselves, conceived on other occasions, are fused together with the new in a single mass, in the same way as we can cast into a melting furnace formless pieces of bronze and choicest statuettes. These choicest statuettes must be melted just like the pieces of bronze, before there can be a new statue. The old expressions must descend again to the level of impressions, in order to be synthesized in a new single expression.

The statuettes as well as the scraps of junk lose their form when melted down for the new statue—all the little pieces are equal, all equally sacrifice whatever form they have. There is a certain sense in which this makes a valid analogy for poetry, where indeed all the elements are employed in such a way as to suffer a transformation into something *more than* their simple, abstracted, and dictionary selves. But there is too a certain important sense in which this is not a valid analogy—a sense indicated in the words *more than* of my last sentence. For the words which are fused into a poem have their new value not by losing their first or ordinary meanings but only by retaining these. And this is also true of the various labels, proverbs, maxims, epigrams, conceits, and verse forms which in a more conspicuous and rococo sense make up the repertoire of conventions and ready-made meanings which the poet uses. It would be much more appropriate to liken these to the gargoyles, finials, monuments, and other carved ornaments of a cathedral, than to statuettes whose form disappears as they enter the statue. The proverb, the verse form, may have poetic virtue in its new context only by some ironical twist—but it has to retain its original character in order to be twisted.

$\lfloor 3$

. . . ὅταν δὲ τί ἐστιν οὐ λευκὸν οὐδὲ θερμὸν
οὐδὲ τρίπηχυ, ἀλλ᾽ ἄνθρωπον ἢ Θεόν.

—Metaphysics, Z, 1

THE SUBSTANTIVE LEVEL

MY ARGUMENT begins with a respectful but inquiring glance at the schoolbook rule that verbal discourse, and especially description, ought to be particular or concrete. This counterpart of such anciently honored figures as vividness (*enargeia*) and amplification, formulated for the English tradition during the second half of the eighteenth century as Scottish associational rhetoricians moved away from the more Platonic forms of neoclassicism, appears to be one of the most axiomatic of all modern rhetorical rules. At the same time it is, I believe, one of the most reluctant to yield its modicum of real meaning.

"Men jostled one another in the street" is less vigorous than "Butcher elbowed banker in Threadneedle Street."

In the beginning of 1752 the London theatres offered enviable entertainment. At Covent Garden the highly educated Susannah Maria Cibber and the ex-silversmith Spranger Barry excelled in *Romeo and Juliet* and other tragedies.

The first of these passages is from a school manual of composition, the second from an exercise in higher studies which has apparently aimed at putting elementary principles into practice. The conjunction of the two may suggest that the schoolbook thesis enjoys its degree of plausibility not only for the special reason that the very meaning of the example used favors the decorum of congestion but for the more usual reason that the example is so far stripped of context that we cannot really form a judgment about it. In the second passage the meaning has no such special affinity for concreteness, and the exposition is complete enough to let us see readily that though the first of the conspicuous qualifiers, "highly educated," has perhaps something to do with the business in hand, the second, "ex-silversmith," is present mainly because it stands for a fact, or because the author wished to be concrete. If these two ornaments conspire at a sort of half-hearted antithesis, this again is little to the point.

The examples given in the schoolbooks usually suggest prose fiction. But if we turn to the canon:

On the strength of Darcy's regard, Bingley had the firmest reliance, and of his judgment the highest opinion. In understanding, Darcy was superior. Bingley was by no means deficient, but Darcy was clever. He was at the same time haughty, reserved, and fastidious, and his manners, though well-bred, were not inviting.—*Pride and Prejudice,* ch. IV

A sudden suspicion of hatred against him, of the nearness of "enemies," seemed all at once to alter the visible form of things, as with the child's hero, when he found the footprint on the sand of his peaceful, dreamy island.—*Marius the Epicurean,* II, x

Wandering through clear chambers where the general effect made preferences almost as impossible as if they had been shocks, passing at open doors where vistas were long and bland, she would, even if she had not already known, have discovered for herself that Poynton was the record of a life. It was written in great syllables of color and form, the tongues of other countries and the hands of rare artists.—*The Spoils of Poynton,* ch. III

It has never been quite clear to me that the first of these ex-

amples might not have been more interesting than it is. But at
least it is the opposite of opaque. Its light penciling is part of
a dramatic plan and style, a field of feminine thought and
genteel appraisive generalizing which makes the peculiar and
right preliminary for the story which is unfolding. The second
is a much more curious example. There is the obvious proper
name (so significant in fact as to be generic) which calls out
for mention, but it is only by refraining from this concreteness
that Pater can assimilate the gross anachronism to the theological twilight of his Roman story. It is somewhat the same
kind of reticent virtuosity which appears in the suppressions
managed so often by Henry James, as of the indelicate reasons
behind a social crisis or irritation—Mrs. Medwin's past (we are
never told what, simply that she was "impossible") or the
certain vulgar household object (never named) which was
manufactured by the Newsome family at Woollett, Massa-
chusetts, and was the source of their affluence. It happens that
James has left writers of fiction some earnest advice about "the
color, the relief, the expression, the surface, the substance of
the human spectacle"—"solidity of specification." But he may
be adduced as the master of several systematic forms of abstractness. The third passage which I have quoted above is a
striking instance of what one may call the postponement, the
rule of nothing too much and nothing too soon. *The Spoils of
Poynton* is about furniture. Furniture *is* the spoils. The passage quoted describes not something incidental but the symbolic center of the story. It gives us our first glimpse of that
center—after considerable anticipation—a spacious and well
lighted purview, with almost nothing in it. Later in the same
paragraph we hear cursorily of "brasses," "Venetian velvets,"
"enamels," "cabinets," "panels," "stuffs." But it is not until four
chapters later, when Poynton has been despoiled and the furniture set up in another house, that we find a "Venetian lamp" in
a "plain square hall," showing "on either wall, the richness of
an admirable tapestry," and from "a sofa in the drawing room"
observe "the great Italian cabinet that, at Poynton, had been in
the red saloon." Since the same things may have to be men-

tioned many times in the course of one story, he is doubtless a
wary craftsman who makes the first description a promise or a
threat.

II

A fairly obvious theoretical objection to the schoolbook rule
might be derived from the fact that while it is possible to say
definitely what is meant by "abstract" in the absolute or second-
level sense, this is not so for the other frequent sense of the
"very general," or for its opposite the "concrete" or "specific."
We have only more or less specific, more or less general. What
is the right word for anything,[1] the right degree of specification? One would gather that the answer is to be determined
by the decorum of the level at which the writing proceeds.
Nevertheless, it would appear that somewhere in the range of
our generalizing a kind of line is crossed. The problem is one
inherited from Aristotle, who long ago left it not quite clear in
certain passages whether he was talking about that in virtue of
which a thing is a thing or about that in virtue of which a thing
is a certain kind of thing. The two concepts, in Aristotle's system at least, seemed to require each other.[2] The *Iliad* was not
an essence, nor was *white man,* nor *white.* These were not first-
rate answers to the quesion: What is it? "When we say *what*
it is, we do not say, 'white' or 'hot' or 'three cubits long,' but 'a
man' or 'a god.' "[3] That is to say, *man* and *god* are at a level
of classification where specific and concrete are mutually impli-
cated. We may describe this as a kind of critical or vaporizing
line in the scale of generality. Above this level, what is abstract in a relative sense (not very specific) accommodates itself so readily to what is abstract in the absolute sense (not
concrete) that it tends to leave concreteness behind. Solidity
of substance abstracts into mere quality. Below this level, on
the contrary, there is excrescence of detail. The Aristotelian
mind (and it is, habitually, all our minds) accepts *man* as a
better name of a thing than either *vertebrate* or *white man* and
a better answer to the question: What is it? The tree of Por-
phyry reached down to the species. It is possible that a sci-

entist would decline to countenance this discussion. Metaphysicians would differ about it. It will suffice for the argument if we speak in practical and approximate terms or in linguistic and psychological—that is, in terms which refer to common speech and thought. Whatever the relation of verbal art to the outer world, it is a highly reflexive art, the projection of our very minds.

We speak of calling a spade a spade—giving it its right name —something more than merely alluding to it, and less than describing it. Some such conception as this is what the Gestalt psychologists have been telling us about—what we find when we get back to naive perception undebauched by analytic learning, not assemblages of sensations, but identifiable wholes, ailanthus, cow, and chickencoop. There is the phenomenon of what is called in our day "abstract" or "nonrepresentational" art. How, the post-Lockean logician would have to ask, can a line, a shape, a color be nonrepresentational? Nonrepresentational of what? Red is like a sunset, an oval is like an egg or like something like an egg. No visible thing is so unlike all else that it is invincibly a symbol of nothing. But neither the artists nor the common lookers have seen it that way—the latter plaintively missing something which the former have avoided with an intensity which Ortega has well described as Manichaean. *Omne corpus fugiendum est.* "Arts of sound and arts of movement divide according to whether they rouse determinate or indeterminate images."[4] Cézanne's "Old Woman with Rosary" drew "instant praise because everyone could tell precisely what it was."[5] A magazine cover is representational or naturalistic for the reason that it presents in a determinate, or specific, way: men, houses, sofas, pumpkins, cows, and chickencoops. The landscape of such art is filled with objects identifiable in the vocabulary of our substantive discourse.

III

It may well be that the pattern of this discourse is not strictly Aristotelian or "essential." The notion of the specific or fixed

rides well with various subspecies—with those, for example, of
man: businessman, housewife, postman, barkeeper, schoolboy,
and all the others that make up the modern gallery of Theo-
phrastan or Horatian characters. There is likely to be difficulty
in saying whether a given adjective is "accidental" and detach-
able, or whether it in fact forms a substantive blend with its
noun, a difficulty often attested by our uncertainties about hy-
phenation. In many areas of vocabulary the substantive line
which we wish to defend may be not so much a line as a belt.
It is true also that predication inevitably sophisticates the status
of specific nouns used in subject positions, so that all discourse
is to some degree mixed.* Yet something may be said along the
lines we have been preparing.

For neutral purposes of analysis and description, it might be
convenient to construct a new table of styles or genres in description—not the ancient genera, *grande, medium,* and *tenue,*
nor yet the *sublime,* the *picturesque,* and the *beautiful* of a
more recent day—but three main styles arranged in a scale with
reference to the concept of species and implicitly to that of
substance:

1. The abstract or less than specific-substantive style: e.g.,
    implement.
2. The minimum concrete or specific-substantive style: e.g.,
    spade.
3. The extra-concrete, the detailed, or more than specific style:
    e.g., *rusty garden spade.*

It will make some difference, at the third level, whether the
epithet is logically inseparable and hence gratuitous, merely
unfolding what is part of the definition of the specific name (as
if Homer had found occasion to say "the digger spade"), or
is (like "rusty") an increment or extra-specification. Yet it may
be difficult to draw a line. Most adjectival elaboration shows

---

* Even here perhaps certain levels analogous to specificity may be traced,
certain arterial lines of conceptual traffic—for instance, the primary colors, contrasted in one direction to *hue, color* itself, or *shade,* and in the other to refined
observations like *mauve, ocher, vermilion.*

at least a tendency toward the more than specific—"violets dim" and "lady-smocks all silver-white" only somewhat less than "cowslips wan that hang the pensive head" and "the coming musk-rose, full of dewy wine," or than even the most characteristic examples of twentieth century imagism, "Rose, harsh rose, marred and with stint of petals," "purple grackles—shining and bulging under leaves." The imagist view of poetry and related modern views have tended to see precisely this level of concreteness as the poetic level. In some sense it may be. At the same time we may observe that this is the level of presentation at which we encounter not only the dismal schoolbook instance of particularity but such opaque pictorial fallacies as the slice of life and local color, the irrelevant reportage of amateur short-story writers, the meticulous chunking of coffee cups on counters in early sound movies.

Examples at the second level, the purely specific or substantial, may be the rarest. A few lines together may be found in a nature poet whose slant is toward the simplicities and honesties of rustic labor. Wordsworth, as it happens, wrote a poem beginning "Spade! with which Wilkinson hath tilled his lands." The style has been employed for effects of a certain classic severity.

> Under some mulberry trees I found
> A little pool; and in brief space
> With all the water that was there
> I fill'd my pitcher and stole home.
> —*The Sick King in Bokhara*

In some of the best known prose examples it serves yet another sort of starkness.

The door of Henry's lunchroom opened and two men came in. They sat down at the counter.—*The Killers*

The kingdom is a peninsula, terminated to the northeast by a ridge of mountains thirty miles high, which are altogether impassable by reason of the volcanoes upon the tops. Neither do the most learned know what sort of mortals inhabit beyond those mountains, or

whether they be inhabited at all. On the three other sides it is
bounded by the ocean. There is not a sea-port in the whole kingdom.—*Gulliver's Travels,* II, iv

The apparently thoughtless style of telling a gangster story, flat
as a cement sidewalk, is a close relative of the complicated Gul-
liverian illusion, that here we have *res* rather than *verba,* albeit
res in apple-pie order. "He had to count ten," said Johnson,
"and he has counted it right."

IV

An earlier stage of the argument has illustrated something
like our first level of descriptive style—the abstract or less than
substantial—from the intellectualist fiction of Austen, Pater, and
James. In describing this style further, I believe it will be
relevant to intimate certain historical lines. "There is nothing
I have," wrote Locke, "is essential to me."

An accident or disease may very much alter my colour or shape; a
fever or fall may take away my reason or memory, or both; and an
apoplexy leave neither sense, nor understanding, no, nor life. . . .
It would be absurd to ask, whether a thing really existing wanted
anything essential to it . . . since *we* have no other measure of mental
or specific but our abstract ideas? . . . I would ask any one, What is
sufficient to make an essential difference in nature between any two
particular beings, without any regard had to some abstract idea,
which is looked upon as the essence and standard of a species?—
Essay, III, vi, 4, 5.

Here, one might say, Locke is defending the dignity and pri-
macy of the individual subsistent thing—against the abstraction
of the species. But the passage in fact leads another way—it
might lead one to speculate, for instance, how we know where
one thing ends and another begins, how we know we have
things at all. This passage shows the intimate historical connection between the denial of proper essences or species and
the general direction of philosophy from Locke to Kant: the
discrimination of secondary qualities and denial of their objectivity, the Berkeleyan being in being perceived, the Humean
dissolution of causal nexus and even of personal substance, the

victory in short of the phenomenal over the noumenal, of qualities over things. When the proper names and essences of things
had been deprived of any special dignity, the things themselves
easily became less impressive than their definitions, their peri-
phrases, their qualitative connotations.

A theologian and scientist who flourished in the time of Swift
and Locke wrote a passage in praise of "glass," saying that it
served "to make Windows for our Houses . . . for Looking-
glasses, Spectacles, Microscopes and Telescopes."[6] During the
enlightenment which followed shortly on these teleological remarks and on the lean, substantive ironies of Swift, appeared
the *Ramblers* of Samuel Johnson, in one of which we find a
description of a substance which is not immediately named, "a
body at once in a high degree solid and transparent, which
might admit the light of the sun, and exclude the violence of
the wind; which might extend the sight of the philosopher to
new ranges of existence . . . and . . . might supply the decays of
nature, and succour old age with subsidiary sight."[7] Johnson
has a reputation as the most advanced abstractionist of his era.
His contemporary John Wesley will scarcely be thought of as
leaning to the same extreme. Yet where Herbert had written:
"Who sweeps a room as for Thy laws Makes that and th' action
fine," Wesley adapted: "If done t' obey Thy laws, Even servile
labours shine."[8] A line in Gray's *Ode on a Distant Prospect of
Eton College* shows the substantive object first geometrized,
then turned into a rate of motion: instead of "roll the hoop,"
"chase the rolling circle's speed." Johnson, Wesley, and Gray
all write as if they had to suppress something. Johnson and
Gray, indulging in a kind of riddle, anticipate the rule of the
symbolist poet: "*Nommer* un objet, c'est supprimer les trois
quarts de la jouissance du poème qui est faite du bonheur de
deviner peu a peu." In the eighteenth century the principle
was described by another Frenchman (not a poet but a scientist) as "care in the matter of expressing things only in their
most general terms."[9]

Or, if the general terms were modified, it might be in a
peculiar way which we may describe approximately, in terms
of our table of styles, as a conjunction of extremes. This was

what made one important species of the now notorious eighteenth century "poetic diction": to leave out the usual class name, to give instead a more generic name plus a note of physical appearance (a "property") adequate to determine the usual name. Although such locutions derived in part from Virgilian antiquity, it means something to say that in English poetry they reached their zenith during the Lockean era. Instead of *fish, scaly breed;* instead of *sheep, fleecy kind;* instead of *birds, feathered troop;* instead of *sea, watery plains.* "The vocabulary," say Wellek and Warren, "requires periphrasis, and periphrasis implies a tension between word and thing." Or one might say the tension is between the more and the less concrete, with the precise point of specific and substantial concreteness unmentioned but present between.

It is worth while to note the difference between such periphrastic formulas and those which, in a more Homeric way, *include* a specific name: *liquid air, rosy-fingered dawn, wine-dark sea.* These latter are instances of our third level, but even there they are special instances, inasmuch as a tendency of the epithet to inseparability is strongly fixed and accentuated by the very fact of formulary repetition. The stereotypes of the Homeric style, says C. S. Lewis, "emphasize the unchanging human environment." They "make it appear that we are dealing not with poetry about the things, but almost with the things themselves." They are a way of conferring on the names of things, on the specific and essential labels of our experience, a special plumpness and sleekness. Our specific concepts become more than usually substantive, weighted, and palpable. To speak more broadly: the kinds of concreteness sometimes achieved within the general decorum of "poetic diction" may be distinguished not only from periphrase, by the presence of the specific name, but from other forms of third-level description, by a tendency to stay near the beginning of the list of examples which we have quoted above—the "lady-smocks all silver-white" rather than the marred and stinted rose. Pictorial notes might be gorgeous or even lavish, but they tended to be typical. That in fact was the point. Even concreteness had to stay within lines.

> The bright-eyed perch with fins of Tyrian dye,
> The silver eel, in shining volumes rolled,
> The yellow carp in scales bedropped with gold,
> Swift trouts, diversified with crimson stains,
> And pikes, the tyrants of the watery plains.
>   —*Windsor Forest*

This is detail substantively centered.

The more abstract and periphrastic ways of naming seem, as we have been suggesting, to have a hole in their center. They show a bashful reticence and have always been ready to slip into the comic—as in a modern synthetic version of the language of canny mobsmen and molls. " 'He knocks me down with something, I do not know what.' 'The chances are,' I say, 'it is a blunt instrument.' " The same story refers at another point to "bits of jewelry and other portable merchandise."[10] This kind of humor (by conspicuous exclusion of the spade-level word) may appear in a more cumbrous form of parody.

> Metallic blade wedded to ligneous rod,
> Wherewith the rustic swain upturns the sod.

Here it is perhaps impossible to say of certain elements whether they belong at the first or at the third level. We have the kaleidoscope of qualities, parts, and functions, whirled about the empty center.

V

The revolt against the fixity of epithets was a feat of romanticism. But romanticism itself moved on the flood of phenomenalism which was throwing up the faerie spray of its crest in the realm of metaphysics. Twentieth century critics have spoken about a poetry of atmosphere, a loss of interest in diction as such, a "deliquescence" of language. Even Wordsworth could (like Gray) be reticent about naming a child's toy and children's games. "All shod with steel we hissed along the polished ice in games confederate." The well conceived title of a recent essay is "The Abstractness of Shelley." Not only his choice of starlight and moonbeam symbols, the swirl of leaves, the rainbow, the electric fire, the cloud, but the slight role played by ordinary substantial names in his poems accounts for the highly colored yet vaporous, the strangely aetherial, shadowy, airy, and iridescent character of the Shelleyan expression. "The deep truth is imageless." Not quite. But the vortex of elements, the color on the surface of we conceive not what, the stained white radiance of eternity, the shadow of the dream are his hallmarks. "The imagery which I have employed will be found, in many instances, to have been drawn from the operations of the human mind, or from those external actions by which they are expressed." The recent analyst of Shelley's imagery speaks of "the ambiguous relationship which . . . obtains between the physical and mental," and from the lyric "Life of Life" (at the heart of which lies the "finite-infinite image") he strips "off layer after layer without arriving at any solid certainty." This style, when joined with the use of explicit, or second-stage, abstractions, produces an inspirational *Erhebung* which is one of the peculiar romantic feats.

> He has outsoared the shadow of our night;
> Envy and calumny and hurt and pain
> And that unrest which men miscall delight
> Can touch him not nor torture him again.
>   —*Adonais*, Stanza 40

The substantive image to be underpainted here is doubtless that of the skylark (the soaring poet) who rises beyond the reach of the vultures and kites (envy and calumny and hurt and pain). But we are not required by the passage itself to descend to the substantive level. It is rather the strength of the passage (and of much romantic poetry) that it forbids us to do so.

Both the more than substantive style and the less than substantive are pre-eminently internal and reflexive modes of description—expressing on the one hand the intricately sensitive, Proustean awareness of experience in detail, and on the other the dreamy abstractness, the suffused vagueness of revery. The latter style has something to do also of course with the sublime (which Kant said was subjective). These facts make it impossible to argue for a stylistic standard of simple fidelity to external specific classes. I incline indeed to the view that both the inflation of the abstract style and the solid minutiae of imagism are best when they cut fairly close to the substantive level of discourse. I am not, however, bent on arguing this. The main point is to show what the abstract and concrete in description are, or how these concepts make more sense in the light of the more precise concept of specific substance—and hence how criticism of poetry as "abstract" or "concrete" makes more sense in the same light. The concept, so far as I know, has not usually if ever been invoked by those who have objected to the abstraction of romantic poetry, though much of their criticism it seems to me has really centered here.

The classical view of man as a "fixed and limited animal," against the romantic "infinite reservoir of possibilities," was baldly re-presented in T. E. Hulme's famous essay "Romanticism and Classicism." Hulme predicted a new era of "accurate, precise and definite description," "the light of ordinary day."[11] He alluded to Bergson's intuitive and "intensive" complexity and the opposed "extensive" or intellectual multiplicity, and he wrote another essay on just that theme. In the criticism of our day, especially in those branches which stem from Hulme, we have had an epidemic appearance of two other terms, "connotative" and "denotative," the relation of which to "intensive" and "extensive" seems to me a curious thing. "What it comes to," says F. W. Bateson, "is that words are double-sided. They possess both a denotation and a connotation." And T. S. Eliot adds:

Swinburne was also a master of words, but Swinburne's words are all suggestion and no denotation; if they suggest nothing, it is because they suggest too much. Dryden's words, on the other hand, are precise, they state immensely, but their suggestiveness is almost nothing.

Here "suggestion" takes (happily, as I shall argue in a moment) the place of "connotation," the more usual completion of the antithesis. The irony of the petard is no relevant part of my drift if I next present the same terms used against the school of Pound by an even more classical critic, Yvor Winters.

Since only one aspect of language, the connotative, is being utilized, less can be said in a given number of words than if the denotative aspect were being fully utilized at the same time. . . . When the denotative power of language is impaired, the connotative becomes proportionally parisitic upon denotations in previous contexts, for words cannot have associations without meanings.

At this point it is necessary to intrude and say firmly that, whatever overtones of technicality and subtlety may accrue in these contexts from use of the terms "denotative" and "connotative" and their cognates, they do not here mean what they mean in books of logic. By "denotation" Eliot and Winters apparently mean stated, explicit, definable, or dictionary meaning. By "connotation" they apparently mean what may be distinguished from the former as suggested, implicit, or intimated meaning. "Statement" and "suggestion" would be clearer terms.

"Denotation" (in the sense common with English logicians since J. S. Mill) is "that which a word *denotes* . . . the aggregate of objects of which a word may be predicated; extension." "Connotation" is "the attribute or aggregate of attributes connoted by a term."[12] Obviously it makes no sense to say that either denotation or connotation in these senses is either absent or weak in a given poem, or present or strong. Modern critics might readily appeal to less technical meanings in the *Oxford English Dictionary* ("denotation" 4 and "connotation" 1) to support their use of these terms to mean approximately statement and suggestion. But the appeal would hardly explain why the critics have been so much given to these logical-sounding terms, with their actually obscure, if not incorrect, intimations. The explanation I believe is that their use of these terms does make an implicit if vague appeal to technical logic and really is a struggle to indicate more than the fairly easy and not always reliable distinction between statement and suggestion. The point appears strikingly in an essay by Allen Tate, "Tension in Poetry," in which the terms "denotation" and "connotation" are used interchangeably with the clearly technical terms "intension" and "extension," and which may be read as a culmination of the critical trend which we have been considering. Tate's essay is difficult to synopsize but means I believe essentially this: The following is a bad example of romantic poetry:

> The wine of love is music,
>   And the feast of love is song:
> When love sits down to banquet,
>   Love sits long:
>
> Sits long and rises drunken,
>   But not with the feast and the wine;
> He reeleth with his own heart,
>   That great rich Vine.

The reason this is bad is that although it has a sizable "intension" or "connotation," that is, suggestive power, it has no logic, no "denotation," no objective content. The following stanza of a hymn to light is, on the other hand, a bad example of metaphysical poetry.

> The Violet, springs little Infant, stands,
>   Girt in thy purple Swadling-bands:
> On the fair Tulip thou dost dote;
> Thou cloath'st it in a gay and party-colour'd Coat.

The reason this stanza is bad is that it proceeds only by logical "extension" or "denotation." It fails in "intension" or "connotation." We can unify the "connotations" only by forgetting the firm "denotations" of the main terms. We have to ignore the denoted diaper in order to take seriously the violet which it pretends to swathe. What then is good poetry? That which avoids both these extremes—an organized body of *extension* and *intension,* where "the remotest figurative significance that we can derive does not invalidate the extensions of the literal statement." For example:

> Our two soules therefore, which are one,
>   Though I must goe, endure not yet
> A breach, but an expansion,
>   Like gold to ayery thinnesse beate.

In short, the feat of poetry is that of pushing *intension* and *extension* toward each other so as to have the fullest measure of both.

The terms "intension" and "extension" as they are used here suggest a technical, logical sense, both for themselves and for their equivalents "connotation" and "denotation." But the precise technical senses, as we have said, are impossible. Extension and intension have an inverse relation. The wider the first the shallower the second. There are more boats than steamboats. But there is less in "boat" than in "steamboat." If we try to push these notions together, we find that it cannot be done. There is simply no kind of term or set of terms which maximizes both. Tate's meaning actually leans a good deal toward the simpler antithesis of statement and suggestion, one which makes good enough sense. But, as I have already indicated, we may wonder: Why all the complication of apparently technical terms to get this said?

The answer, I believe, is that, although the technical concepts intension-connotation, extension-denotation do have some place in the argument, their operation is not clear without explicit invocation of that other technical concept, logical or ontological, with which we have been concerned in this essay—that of specific or substantial essence. What makes this instance especially instructive is the fact that we now cope with a situation greatly complicated beyond the simple naming of objects. We deal with metaphor—the confrontation and mutual reflection of objects. And here the force of substantive discourse is either multiply felt, by reverberations, or its absence multiply missed. We find: wine (of love)=music; feast (of love)= song; heart (of love)=vine. Here are good dictionary, definable names (denotative enough in the simple sense of denotative as opposed to suggestive). Something, however, robs them of their substantive power—the concealed and chaotic abstractions of the second level, "love" and its duplicate "heart." It is not possible to state *what* is confronted with *what*. We have a wild concourse of vehicles. No tenor. (If the concrete, specific substances behind "love" were brought to light—that is, man or woman in love—the vehicles would be discountenanced.) In the second example of bad poetry, on the contrary, there is complete substantive firmness—the violet, the infant in swaddling-bands—but their resemblance is so stretched (so "over-extended") that they discountenance each other even without analysis. It remains that in the two souls (a synecdoche for the two lovers parting) and beaten gold we have that rare situation where two clearly and substantially named objects (denotation) are brought into such a context that they face each other with fullest relevance and illumination (connotation). In such a structure of substantial meaning there is indeed precise extension of specifically named concrete objects and deep intension of radiated relation or symbolic significance. Or, since the terms are used here by a kind of analogical courtesy and stretch of their technical meaning, there is just the reverse: deep intension of specifically qualified literal objects, and wide extension of objects touched by symbolic radiation. This may be what it means to say that extension and intension are pushed toward each other. A closely related truth, I suspect, is that poetry is that type of verbal structure where truth of reference or correspondence reaches a maximum degree of fusion with truth of coherence—or where external and internal relation are intimately mutual reflections.

VI

It is possible of course to have metaphor at levels of discourse other than the substantive. It is possible to say redness is anger, blackness is death. A large number of our best known metaphors, famous instances or Bartlett quotations, actually have an abstraction of the second level as their tenor. They are personifications, or nearly so. "Sleep that knits up the ravelled sleave of care," "Unregarded age in corners thrown," "Laughter holding both his sides," "Close bosom-friend of the maturing sun." Nevertheless, I believe that metaphor has a fairly important affinity for the concept of the specific and substantive. It is by means of this concept, in fact, that one ordinarily distinguishes between metaphor (or simile) and certain less imaginative similitudes which are likely to be called analogies or merely comparisons. A certain traitor is like Judas; a certain tyrant is like Caesar. The two sides of the *analogy* belong in the same specific class. But when a man is called a skunk, specific difference as well as similarity is involved, the predication is concrete, there is *metaphor*. A notion that seems invited is that the modern desire for metaphysical metaphor may be more analytically described as a desire for metaphor in which both vehicle and tenor are objects named specifically and substantively. There has been some tendency to relegate the metaphor with abstract tenor to the class of didactic allegory. Whatever the justice of this position, it would appear to me that metaphysical metaphor may indeed be described as metaphor in which both vehicle and tenor are specifically named objects —and furthermore, that this kind of metaphor is a sort of special fulfillment of the essential direction of metaphor, toward concrete rather than abstractive predication. The fact may be illustrated by both more and less serious instances.

> *Written in Juice of Lemmon*
> But if her wisdom grow severe,
>
> . . . .
> Be not discourag'd, but require
> A more gentle Ordeal Fire,
> And bid her by Loves-Flames read it again.

> On a round ball
> A workman that hath copies by, can lay
> An Europe, Afrique, and an Asia,
> So doth each teare
> Which thee doth weare,
> A globe, yea world by that impression grow
> Till all my tears mixed with thine do overflow
> The world, by waters sent from thee, my heaven dissolved so.

One notices here the infrequency of both abstractions and attributive adjectives. The originality of these passages does not lie in the refinement with which given objects have been observed and delineated (imagism) nor in the depth, height, or shadowy suggestion of abstractive categorizing. It lies rather in relations. Given the condition that the metaphysical poet was to deal in simple species of objects, as he found them named in the dictionary or treatise, the source of his originality and individuation had to lie in the relations he was able to set up between objects. This is another way of getting at the celebrated *discordia concors,* the ontological distance between the objects which the metaphysical poet yoked by violence together. Originality of relation is distance. And a kind of circuit of dependencies is completed if we observe that when objects are pulled from such distances so violently together, a certain firmness in their naming is requisite if they are to survive as objects, not be melted or dissipated—or, to change the figure, if the focus of one upon the other is to remain intelligible. There is no room here for iridescences or fretwork, nor for abstractive expansion. Almost all that is descriptive or minutely qualificative in such poetry takes the form not of streak, shade, or inscape, but of external relationship between distinctly conceived objects: juice from a lemon, fire that is used for ordeal, flames that proceed from a lover, maps which a workman can apply to a sphere, objects reflected in tears, the world overflowed by waters. The relationships subdivide within each side of the main relation or analogy. For with concreteness or substance relationship is multiply invited. With the concreteness of metaphor, predication is solid or indefinite, and meditation limitless.

These remarks are not enough to account for metaphysical metaphor, define its virtue, distinguish the true from the false, tell when or when not the "violence" has been justified. The violet and the swaddling bands, the relatively frivolous juice of lemon in love's flames, these, like the metaphors of Donne, will only be more or less accounted for by the help of the concept which I have been proposing throughout this essay. But the same disability for criticism inheres in all logical formulas. I am interested in maintaining no more than that the concept of specific substance, as it may help to map many simpler provinces of descriptive technique, distinguishing the style of Swift, for example, from that of Johnson and that of Keats, is also a concept through which some insight may be had into the more dimly lit mirror relations of the realm of metaphor.

Vous ferez rimer ensemble, autant qu'il se pourra, des mots très-semblables entre eux comme SON, et très-differents entre eux comme SENS.—THÉODORE DE BANVILLE, Petit Traité de Poésie Française

ONE RELATION
OF RHYME TO REASON

THE VIEW of rhyme which I wish to discuss in this essay has been formerly advanced[1] but has never, I believe, been widely entertained. It seems never to have been expounded in English and has never become a part of English literary theory in the sense of being illustrated from English poetry. English prosodists have discussed rhyme as a degree of likeness in word sounds and have catalogued its approximations: alliteration, assonance, slant rhyme, eye rhyme, analyzed rhyme, dissonance, and so forth. But about the meaning of rhyme words they have had little to say. In this essay I wish to develop the idea that verse in general, and more particularly rhyme, make their special contribution to poetic structure in virtue of a studiously and accurately semantic character. They impose upon the logical pattern of expressed argument a kind of fixative counterpattern of alogical implication.

II

It would be only an exaggeration, not a distortion, of principle to say that the difference between prose and verse is the difference between homoeoteleuton and rhyme. "Non modo ad salutem ejus exstinguendam sed etiam gloriam per tales viros infringendam," says Cicero, and Quintilian quotes[2] it as an example of homoeoteleuton or like endings. Here the -*endam* and the -*endam* are alike, logically and legitimately alike; each has the same meaning, or is the same morpheme, and each supports the logic of the sentence by appearing in a certain place in the structure. Stylistic parallels or forms of meaning of this sort seem to come fairly to the aid of logic; they are part of the normal framework of prose. The difference between these and rhyme in prose may be illustrated by the following examples from St. Augustine: "Lingua clamat, cor amat"; "Praecedat spes, ut sequatur res." Here not only the endings but also the roots rhyme, and the result is an effect of alogicality, if not of excess and artificiality. It is not really to be expected that the roots should rhyme. The same may be said for all parallels of sound which do not inhere in some parallel meaning of the words themselves, but acquire their parallel merely through being placed in parallel structures. Such, for example, is the transverse alliteration of Lyly,[3] where the series of parallel consonants has logically nothing to do with the antithetic parallel of the words. Of somewhat the same character is the cursus or metrical ending. And if a prose writer were to reinforce a pair of parallel or antithetic clauses by making each one an iambic pentameter, we should say that this was decidedly too much, that the metrical equality was hardly interesting unless it combined with a vein of logic that ran differently.

It is possible to point out examples, in balladry and in other primitive types of poetry, where the equalities of verse coincide with the parallels of meaning. Even in sophisticated poetry such as Tennyson's *In Memoriam* one may find some stanzas where a high degree of parallel is successful.[4] But on the whole the tendency of verse, or certainly that of English verse, has been the opposite. The smallest equalities, the feet, so many syllables, or so many time units, are superimposed upon the linear succession of ideas most often without any regard for the equalities of logic. Two successive iambs may be two words, or one word, or parts of two words, and so on. The larger units, the lines, also are measured without reference to logically parallel sections of sense. Even in heavily end-stopped verse, such as that in Shakespeare's early plays, the complete phrase of which each line is formed stands in oblique relation to the lines before and after. The lines do not parallel one another but spring ahead, one from another, diversely.

The more primitive and forthrightly emotional the poetry, as in balladry, the less it may demand the sensory resistance of verse nonparallel to logic. The more sophisticated and intellectualized the poetry, the more it will demand such resistance. The point is worth illustrating from the blank verse of *Paradise Lost*—one of the most artful verse forms in the range of English literature. An important phrase in Milton's own prescription for blank verse is "sense variously drawn out from one verse into another." This various drawing out he accomplishes for the most part by his ever various, subtly continuous, confused, and tenuous syntax, by which the sense drips down from line to line and does not usually run parallel in any successive lines. But if it does run parallel, there will be certain careful and curious dislocations that prevent the lines from seeming to be the unit of logical measure.

> Abhorred *Styx*, the flood of deadly hate;
> Sad *Acheron* of sorrow, black and deep;
> *Cocytus*, named of lamentation loud
> Heard on the rueful stream; fierce *Phlegethon*,
> Whose waves of torrent fire inflame with rage.

It is I who have italicized the names of the four infernal rivers. These are the four heads of the parallel—moving back toward the front of the line, from Styx to Cocytus, then leaping to the end with Phlegethon. The modifiers of the first two are of about the same length and place in the line; that of the third is longer and runs through two lines; that of the fourth fills just one line. Thus comes the sense of weaving back and forth, of intellect threading complexity, rather than a cool, simplifying triumph of classification.[5] The same handling of parallel can sometimes be seen in single lines.

> *Unres'pited', unpit'ied, un'reprieved'*

*Un*shak'en, *un*'seduced', *un*ter'rified'

Thou' art' my fa'ther, *thou'* my au'thor, *thou'*
My being gavest me.

The italicized syllables escape a prosaic parallel by falling in
different metrical positions, now in thesis, now in arsis. The
third "thou" is thrust out alone at the end of the line. The
verse runs sinuously, intertwining with the sense and making
a tension and resilience.

III

We come then to rhyme, the subject of our argument. And
first it must be admitted that in certain contexts a high degree
of parallel in sense may be found even in rhyme. Even identical
words may rhyme. In the sestina, for example, the same set of
rhyme words is repeated in six different stanzas. But here the
order changes, and so does the relation of each rhyme word to
the context. That is the point of the sestina. Somewhat the
same may be said for a refrain when it does not rhyme with
any other line of the context. In the broadest sense, difference
of meaning in rhyme words includes difference of syntax. In
fact, words have no character as rhymes until they become
points in a syntactic succession. Hence rhyme words (even
identical ones) can scarcely appear in a context without showing some difference of meaning. The point of this essay is
therefore not to prove that rhyme words must exhibit difference of meaning, but to discuss the value of the difference and
to show how a greater degree of difference harmonizes with a
certain type of verse structure.

Under certain conditions (much more common than the
sestina or refrain mentioned above) the opportunity and the
demand for difference of meaning in rhyme may be slight.

> Scogan, that knelest at the stremes hed
> Of grace, of alle honour and worthynesse,
> In th'ende of which strem I am dul as ded,
> Forgete in solitarie wildernesse,—
> Yet, Scogan, thenke on Tullius kyndenesse.

The three identical "nesse" rhymes could be mere prosy homoeoteleuton if the three words occurred in positions of nearly
parallel logic or syntax. But Chaucer's sense, meandering like
the stream through the stanza, makes no great demand upon
these rhymes, and weak though they are, they are strong
enough. Even in Chaucer's couplets the same continuity of
sense through the verse may be discovered, and the same
tendency in rhyming, as we shall illustrate in the comparison
which follows.

Pope is the English poet whose rhyming shows perhaps the
clearest contrast to Chaucer's. Chaucer found, even in Middle
English, a "skarsete" of rhyme.[6] There would come a day when
an even greater scarcity of easy rhymes would create a challenge to the English poet and at the same time indicate one
of his most subtle opportunities. In the course of three hundred
years English lost many of its easy rhymes, stressed Germanic
and Romance endings, *y, ing, ere, esse,* and *able, age, al, aunce,
aile, ain, esse, oun, ous, ure,* so that Pope perforce rhymed
words differing more widely in meaning. The characteristics
of Pope's couplet, as opposed to Chaucer's, are, of course, its
closure or completeness, its stronger tendency to parallel, and
its epigrammatic, witty, intellectual point. One can hardly
imagine such a couplet rhyming "wildernesse" and "kynde-
nesse," or "worthynesse" and "hethenesse," as Chaucer does in
one couplet of the knight's portrait.

Most likely it is neither feasible nor even desirable to construct a scale of meaning differences to measure the cleverness
of rhyme. The analysis which I intend is not in the main
statistical. But an obvious, if rude, basis for classification is
provided by the parts of speech. It may be said, broadly, that
difference in meaning of rhyme words can be recognized in
difference of parts of speech and in difference of functions of
the same part of speech, and that both of these differences
will be qualified by the degree of parallel or of obliquity appearing between the two whole lines of a rhyming pair. The
tenor of the comparison which follows will be to suggest that
Pope's rhymes are characterized by difference in parts of speech

or in function of the same parts of speech, the difference in each case being accentuated by the tendency of his couplets to parallel structure.

A large number of rhymes in both Pope and Chaucer, or indeed in any English poet, are rather neutral to our inquiry.

> Whan that Aprille with his shoures soote
> The droghte of March hath perced to the roote.

Here the rhyme makes its contribution to difference of sense against equality of verse, but because the oblique phrases themselves make a fundamental contrast to the metrically equal lines, and the rhyming parts of speech are a function of the phrases, the rhyme is not likely to be felt as a special element of variation. There is a higher proportion of such rhymes in Chaucer than in Pope.[7] In general Chaucer relies for variation more on continuous sense and syntax than on rhyme, and when his rhyme words are the same part of speech, he is apt to give us a dullish rhyme:

> Me thynketh it acordaunt to resoun
> To telle you al the condicioun.

In similar constructions Pope is apt to find some quaint minor contrast in length and quality of words:

> What guards the purity of melting maids,
> In courtly balls, and midnight masquerades?

It is in couplets of parallel structure, however, that the rhyming of Pope is seen to best advantage. More of these couplets in Pope have rhymes of different parts of speech than in Chaucer, and their effect is more pronounced in Pope because the parallel within the closed couplet of Pope is likely to be smarter. Chaucer will write:

> And everemoore he hadde a sovereyn prys;
> And though that he were worthy, he was wys.

Pope will write:

> Oft, when the world imagine women stray,
> The Sylphs thro' mystic mazes guide their way.

> When Florio speaks, what virgin could withstand,
> If gentle Damon did not squeeze her hand.

In these two examples, though the syntax is oblique, the sense is parallel and antithetic. Pope's couplets, no matter what their syntax, tend to hover on the verge of antithesis and hence to throw a stress upon whatever difference of meaning appears in the rhyme words.

One might expect to find that a parallel both of general sense and of rhyming parts of speech would produce a quality of flatness, a sort of minimum rhyme such as we found in St. Augustine—"Lingua clamat, cor amat"—only the first step beyond homoeoteleuton. One thing that may prevent this and may lend the rhyme a value of variation is that through some irregularity or incompleteness of parallel the rhyming words have oblique functions. Thus Chaucer:

> No deyntee morsel passed thurgh hir throte;
> Hir diete was accordant to hir cote.

And Pope:

> From each she nicely culls with curious toil,
> And decks the Goddess with the glitt'ring spoil.

There are more of these couplets in Pope than in Chaucer, and with Pope the rhyme difference is more likely to seem the result of some deft twist or trick.

> Some are bewilder'd in the maze of schools,
> And some made coxcombs Nature meant but fools.

There is a kind of inversion (from pupils to schools and back to the pupils in a new light) which in some couplets appears more completely as chiasmus, an effect concerning which I shall have more to say.

The two types of rhyme difference which characterize Pope's poetry (that of different parts of speech and that of the same part of speech in different functions) are a complement, as I have suggested, of his tendency to a parallel of lines. To recognize this may affect our opinion about how deliberately or consciously Pope strove for difference of rhyme, but it should not diminish the impression which the actual difference of rhyme makes upon us. Such rhyme difference may be felt more clearly as a characteristic of Pope if we examine the rhymes in a passage where the parallel is somewhat like that which Chaucer at times employs. It is difficult to find passages of sustained parallel in Chaucer. The usual narrative movement of his couplets is the oblique forward movement of actions in a sequence. But in the character sketches of the *Canterbury Prologue* a kind of loose parallel often prevails for ten or twenty lines, as one feature of a pilgrim after another is enumerated. The sense is continuous, in that the couplets tend to be incomplete, but the lines are all members of a parallel bundle. A clear example may be seen in the yeoman's portrait.

> And he was clad in cote and hood of grene.
> A sheef of pecock arwes, bright and kene,
> Under his belt he bar ful thriftily,
> (Wel coude he dresse his takel yemanly:
> . . . .
> Upon his arm he baar a gay bracer,
> And by his syde a swerd and a bokeler,
> And on that oother syde a gay daggere
> Harneised wel and sharp as point of spere;
> A Christopher on his brest of silver sheene,
> A horn he bar, the bawdryk was of grene.

"Thriftily" and "yemanly," "bracer" and "bokeler," "sheene" and "grene," rhymes like these (aside even from the use of final syllables, "ly" and "er") I should call tame rhymes because the same parts of speech are used in closely parallel functions. To see the difference in this respect between Chaucer and Pope we may turn to the classic lines of another portrait:

> Bless'd with each talent and each art to please,
> And born to write, converse, and live with ease;
> Should such a man, too fond to rule alone,
> Bear, like the Turk, no brother near the throne;
> View him with scornful, yet with jealous eyes,
> And hate for arts that caus'd himself to rise;
> Damn with faint praise, assent with civil leer,

> And without sneering teach the rest to sneer;
> Willing to wound, and yet afraid to strike,
> Just hint a fault, and hesitate dislike;
> Alike reserv'd to blame or to commend,
> A tim'rous foe, and a suspicious friend.

The parallel of lines is continuous, but the rhymes are always different parts of speech. The portrait continues:

> Dreading ev'n fools; by flatterers besieged,
> And so obliging that he ne'er obliged;
> Like *Cato,* give his little Senate laws,
> And sit attentive to his own applause.

Here the same parts of speech are rhymed, but one verb is passive, one active; one noun is plural, one singular. The functions are different, in each case what he does being set against what he receives.

It is to be noted that in the yeoman's portrait such rhymes as "grene" and "kene," "thriftily" and "yemanly" are of the sort which we described above as minimum rhyme, only one step away from homoeoteleuton. Rhymes of this type often escape the extreme, as we saw, by some irregularity of parallel. But it is significant to add now that even when Pope does not escape the extreme he has resources of piquancy. Here and there he will be guilty of a certain flatness:

> Each motion guides, and every nerve sustains,
> Itself unseen, but in th' effects remains.

Often, however, he conveys some nice contrast in the parallel.

> True wit is Nature to advantage dress'd,
> What oft was thought, but ne'er so well express'd.

Here the two rhyme verbs are not merely parallel examples. One is literal, one is figurative, and in being matched with each other they express in brief the metaphor on which this classic critical doctrine is based, that to express is to dress.

> Th' adventurous Baron the bright locks admired;
> He saw, he wish'd, and to the prize aspired.

Here the difference between "admired" and "aspired," the swift ascent of the Baron's aspiration, is precisely the point.

> One speaks the glory of the British Queen,
> And one describes a charming Indian screen.

> Do thou, Crispissa, tend her fav'rite Lock;
> Ariel himself shall be the guard of Shock.

From "British Queen" to "Indian screen," from "Lock" to "Shock," here is the same bathos he more often puts into one line—"When husbands, or when lapdogs breathe their last."

IV

What I conceive to be the acme of variation occurs in a construction to which I have already alluded, chiasmus. The basis of chiasmus will be a high degree of parallel, often antithetic. The rhyme may be of the same part of speech or of different parts. If it is of the same part, the chiastic variation will be a special case of the "schools"–"fools" rhyme already quoted, where a twist in the meaning gives different functions to the rhyme words. If the rhyme is of different parts, the variation will be a special case of that already discussed, where different parts of speech rhyme in parallel lines.

> Whether the nymph shall break[1] Diana's law,[2]
> Or some frail China jar[2'] receive a flaw.[1']

In the first line the breakage, then the fragile thing (the law); in the second line another fragile thing (the jar) and then its breaking (the flaw). The parallel is given a kind of roundness and completeness; the intellectual lines are softened into the concrete harmony of "law" and "flaw." The meaning is locked in a pattern of inevitability.

> What dire offence from amr'ous causes[1] springs,[2]
> What mighty contests rise[2'] from trivial things.[1']

> Love, Hope, and Joy, fair Pleasure's[1] smiling train,[2]
> Hate, Fear, and Grief, the family[2'] of pain.[1']

Fear¹ to the statesman,² rashness¹ to the chief,²
To kings²′ presumption,¹′ and to crowds²′ belief.¹′

Thus critics of less judgment¹ than caprice,²
Curious,²′ not knowing,¹′ not exact,¹ but nice.²

In the last example the antithesis is tripled, and the order being
successively chiastic, returns upon itself, which is sufficient
complication to make "caprice" and "nice" a surprise. Then
one is an adjective and one a noun, and "caprice" has two
syllables.[8]

The contemplation of chiastic rhyme, the most brilliant and
complex of all the forms of rhyme variation, leads me to make
a brief general remark upon the degree of Pope's reputation
for rhyme. I have relied heavily upon examples of rhyme from
Pope because he takes such clear and frequent advantage of
the rhyming quality with which I am concerned. To that extent, and it seems to me an important extent, he is one of the
finest English rhymers. Yet a critic of Pope's rhyme has spoken
of "true" rhymes and "false" rhymes and "rimes to the eye" and
has been concerned to discover that of 7874 rhymes in Pope
1027 are "false." Another has approved of Pope's "correctness"
in excluding polysyllables from his rhymes, but has found
Pope's repeated use of the same rhyme words "monotonous in
a high degree and a very serious artistic defect." The same
critic has actually spoken of Pope's "poverty of rhyme." One
of the purposes of my argument is to cut the ground from
under such judgments. They can spring only from a limited
view of rhyme as a form of phonetic harmony—to be described
and appraised in terms of phonetic accuracy, complexity, and
variety—in other words, from a failure to connect rhyme with
reason.[9]

V

We have so far considered rhyme as it makes variation
against the parallels of verse. If we think now of the meaning
of the words as the basis of comparison, thus beginning with
variation or difference, we can discuss the sameness of the

rhyme sound as a binding force. Rhyme is commonly recognized as a binder in verse structure. But where there is need for binding there must be some difference or separation between the things to be bound. If they are already close together, it is supererogatory to emphasize this by the maneuver of rhyme. So we may say that the greater the difference in meaning between rhyme words the more marked and the more appropriate will be the binding effect. Rhyme theorists have spoken of the "surprise" which is the pleasure of rhyme, and surely this surprise is not merely a matter of coming upon a similarity which one has not *previously* anticipated. It cannot be a matter of time. Even after the discovery, when the rhyme is known by heart, the pleasurable surprise remains. It must depend on some incongruity or unlikelihood inherent in the coupling. It is a curious thing that "queen" should rhyme with "screen;" they are very unlike objects. But Pope has found a connection between them, has classified them as topics of chat, and then the parallel of sound comes to his aid as a humorous binder.

> The hero William, and the martyr Charles,
> One knighted Blackmore, and one pension'd Quarles.

"Charles" did not actually pension "Quarles," but we are well on the way to believing that he did; the rhyme at least is a *fait accompli.*

The most extreme examples of this kind of humor are the extravagant double or triple rhymes of a Butler, a Swift, a Byron, or a Browning. One stanza from Byron will do.

> He was a Turk, the colour of mahogany;
> And Laura saw him, and at first was glad,
> Because the Turks so much admire philogyny,
> Although their usage of their wives is sad;
> 'Tis said they use no better than a dog any
> Poor woman, whom they purchase like a pad:
> They have a number, though they ne'er exhibit 'em,
> Four wives by law, and concubines "ad libitum."

If Byron had rhymed "philogyny" and "misogyny," it would not be very funny, for one expects these two words to sound alike;

they are formed alike from the Greek and make the end words
of a natural antithesis. They are mere homoeoteleuton. "Mahogany" makes a comic rhyme with "philogyny" because of
the wide disparity in meaning between the words. Mahogany,
the Spanish name of a reddish hardwood, is not a likely companion for the learned Greek abstraction, but once an ingenious
affinity in meaning is established, the rhyme sounds a triple
surprise of ratification. Then comes "dog any," and difference
of meaning in rhyme has proceeded to the point of disintegra-
tion and mad abandon. What convinces us that "dog any" belongs in this stanza is not so much its inevitable or appropriate
meaning as the fact that it does rhyme.

VI

"Rime," says Henry Lanz, "is one of those irrational satellites
that revolve around reason. It is concerned not with the meaning of verse but only with its form, which is emotional. It lies
within the plane of the a-logical cross-section of verse."[10] It is
within the scope of my argument to grant the alogical character of rhyme, or rather to insist on it, but at the same time to
insist that the alogical character by itself has little, if any,
aesthetic value. The music of spoken words in itself is meager,
so meager in comparison to the music of song or instrument as
to be hardly worth discussion. It has become a platitude of
criticism to point out that verses composed of meaningless
words afford no pleasure of any kind and can scarcely be called
rhythmical—let them even be rhymed. The mere return to the
vowel tonic (the chord or tone cluster characteristic of a
vowel) is likely to produce the emotion of boredom. The art of
words is an intellectual art, and the emotions of poetry are
simultaneous with conceptions and largely induced through the
medium of conceptions. In literary art only the wedding of the
alogical with the logical gives the former an aesthetic value.
The words of a rhyme, with their curious harmony of sound and
distinction of sense, are an amalgam of the sensory and the
logical, or an arrest and precipitation of the logical in sensory
form; they are the icon in which the idea is caught. Rhyme and

other verse elements save the physical quality of words—intellectualized and made transparent by daily prose usage.[11] But
without the intellectual element there is nothing to save and no
reason why the physical element of words need be asserted.
"Many a man," says Dr. Lanz at the close of his book, "was
cruelly put to death for a 'daring rhyme.'" And he regards it
as a "triumph of modern science that, instead of marveling at
the mystery of this force, we can 'dissect it as a corpse.'" These
notions seem set up to provoke the retort that men are cruelly
put to death not for melodies but for ideas, and that it is only
when reduced to a purely "physical basis" that rhyme becomes
a "corpse."

> When Adam dalf and Eve span,
> Who was then a gentilman?[12]

If there is something daring in this rhyme of John Ball's, it is
certainly not in the return to the overtone of 1840 vibrations
per second characteristic of ă [æ], but in the ironic jostle by
which plebian "span" gives a lesson in human values to aristocratic "gentilman."

. . . οἷον εἰ καὶ τὰ ὀνόματα μεταφορὰ εἴη καὶ μεταφορὰ τοιαδὶ καὶ ἀντίθεσις καὶ παρίσωσις.
—Rhetoric, III, xi

RHETORIC
AND POEMS

ALEXANDER POPE

WHEN WE seek to confront two such elusive entities as a theory of poems and poems themselves and to determine relations between these two, I think there is much to be said for placing them first, tentatively, in their most generic and noncommittal relation. There is much to be said for the conjunctional form of title commonly given to the academic paper: X *and* Y, Shakespeare *and* Hall's Chronicle, Theory *and* Poems. I for one find it convenient to distinguish five main types of relation between theory and poems, all five of which are frequently to be observed in critical and historical studies, though often more or less confused.

I. There is for one thing the kind of relation between theory and poems with which we are concerned when our interest is chiefly in the theory itself, that is, when we try to describe and assess a given theory as objectively as we can with reference to whatever general norms for poems and hence for theory we possess. Is the classical theory of imitation in any sense a good

Reprinted from *English Institute Essays, 1948.* Copyright 1949 by Columbia University Press.

or fruitful theory of poems? Or the classical theory of ornament
and system of rhetoric? Or do these deserve to be completely
demolished, as in the Crocean history of Aesthetic? Is Matthew
Arnold's view of the high seriousness and critical function of
poems the right view? Or, does it, as Tate and others have
argued, deliver poems into the hands of science and morals?
My purpose at the moment is not to maintain the importance
of such questions, but merely to note their occurrence.

II. It may at times be difficult to distinguish between such a
general evaluative interest in theory and what I consider a
second kind of interest, that with which we approach a theorist,
especially a technical or rhetorical theorist and his cousins of
the trivium, the grammarian and logician, for the purpose of
borrowing tools which we shall put to the partly unpredictable
uses of our own analysis: *fable*, or *character*, or *metaphor* from
Aristotle, *antithesis* or *parallel* from the rhetoricians, *sentences*,
for that matter, and *nouns* and *verbs* from the grammarians.
To do this may imply that we think a theorist a good theorist
of poems, and yet I believe it may come short of that, in so
far as concepts themselves may come short of integrated or
achieved theory, and also in so far as this borrowing extends
readily, and perhaps most profitably, to the less literary philosophers, the grammarian and logician.

To look in the historical direction, I should say that when we
take up the more generic concepts of rhetoric, grammar, and
logic, we ought to be on our guard against imputing to them
special connections with the poems of any specific period—as
would happen if one were to note the Aristotelian "categories"
in Renaissance logic and read in them an influence on the
imagery of Drayton or Donne. Richards in his *Philosophy of
Rhetoric* has found the concept of the morpheme as defined by
Bloomfield a useful one for explaining certain powers of words.
But it would be somewhat wide of the mark to learn that Auden
had read either Richards or Bloomfield and from that go on to
discover such elements as morphemes in Auden's poems. The
idea of the circulation of the blood was expounded by Harvey
in 1616, but we do not conceive that it was about that time
that blood began to circulate in the human body.

III. A third relation between theory and poems is that which obtains when a given theory does have a specific, historical relation to a poem, but has this in virtue of the special fact that it appears in the poem as part of the poem's meaning or content. One will recall numerous instances in the history of English poetry: Chaucer's burlesque of Geoffrey of Vinsauf in the mock heroic of the cock and the fox, Stephen Hawes' celebration of "golden" words in his *Pastime of Pleasure,* the Horatian arts of poetry (especially that of Pope), Mark Akenside's *Pleasures of the Imagination,* Wordsworth's *Prelude,* and Shelley's *Ode to the West Wind* (where the sparks from the unextinguished priestly hearth mingle with the sparks of "inextinguishable thought" which appear twice in his prose *Defense of Poetry*). This relation between theory and poems is that which for the most part obtains in historical studies of the neutrally observational type—but often with some implication that the relation established is of a more formal, or actually theoretical, sort.

IV. A fourth relation between theory and poems which I believe it worth while to distinguish is again a specific historical relation, that which obtains when in a given era a theory helps to determine poems not as subject matter but as an influence or cause why they are written in a certain way. Perhaps the most important thing to note about this relation is that (like number III) it does not require that the theory as theory be an adequate account of the poems. The classic theory concerning imitation of models, for instance, had a close bearing on the Augustan vogue of translations, paraphrases, and "imitations." Yet a theory of models is never really a literary theory, only a practical rule of inspiration. And the classic theory in particular seemed almost unconscious of the paramount factor of parody, or allusiveness, which worked in the most lively Augustan instances. Again, the massive theory of epic which prevailed in that day might be taken as a partial cause of Blackmore's *Prince Arthur* or, in jocular reversal, of *The Rape of the Lock,* or *The Dunciad.* But there are no successfully serious epics with which the theory can be compared. During the same period, the doctrine *Ut pictura poesis* may have joined with empirical views of imagination to determine the subject matter of some poems; it may have been responsible for certain instances of the pictorial fallacy or opaqueness in word painting; but, as Lessing was partly to show, the analogy between words and marble or paint is of limited service for analyzing the positive qualities of verbal art.

V. A fifth relation between theory and poems, that which will be the final focus of our argument, is that which obtains when in any historical era we can discern a specific affinity between theory as such and poems; that is, when what the theory says seems to be a specially appropriate description of what the poems are. Such a relation may of course coincide with the causal relation which we have just considered. There may be instances of a close causal connection between theory and poems and at the same time a high degree of validity for the theory as theory. A successful poet may be shown to have read a certain theory with profit, or he may even, though this I believe is rare, succeed in uttering a theory which explains his own poems. But these are matters for another sort of inquiry. It is only by keeping clear of such intentionalistic complications that we can focus upon the literary and critical issue: that is, the degree of resemblance between the theory and the poems or the adequacy of the theory to describe the poems.

To show a real correspondence between the theory of an era and the poems of the era would be, I take it, one of the most proper concerns of the student of criticism in its historical aspect, and to show that the theory gave an adequate account of the poems would be his masterpiece. Such an achievement, we ought at the same time to note, would be a special challenge to the student of either theory or poems who was interested in universal definitions or norms. Poems in different eras, it is assumed, will be to some extent different. But theory deals with universals. It is more disconcerting to find the theory of successive ages different than to find the poems different. No matter how well we, with our historical desires, succeed in localizing the theory or assimilating it to the poems of its own age, we can still see that the theory itself aims at the universal. If the poems and the theory vary in step with each other, then I suppose a great appearance of support is offered to historical relativism—unless indeed one's dialectic rises to reconciling certain valid special theories of poetry, say the metaphysical theory of wit and the romantic theory of imagination, in a more inclusive harmony. Or unless one is brave enough to decide in a given case that both poems and theory are bad—as Yvor Winters has not scrupled to say the poems of Poe are bad because they perfectly illustrate Poe's theory, a deliquescent version of romantic imagination.

Not every theory found in a given age is equally relevant to describing the poems of that age. There are not only bad theories which have no special bearing on any kind of poems, but another and more important kind, those of such general significance (if not complete truth) that they transcend a special application to the poems of their age. Such, for example, I should call the neoclassic doctrine that poetry reveals the generic or universal. Despite the game of omber and the all too specific and solid Dunces, the doctrine of the universal is if correctly interpreted a valid doctrine, and furthermore it is itself universal, that is, neither more nor less true of good neoclassic poems than of good poems in any other mode. Or the related doctrine that "Style is the dress of thought"[1]—true poetry is "nature to advantage dressed." This would appear to be the Augustan version of a paradox which literary criticism has so far by no means solved. Today we speak of art signs as iconic or as calling attention to their own excellence, or we speak of poetry as intensely realized meaning, or as dramatized meaning, or perhaps as structure of meaning. Poetic meaning still seems to contain other meanings and to make use of them, but seems not to be tested in the end by the same norms. The doctrine that style is the dress of thought is as much our concern as it was Pope's, and, whatever its degree of truth, it applies no more specially to Augustan poems than to any other kind.[2]

In somewhat the same way I believe we should have to discuss the whole classical theory of imitation and the antitheses deriving from the theory and flourishing in Pope's time, between art and nature, between invention and imitation of

models, between wit and judgment, between genius and the
rules. Or perhaps some of these theoretical formulas do show a
special relation to the poems of the age, though one which will
make acceptable sense to us only after a certain adjustment.
One such example seems to me of importance here as a partial
frame of reference for the more specific rhetorical ideas which
I wish to discuss. I have in mind the Augustan concept of "correctness," which, distinguished from greatness or "genius,"
sometimes took the form of an ideal, as in the well known advice of Walsh to Pope: that there had been *great* English poets,
but no great poet who was *correct;* but sometimes also was conceived as a fault or limitation, as in Addison's *Spectators*, Nos.
160 and 291, where the untrammeled productions of ancient
Genius are preferred to the scrupulous nicety or correctness of
the moderns. As Sir Joshua Reynolds was later to phrase it: "So
far, indeed, is the presence of genius from implying an absence
of faults, that they are considered by many as its inseparable
companions."[3] The paradox was still vital in the next century,
when Ruskin preferred the *imperfections,* that is, the irregulari-
ties, of Gothic architecture to the *perfection,* that is the regu-
larity, of geometric ornaments in Greek architecture. This bizarre critical tradition seems to arise from the capacity of the
term *correctness* to be taken not only (1) as a general term of
value (certainly what is "correct" is right and good), but (2)
as a more specially descriptive term, meaning something like
symmetry and something like restraint and precision. It is in
the latter sense of course that we shall have to take it if we
apply it to Augustan poems—if we wish to say that Pope followed the advice of Walsh and became a *correct* poet. The
other sense will hardly go with the liberal and usually accepted
view that Shakespeare's verse and rhetoric fit what Shakespeare
is saying, just as Pope's fit what Pope is saying. In the final
sense of poetic value, each kind of good poetry is correct.

II

It is under the head of correctness in its limited sense that
the most precise resemblances between neoclassic theory and

neoclassic poems seem to be available—I mean in the rhetoric of the closed couplet. Perhaps it is not too much to say that the resemblance between theory and poems which obtains here is one of the most precise in the history of literature and criticism—that the hexameter couplets of Boileau and Racine and the pentameters of Dryden and Pope represent the maximum fulfillment of a classic technical theory. Yet the relation between theory and poems which obtains even here is not, as we shall see, strictly a synchronous one.

The year 1935 gave us two highly competent studies, one by Professor Williamson, concerning the history of English couplet theory from Puttenham in 1589 to Edward Bysshe in 1702; and one by Miss Wallerstein, concerning the practice of English couplet writers, from the poems of Grimald in Tottel's *Miscellany* to Denham's lines on the Thames in 1655. Professors Williamson and Wallerstein, writing from these different directions, theory and poems, produced notably harmonious accounts of couplet rhetoric: the sententious closure, the balanced lines and half-lines, the antithesis and inversion, the strict metric and accordingly slight but telling variations, the constantly close and tensile union of what are called musical with logical and rhetorical effects. The dates embraced in the works of these two writers may, however, invite the reflection that so far as the couplets of Alexander Pope (at the English neoclassic zenith) conform to a theory of rhetoric, it is to a theory which had reached its full development a generation or two earlier. For a good account in English of the figures of speech and thought to be found in Pope's verse one will perhaps go even as far back as Puttenham's *Arte of English Poesie*. In Puttenham one will find too the main metrical rules and even the important emphasis on the caesura. Edward Bysshe's *Art of English Poetry*, which may plausibly be taken as representative of what had happened to English poetics by the time Pope was a youth, says nothing at all of the figures, though it carries the metrics to a far greater degree of rigidity than Puttenham and includes the now famous dictionary of rhymes. The classical figures of speech and thought, joined with poetics during the Middle Ages, had by Bysshe's time been reseparated from

poetics and confined again in the treatises on prose rhetoric—
such as that of Thomas Blount, *The Academie of Eloquence*
(1654) or that of John Smith, *The Mysterie of Rhetorique Un-vail'd* (1657).[4] Puttenham's *Arte* of 1589, though it is only one
of many English accounts of rhetorical figures up to Pope's day,
remains the most lively and informative and the most precisely
focused upon poems.[5]

Pope himself in Chapters X and XI of *Peri Bathous* wrote a
comic treatment of "Tropes and Figures" (including "The Antithesis, or See-Saw"), and he once observed to Spence that the
"stiffness of style" in Wycherley's plays was "occasioned by his
always studying for antithesis." But neither in his *Essay on
Criticism*, nor in his remarks to Spence, nor in his letters, even
the elaborate letter on versification to Walsh, has Pope anything
substantial to say about the system of artful figures which later
critics have considered characteristic of his couplets. Pope
talks of the metrical "niceties," of suiting the sound to the sense,
of caesura, of expletives, and of hiatus, or of avoiding extravagance in diction. The rhetorical sinews of the kind of verse in
which he was the champion—the essential patterns where Wal-
ler's strength and Denham's sweetness joined, where Dryden
had achieved the long resounding march and energy divine[6]
—these perhaps had been learned so well by Pope as a boy that
he could forget them. "It was our family priest," he told
Spence, "who taught me the figures, accidence, and first part
of grammar." In later life perhaps the figures were assumed by
Pope under the general head of "correctness." At any rate he
seems to have been able to take them for granted.

Among the hundred odd figures, "auricular," "sensable," and
"sententious," presented by Puttenham, there are certain ones,
a rather large number if all subdivisions of the main types are
counted, which would seem to be fundamental to the logic of
the formally ordered verbal style. Thus, "*Parison*, or the figure
of even [clauses]," "*Omoioteleton*, or the figure of like-loose
[like endings]," and "*Anaphora*, or the figure of report" (that is,
repetition of a word at the beginning of successive clauses) are
the figures in Puttenham which refer to formal parallels and

which under one set of terms or another are a constant part of
the rhetorical tradition from Puttenham back to Aristotle. Contrast or antithesis is the natural accompaniment of parallel.
This appears in Puttenham as "*Antitheton,* or the quarreller,
otherwise called the overthwart or rencounter." Wherever
there is a parallel, there is a distinction, and wherever a distinction, the possibility of a paradox, an antithesis, or at least a
modulation. Thus, to illustrate now from the verse of Pope:

> Who sees with equal eye, as God of all,
> A hero perish, or a sparrow fall.
>
> Favours to none, to all she smiles extends;
> Oft she rejects, but never once offends.
>
> Survey the WHOLE, nor seek slight faults to find
> Where nature moves, and rapture warms the mind.

This brings us, still quite naturally, to a third group of figures,
those distinguished by Puttenham as "*Zeugma,* or the single
supply" and "*Sillepsis,* or the double supply." Zeugma is further distinguished by Puttenham into *Prozeugma* (or the Ring-
leader), *Mezozeugma* (or the Middlemarcher), and *Hypozeugma* (or the Rerewarder), accordingly as the zeugma, or
yoking word, occurs at the beginning, the middle, or the end
of a total construction. He treats zeugma among the figures
"merely *auricular* in that they reach no furder than the eare,"
and among figures "that work by defect," that is, by the absence of "some little portion of speech." He does not say anything about the relation of zeugma to parallel. But we might
observe that zeugma or ellipsis[7] is almost the inevitable effect
of a tightened and precise economy of parallel. If A, B, C and
X, B, Z are presented, then A, B, C and X, Z is an easy result;
or if A, B and X, B, then A, B and X—in the more usual case,
the parallel of two elements. Thus, in Pope's verse:

Who could not win the mistress, wooed the maid. (Prozeugma)

And now a bubble *burst,* and now a world. (Mezozeugma)

Where nature moves, and rapture warms the *mind.* (Hypozeugma)

And, to note a special and significant kind of zeugma that occurs in Pope's verse, such examples as these:

> Or lose her heart, or necklace, at a ball.

> Or stain her honour or her new brocade.

This is metaphor. I mention it here not simply to list the figure of metaphor among Pope's accomplishments. Puttenham also duly lists "*Metaphora*, or the figure of transport." But here it seems to me curious, and worth noting, though it is not noted by Puttenham, that a series of several logical steps, distinction, parallel, then simplification or canceling a common element, has led us to metaphor, something that has often, and notably by some in Pope's day, been considered the very essence of the irrational or merely imaginative in poetry. Let us carry our series to its conclusion, returning to Puttenham for help. Consider the figure of "*Sillepsis*, or the double supply," which occurs according to Puttenham when a verb is used either with a double grammatical congruity, or in a double sense.[8] The latter may be thus illustrated from Pope's verse.

> Here thou, great Anna! whom three realms obey,
> Dost sometimes counsel take—and sometimes tea.

> With earnest eyes, and round unthinking fa ;e,
> He first the snuff-box opened, then the case.

Worse and worse. We have now descended from logical parallel and ellipsis, through metaphor, into pun. In short, by starting with what might have been thought the most log;cal and prosaic aspects of Pope's verse (both *Antitheton* and *Parison* were mentioned by Puttenham as figures specially related to prose), and by moving through a few shades of meaning we have arrived at the very things which the modern critic Empson noticed first in looking for the shiftiness or ambiguity of this kind of verse. We may note too, as we pass, that the distinction between the two figures last described, the metaphoric zeugma and the punning syllepsis, is not alwa :s easy. Take the couplet preceding that about counsel and tea:

> Here Britain's statesmen oft the fall foredoom
> Of foreign Tyrants and of Nymphs at home.

It depends on how technically and specifically we are accustomed to think of a "fall" from virtue, whether we take "the fall of tyrants and of nymphs" as metaphor or pun.

But now I should like to backtrack into an area of rhetoric different from antitheses and parallels, though joining them or branching off from them, in Puttenham's *Arte*, under the figure *Anaphora*, the word or phrase repeated at the beginning of successive clauses. Puttenham supplies a large battery of figures in this area: "counterturns," "redoubles," "eccho sounds," "swifte repeates," "rebounds," and "counterchanges," among which the pick is "*Traductio*, or the tranlacer." This, says Puttenham, "is when ye turne and tranlace a word into many sundrie shapes as the Tailor doth his garment, and after that sort do play with him in your dittie." The principle of these figures is that a word or root is repeated in various syntactic positions, and sometimes in various forms, with a consequent shifting, version, turning, or translacing of the sense. These are the figures which Dryden in 1693 calls "turns, both on the words and on the thought," and which, despite a report by Dryden to the contrary, are nowhere better illustrated than in Milton's *Paradise Lost*. The turn is one of the main sinews of the sense variously drawn out from line to line. "So Man . . . Shall . . . die, And dying rise, and rising with him raise His Brethern, ransomed with his own dear life." Toward the end of the seventeenth century this kind of wordplay had fallen into comparative disfavor.[9] We need not be surprised that in Pope's verse it is less heavily underscored.

> Yet graceful ease, and sweetness void of pride,
> Might hide her faults, if Belles had faults to hide.
>
> Jilts ruled the state, and statesmen farces writ,
> Nay wits had pensions, and young lords had wit.

These are lighter turns than Milton's—and at the same time wittier turns. By a different route we have arrived at somewhat the same terminus as when we pursued the forms of logical parallel, that is, at something like illogical pun—a difference being that whereas before we found the single word of two meanings, we find now two or more words of similar sound and one or another kind of play between their meanings.

In the couplet rhetoric which we have been examining, the abstract logic of parallel and antithesis is complicated and off-set, then, by the turn and by the metaphoric zeugma and the punning syllepsis. It is complicated also by one other element of alogical counterpattern—the most important by far and, I believe, the apex of all the rhetorical phenomena which we have been considering—that is, rhyme. "Symphonie" or "cadence," says Puttenham, meaning rhyme, is "all the sweetnesse and cunning in our vulgar poesie." And here we have too, as it happens, a theoretical statement by the master of practice. Pope told Spence:

I have nothing to say for rhyme but that I doubt whether a poem can support itself without it in our language, unless it be stiffened with such strange words as are likely to destroy our language itself. The high style that is affected so much in blank verse would not have been borne even in Milton had not his subject turned so much on such strange, out-of-the-world things as it does.

Rhyme, in this offhand statement, seems to be something like a stiffening or support of verse, rather than the commonly conceived music. Puttenham remarks that the Greeks and Latins "used a maner of speach, by clauses of like termination, which they called *homoioteleuton*," a thing somewhat like vernacular rhyme, yet different. The difference between *rhyme* and *homoeoteleuton* is, in fact, one of the most profound of rhetorical differences. For *homoeoteleuton*, the repetition of inflected endings (morphemes) to support logical parallels of statement, is that which added to parallel and antithesis makes the rhetoric of pointed prose. But rhyme, the use of alogical or accidental sound resemblances between different morphemes, is that which added to parallel and antithesis makes the rhetoric of the pointed couplet. As the turn was the characteristic stiffener of classical Latin verse and of its English counterpart the blank verse of Milton, so rhyme was the characteristic stiffener of vernacular verse and especially of the couplet.

> Whatever Nature has in worth denied
> She gives in large recruits of needful Pride.

The music of the rhyme is mental; it consists in an odd, almost magic, relation of phonetic likeness which encourages us to perceive and believe in a meaning otherwise asserted by the words of the couplet. The nonparallel or chiastic[10] chime (worth[1]-denied,[2] gives[2']-Pride[1']) is the phonetic expression of the unhappy receptivity of the mental void. The principle is well illustrated in a few of Pope's proper-name rhymes, where we may note an affinity for a certain old-fashioned and childish form of riddle to be found in the pages of *The Farmer's Almanac.* Why is A like B? Because the name of A or of something connected with A means B or something connected with B. Why is a dog dressed warmer in summer than in winter? Because in winter he wears a fur coat, and in summer he wears a fur coat and pants. Why is a certain poet a dangerous influence upon married women? Because his name sounds like something.

> Poor Cornus sees his frantic wife elope,
> And curses Wit, and Poetry, and Pope.

Why is a certain scholar a graceless figure? Because his name shows it.

> Yet ne'er one sprig of laurel graced these ribalds,
> From slashing *Bentley* down to pidling *Tibbalds.*

Here the words *sprig* and *pidling* play a part too in proving what it means to have a name like that. *Paronomasia,* "*Prosonomasia,* or the Nicknamer,*" is Puttenham's name for this figure. "As, *Tiberius* the Emperor, because he was a great drinker of wine, they called him by way of derision to his owne name, *Caldius Biberius Nero,* in steade of *Claudius Tiberius Nero.*" But Puttenham, I admit, does not connect this figure with the "symphonie" or "tunable consente" called rhyme.

Poetry, it would appear, is not an affair of pure ideas—where X or Y could by agreement be substituted for any given word —nor strictly speaking is it an affair of sound as such or verbal music. Poetry is both sense and sound, and not by parallel or addition, but by a kind of union—which may be heard in onomatopoeia and expressive rhythm and in various modes of suggestion, extension, and secret verbal functioning. Of these the pun and its cousin the rhyme are but the most extravagant instances. Poetry exploits the *facts* of language, that words *do* mean so and so and acquire a kind of prerogative to do this.

English critics of the Renaissance, among them Milton and latterly even Dryden, were inclined to be hard on rhyme, calling it a jingling bondage, rude, beggarly, and Gothic. (Even Puttenham remarks that rhyme was brought into Greek and Latin by "barbarous souldiers out of the Campe.") The Earl of Roscommon in polished couplets recited the bardic and monkish history of rhyme and hailed the glorious day when the British Muse should put on the rhymeless majesty of Rome and Athens. Critics of Pope's day—Dennis, Felton, and Gildon —took the same cue and called rhyme "soft," "effeminate," "emasculating."[11] At the same time, as we have seen, the basic figures of parallel and antithesis originated as prose figures and by their nature tended to abstraction, order, and regular lines. Other factors too in the latter half of the seventeenth century —the scientific mistrust of inventive imagination, the plain style of scientists and pulpit orators, a refined and moderate way of talking adopted by society—are sometimes supposed to have helped in making the Augustan couplet poems the nearest things to prose poems in our language. Dryden and Pope, we remember Arnold said, are "classics of our prose." This of course we do not fully believe any more. Yet I suggest that we are confronted by an extremely curious and challenging situation in the heroic couplet of Pope: where a verse basically ordered by the rational rules of parallel and antithesis and showing at least a certain characteristic restraint of imagination, as contrasted say with metaphysical verse, at the same time is found to rely so heavily for "support" or "stiffening"—to use again the terms of Pope—on so barbarous and Gothic a device as rhyme.

In tracing the parallel between Puttenham and Pope we have observed perhaps the maximum degree of resemblance that obtains between the poems of Pope and any contemporary or nearly contemporary set of poetic rules. At the same time we have scarcely been able to refrain at each step from noting the incompleteness of Puttenham when compared to the fullness of the poetic actuality, even at the level specifically cited from Puttenham, the rhetorical. How far, we may now return and ask, does Puttenham or does any other rhetorician take us either in stating the main principles of couplet rhetoric or in exploring them? The answer, I believe, is: Not far. Puttenham can list and to some extent describe our figures of speech for us. He does little to show their interrelation or total significance. We can improve on Puttenham by going back to antiquity, where in the third book of Aristotle's *Rhetoric* we find a chapter (XI) saying that the smartest expressions consist in a concurrence of antithesis, parallel, metaphor, and "metaphor of a special kind"—by the last of which it would appear that Aristotle means "homonym." All this may seem to relegate the rhetorical theory of Pope's age or that of earlier ages to the status described under the second heading at the start of this paper: rhetorical, grammatical, or logical theory upon which we draw merely for tools that we shall turn to the uses of our own analysis. Perhaps this is what happens. I do not know the remedy—unless in the interests of Puttenham and his fellows, we are to cut our criticism off from all that subsequent linguistics and rhetoric and our own insight may tell us.

"Rules," said Sir William Temple and was paraphrased by Sir Thomas Pope Blount in his *De Re Poetica* of 1694, "at best are capable only to prevent the making of *bad Verses*, but never able to make men *good Poets*." This might have been interpreted in Pope's day and by Pope himself according to the well known doctrine of the *je-ne-sais-quoi*, the "grace be-

yond the reach of art," the Longinian concession to genius and
the element of the unpredictable in art. It ought to be interpreted by us in the further sense that the rules of a given
age never contain even all that can be subsequently formulated
about the poems of the age and hence are never able to pre-
scribe our interpretation or limit our understanding of the
poems. Poems, if not always prior to theory—in the case of the
couplet they seem not to be—are certainly always more concrete than theory.

III

What I have just said is the logical climax and completion
of my argument. What I shall say now, briefly, may be taken
as a kind of tailpiece. In the part of this essay where I made a
brief survey of rhetorical theory in Pope's age and the preceding, I suppressed one curious facet of that history, for the purpose of introducing it at this point. It is a noteworthy fact that
some of the most penetrating technical remarks made by critics
during the age of Pope were made by those who disapproved
of the devices they were describing. One will no doubt recall
Addison's *Spectator* No. 62, where he mentions doggerel rhymes
and puns as instances of that "mixt Wit" which consists "partly
in the Resemblance of Ideas, and partly in the Resemblance of
Words." Addison also promises to tell us something, on another
day, about the "wit" of antithesis. Far more spectacular are
some of the analyses made by Pope's preromantic enemy John
Dennis. "Rime," says Dennis in a Miltonic demonstration pre-
fixed to one of his own blank verse poems, "is the same thing
in Relation to Harmony that a Pun is in Relation to Wit. . . .
Rime may not so absurdly be said to be the Pun of Harmony."[12]
And so far as puns proper and ambiguity are concerned, Empson was not the first to detect their presence in the poetry of
Pope.

> Nay wits had pensions, and young lords had wit.

"Here," says Dennis, "in the compass of one poor line are two
devilish Bobs for the Court. But 'tis no easy matter to tell

which way the latter squinting Reflection looks."[13] Cleanth
Brooks has noticed the indecent pun upon the word "die" in
the Fifth Canto of *The Rape of the Lock*. It is not to be supposed that this had been overlooked by Dennis. "That is to
say," observes Dennis, *"He wish'd for nothing more than to
fight with her, because he desired nothing more than to lie
with her*. Now what sensible Meaning can this have?" Puns,
says Dennis, are everywhere in *The Rape of the Lock*. "Puns
bear the same Proportion to *Thought*, that *Bubbles* hold to
Bodies, and may justly be compared to those gaudy Bladders
which Children make with Soap." Nor is it to be supposed
that Dennis had overlooked the kind of pun hinted by Puttenham in the figures of syllepsis and zeugma. "A Receipt for
dry Joking," says Dennis. "For by placing something important
in the Beginning of a Period, and making something very
trifling to follow it, he seems to take pains to bring *something*
into a Conjunction Copulative with *nothing*, in order to beget
nothing."[14] Perhaps it is needless to add that Dennis chooses
for illustration of this formula the same examples which I have
quoted in my own admiring analysis—those about staining her
honor or her new brocade, and taking counsel and tea. At a
certain level, Dennis saw very well what Pope was up to. Not
an innuendo got past him. This, however, was not the kind of
poetry which Dennis prescribed. These were not the rules he
would write. We are confronted in our final exhibit with a
relation between theory and poems which we have up to now
scarcely canvassed. In this version of the critic's role there is
a marked correlation not between poems and contemporary
poetics but actually between poems and contemporary anti-
poetics.

Quand dans un discours se trouvent des mots répétés, et qu'essayant de les corriger, on les trouve si propres qu'on gâterait le discours, il les faut laisser.—PASCAL, Pensées

WHEN IS VARIATION "ELEGANT"?

THE TERM "elegant variation" is one which I believe we owe to *The King's English* of H. W. and F. G. Fowler. Their analytic wit and readiness with example seem to have brought recognition and a name to a rhetorical fault which formerly one shunned or cultivated only by intuition. Sir Arthur Quiller-Couch in his essay "On Jargon" has written humorously of the same fault. For some time now it has been a topic in textbooks for college English composition. H. W. Fowler's treatment in his *Modern English Usage* is perhaps the most concise and orderly. Here under the headings "Elegant Variation" and "Repetition of Words and Sounds" he illuminates complementary principles, which one may recall by considering only two of his examples.

> They dug their *own* clay, often in *front* of their *own front* doors.

> They spend a few weeks longer in their winter *home* than in their summer *habitat*.

"Diametrically opposed" faults, says Fowler, one of which consists in "carelessly repeating a word in a different application," the other in "carefully not repeating it in a similar application." Or, one might draw up two rules of thumb: When you mean different things, use different words. When you mean the same thing, use the same word.

To phrase the rules this way suggests at once a speculation which, I believe, can lead deep into the question of style and hence have a bearing on more central matters of rhetoric and poetry. "When do I mean different things?" "When do I mean the same thing?" In Fowler's words, when is the "application" different? When is it similar? Both these ways of phrasing harbor an ambiguity which must be resolved before the questions can be answered. A term means a thing, denotes it, refers to it. But also there is to be taken into consideration the class conception which usually accompanies the denoting, the aspect or quality under which the thing is denoted.

In examples of "elegant variation" one has always to consider not only the number of references or aspects but the number of things. There are examples of variation where several physically separable things (a southern part of the earth and a northern) are denoted under slightly different aspects (home and habitat), while the context indicates that the things are really thought of under one aspect (call it either home or habitat). But there are also examples where under different aspects only one thing is denoted. Fowler does not distinguish these two kinds, presenting examples of both but many more of the first kind, where two or more things are denoted. The second kind, however—the one-thing kind—is a better starting point for analysis. It is simpler and, as it appears to me, less frequently deserving of the derogatory name "elegant." One of Fowler's clearest examples of one-thing variation is this:

> Dr Tulloch was for a time *Dr Boyd's* assistant, & knew the *popular preacher* very intimately, & the picture he gives of the *genial essayist* is a very engaging one.

His name was Dr. Boyd; he was a popular preacher and a genial essayist, and he had certain relations with Dr. Tulloch. All this is predicated of a certain *him,* or, to cleanse our term

as far as possible of residual predication, of a certain *it*. It is
true that the predications are made in various ways; they are
hung like Christmas-tree ornaments on various branches of a
syntactic structure. But what then?

Predicates of propositions are not the only parts that have a
predicative function. Almost all terms in a discourse manage
to betray some predication, to assert something of something.
"The barn is big. It is red." "Barn" predicates as much as and
more than "big" and "red." Only the "it" is a pure subject,
algebraically an x, a pointer to the thing under discussion.

The usefulness of naming one thing under any number of
aspects—asserting that it has these aspects—is, of course, not to
be questioned. Such treatment of things is thinking; it is the
basis of reflective and poetic discourse. Not to be questioned
either is the logic and propriety of listing these aspects as a
series, in formal parallel predicative positions. I find this noted
in one textbook treatment of repetition. A "variation of emphatic repetition consists in repeating the idea but changing
the words [rather in repeating the thing but slightly changing
the idea]. 'The boys were tired—completely done up—dead on
their feet.'" Furthermore, the subject of a proposition too may
be a place for special deposits of predication—as in Homer or
in our own *Time* magazine. "Much-enduring noble Odysseus
heard him not." "Last week roly-poly (200 lb., 5 ft. 8 in.)
Harry Gokey, 71, retired vaudeville trouper, made his bid for
No. 1 U.S. professional Santa." Sentences in *Time* tend to become a string of appositional predications with somewhere a
finite verb which makes an assertion that does duty for the
whole. What looks like a heavily weighted subject, all that
comes before the assertion or copula, may turn out to be more
of a predicate than what comes after. "A talented private secre-
tary who, at 37, after her employer's wife died, finally married
her 70-year-old boss not long before his death is the Dowager
Marchioness of Reading."[1]

Neither of these uses, the multiple predicate and the epi-
thetical cumulative subject, produces the effect of variation,
for there is only one proposition, one copula or main finite verb.

But the nearness of these to variation may be seen if one reflects how the various predications might be distributed through
two or more propositions; that is, there might be two or more
propositions where the subjects denoted the same thing, but
either the subjects or predicates or both made different predications about this thing. Something like this, as a matter of
fact, occurs in the Dr. Boyd example from Fowler. If we leave
out of account parts of speech and varied syntax or think of
them as reducible to the subject, copula, and predicate of
propositions, we may find that something like variation occurs
in many forms in many places. Poetry is a good place to look.
And one of the best places that I have found is near the beginning of English poetry, in the Old English epic *Beowulf*.

> To *Hondscio* happened a hopeless contention,
> Death to the *doomed one,* dead he fell foremost,
> *Girded war-champion;* to him Grendel became then,
> To the *vassal-distinguished,* a tooth-weaponed murderer,
> The *well-beloved henchman's* body all swallowed.

>   The *sea-boat* resounded,
> The wind o'er the waters the *wave-floater* nowise
> Kept from its journey; the *sea-goer* traveled,
> The *foamy-necked vessel* floated forth o'er the currents,
> The *well-fashioned vessel* o'er the ways of the ocean.
> . . . .

>   The *wave-goer* hastened

> . . . .
> He bound to the bank then the *broad-bosomed vessel*
> Fast in its fetters, lest the force of the waters
> Should be able to injure the *ocean-wood winsome.*[2]

There are places in *Beowulf* where one might attribute a
variation to metrical or alliterative necessity. But surely not
here in these eight ways of naming the boat. Nor was the poet
here merely afraid of a taboo, scrupulously observing a schoolboy's rule against using the same word in so many sentences or
lines. Nor was he at Fowler's second stage, delighted with an
ingenuity in kennings developed by observing the rule. He was

delighted with the boat. He was eager to tell about it, as much about it as possible while telling what it did. Not only did it go, but it was a wave-floater and well fashioned and foamy necked. An opportunity for such interesting predications came each time the boat was denoted. So it was well to denote it many times, to repeat the fact that it went. (Better than piling all the predications in one proposition, because this other way the boat is kept moving.) Nay, the going itself has interesting aspects. The boat traveled, it floated, it hastened. Quite often, in fact, the poet of *Beowulf* has on his hands two or more variations at once. Not only the man but the sword he is wielding, or not only the swords but the monster they cleave. Not only the waves and the sea but the men and the boat.[3] And the effect of these multiple predications throughout this poem is much the same whether they appear in one proposition or in several. One of the most constant characters of the poem is the incrustation of ideas around single objects. An extreme example, in several propositions, like that of the boat, is felt as only a concentration of what occurs more casually on every page.

The contexts in which variation may function expressively are perhaps of as many kinds as one cares to discover or illustrate. Another example from *Beowulf* will suggest a widely familiar form.

> Lo! we blithely have brought thee, *bairn of Healfdene,*
> *Prince of the Scyldings,* these presents from ocean.

Here is multiple predication in the vocative—as in a litany. In a formal liturgical litany, like that of the Blessed Virgin in the Roman breviary, there may be more than forty predications, the same petition repeated after each. It would be impossible, of course, to think of this as elegant variation. In certain whimsical or emotional veins the essayist, showing his kinship with the poet, may offer us elaborate examples of variation. Lamb, for instance, begins "A Chapter on Ears" with ingenious playfulness:

Nor imagine that I am by nature destitute of those exterior twin appendages, hanging ornaments, and (architecturally speaking) hand-

some volutes to the human capital. . . . I am, I think, rather delicately than copiously provided with those conduits; and I feel no
disposition to envy the mule for his plenty, or the mole for her
exactness, in those ingenious labyrinthine inlets—those indispensable
side-intelligencers.

Or the novelist may employ variation to show the progress of a
conception in the mind of a character.

The distraught young man stood in the middle of the road and
glared back at the town. He did not know the *reporter George Willard* and had no special feeling concerning the *tall boy who ran
about town gathering the town news.* The *reporter* had merely
come, by his presence in the office and in the printshop of the
Winesburg Eagle, to stand for something in the young merchant's
mind. He thought the *boy who passed and repassed Cowley and
Son's store and who stopped to talk to people in the street* must be
thinking of him and perhaps laughing at him.[4]

One of the kinds of variation ridiculed by Sir Arthur Quiller-
Couch is that employed by sports writers, and doubtless the
ridicule is largely justified. An account of a football game is
perhaps not often improved by the appearance of an "oval," a
"pigskin," a "spheroid," a "big leather egg." But I believe that
examples of condonable variation may easily be found. Let us
consider an extreme and classical instance, the sports pages
after the fight in June, 1935, between the Negro boxer Joe Louis
and the giant Italian Primo Carnera. The writers had already
exploited a great opportunity for antonomasia in each of these
figures. Carnera was "ambling Alp," "Italian mastodon," "rudderless mammoth," "robot of the racketeers." Louis was "brown
bomber," "dark destroyer," "black blizzard," "beige butcher,"
"sepia slugger," "dark dynamiter," "tan terror," "dusky Detroiter," "dark detonator," "killer from the cotton fields." And
when these two met:

The *frozen-faced, sloe-eyed Negro's* defeat of Carnera was enacted before 57,000 pairs of eyes red with blood lust. [Carnera]
lacked only one thing—natural fighting ability, of which the *black
Beowulf* had more than an abundance. The *imperturbable brown
bear* . . . had whanged away under Carnera's guard . . . until the

jittery giant had become very weary indeed. . . . The *sensational Senegambian* was pinned in a corner . . . the *lad with the petrified puss* was upon Carnera as he rose as wobbly as a punch-drunk fighter on stilts. . . . Crack, crack! went the right and left of this *calmly savage Ethiopian* to the head of the *battered derelict*. . . . He reeled along the ring ropes, obviously begging that someone stop this *brown mechanism* that was so surely destroying him. . . . He feinted with his hands and the *vast Venetian* threw up his hands widely as his wits scattered.[5]

"Surfeit!" one cries (even though I have omitted a great deal), and one finds a certain crudity, an excess of horror and of alliteration. It is not always clear that expressiveness is put ahead of cleverness. Nevertheless, I submit that these bizarre variations do on the whole express something, that they are relevant to the violent conception, the picture of power and slaughter, which the writer certainly conveys. Without them the account would be much duller. These are his comments of admiration, of pity or contempt, as he tells the facts. These and similar devices (his variation is only part of a wild flair for metaphor) make him the bard, the popular narrator of heroic conflict. Another writer, on the same page, describing the same fight in a somewhat different style, exclaims: "Here was a two-fisted fighter, dealing out dynamite." Ðaet waes gōd cyning! O Black Beowulf!

It would seem safe to say that variation is indigenous to and flourishes in writing that is dramatic and poetic. In poetry there is predication at every point. Every rift is to be packed with ore. The tone is that of trying to say as much as possible with every syllable. The more poetic a writing the more likely it is to employ variation of some sort. Even in more relaxed narrative prose, some more obvious form of variation is likely to crop out. One hardly objects to Meredith's occasional humor in calling one-legged Uncle Algernon "the dismembered Guardsman," or Tom Bakewell "Speed-the-Plough," or Richard Feverel "the hope of Raynham."

On the other hand, the less poetic a writing, the more logical and expository, the more likely an obvious or ingenious variation is to seem "elegant." Fowler's Dr. Boyd example was probably quite offensive in its context. In a purely scientific writing variation would be altogether out of place and incompatible with the purpose of the writing—which is to proceed from step to step with complete security as to what object or what aspect or abstraction is referred to. In a treatise on algebra, variation in verbal exposition would be as chaotic as the indication of a same quantity now by x and now by y. In philosophy the same would be true—or sometimes is. And a determination to avoid the fault makes some philosophers produce pages of a severely repetitious, mathematical character. Like algebraists or philosophers—though with a difference too—the masters of the plain prose style have almost never resorted to poetic variation. Swift, for example, is scrupulous in this regard, especially in his satires, where the ironic effect depends on his sober, chill precision. So to a lesser degree are Dryden, Addison, and Steele. To study their prose is to see how variation may be avoided and how from this discipline a special prosaic beauty is achieved.

H. W. and F. G. Fowler have described a kind of variation which I believe may be legitimately distinguished from either the poetic or the elegant. This may be called "pronominal" variation, a usage by which the plain prose writer can sometimes solve the problem of how to secure reiterated reference without the reiterated emphasis commonly called "monotony" or "repetition." An object is named under a new aspect, but one more generic and hence less informative and less emphatic than that under which it has already been named. The "volume," the "story," the "author," the "hero," the "action," the "object," the "latter," the "former"—such generic levels regularly appear in unobtrusive instances of this arrangement. Yet the arrangement tends to make a kind of empty space in meaning and is perhaps not ideal. The secret of pure prose would seem to be a kind of economy, such a management of the parts of an argument that objects once named do not need to be named soon again—at least not explicitly and emphatically and as subjects of propositions. Loose thinking, fuzziness, and "elegant variation" go well together. There is a kind of unpre-

tentious, unimaginative "elegant variation" which arises simply
from one's not realizing the relations among objects discussed.
The student of composition (if a pedagogic suggestion may be
inserted here) might be persuaded to write a page on which
the same things were rigorously denoted by the same words.
Then might follow a surprising revelation of what the order
of his thoughts ought to be—where pronouns could be used
and where telescoping and ellipsis were called for.

II

But let us return to the other kind of variation described at
the start of our discussion, that where two or more things are
denoted. H. W. Fowler's examples would suggest that this is
of more frequent and less obvious occurrence than one-thing
variation. Two-thing variation, as Fowler's examples also show,
readily invades all the parts of speech. Not nouns and adjectives only, which are easily seen as referring to the same or to
different objects, but verbs (referring to objects as acting) or
prepositions (referring to objects in their relations) or any
parts of speech (referring to concrete or abstract objects in any
of the possible ways) may readily be varied when two or more
objects are present.

> France is now *going through* a similar experience *with regard
> to* Morocco to that which England had to *undergo with refer-
> ence to* Egypt.

This is the kind of variation which finds its way into one's writing in countless complicated ways, sometimes in clearly isolable
short phrases or words, sometimes in lack of parallel between
phrases or clauses, sometimes in the whole structure of argument or order in which the ideas of a discourse are classified
and presented. If one has in mind fifteen examples which show
that romantic poets were interested in kinetic imagery, one
does not state the case in an introductory paragraph and then
list the examples; one achieves the appearance of complication
by inventing fifteen ways to tie an example to the main theme.
One writes fifteen introductory sentences, or fifteen paragraphs,

which seem to say different things but, with relevance to the theme, say only one thing. Viewed this way, variation and its opposite are intrinsic to the very process of thinking. To avoid elegant variation is to achieve rightness, relevance, unity in the analysis and synthesis of our discourse.[6]

When the difference between things and that between the aspects under which things are thought of are both great, there is not much difficulty in seeing that different words are wanted. That is the case when we mention almost any two things in nonparallel or oblique relation. The difficulty begins when we yoke things by parallel or contrast. Then widely different things may be referred to as alike. But it may also happen that different things are referred to as they are not alike, but almost alike; a more generic aspect in which they are alike is suggested by the naming of more specific aspects in which they are almost alike. Some such arrangement as this is common, particularly in narration and description, where different concepts are used in the mere naming of several objects and where the class concept or likeness is less often named by one general term than suggested by approximations, each approximation taking a variation from the thing to which it is attached. It does not matter to our argument what parts of speech are used to refer to likeness or to difference. In the following example from Conrad's *Heart of Darkness,* nouns refer to different objects under clearly different aspects, while adjectives refer to the same objects under aspects which approach one another and suggest a single generic aspect—for which perhaps there is no single word.

> A *small* flame would dart and vanish, a *little* white smoke
> would disappear, a *tiny* projectile would give a *feeble* screech.

Conrad describes a French man-of-war shelling the bush of the African coast. The action is futile—small and weak. He would make each part of the action contribute to the smallness and weakness in its own way. This is the method of concreteness, of narrative symbol as opposed to abstract science. This is basically the way in which the diverse concrete elements of any fiction gain relevance or unity.

Here is a kind of variation which is demanded by the context. If there is to be narrative, and not essay, the different things must be named and each must be small or weak in its own way, differently small or weak. The difference must be indicated verbally. Nevertheless—and this is a point which one may find it hard to grant—there need not be any clear or explicit propriety in the difference in words. It may be beyond the scope of the language to express such difference explicitly. In the home-habitat example the fault lay in implicit difference. In such an example as the above from Conrad the merit may be of the same sort. "Feeble" indicates exactly the way in which a "screech" is small, and "feeble" would not do so well for "projectile." But it might do for "flame." And "small" might do for "projectile," and "little" might do for "flame." But taken in a series, applied to these different objects, these different words for "small" do suggest accurate application and complete relevance. The reason is that flame, smoke, projectile, and screech really are small and weak in different ways, no matter whether there are words in our vocabulary to distinguish the ways accurately. A difference in the sound of words, a difference in their range of meaning, implicitly means the right difference. Let me lay myself open to a charge of insensitivity by citing a more famous instance:

> St. Agnes' Eve—Ah, bitter chill it was!
> The owl, for all his feathers, was a-cold.

"In the first Stanza," wrote Keats, "my copy reads . . . 'bitter *chill* it was' to avoid the echo cold in the second line." Certainly it is better to have the two words different. The air is cold or chill in one way; the owl in another. What seems more questionable is that the coldness of either could not (aside from the rhyme) be indicated equally well with either word. And somewhat the same can be said for the following line of *Paradise Lost:* "Horrid to think, how horrible to feel." There is a difference between "to think" and "to feel" which may be reflected or extended into the difference between "horrid" and "horrible," but (aside from meter and climax) it is difficult to see why the order of these adjectives might not be reversed.

A clearer propriety in difference of words may be discerned when objects are denoted under aspects that are parallel and nearly the same but nevertheless contrasted or antithetic. Wilde once read to Yeats from the proofs of *The Decay of Lying*.

And when he came to the sentence: "Schopenhauer has analysed the pessimism that characterizes modern thought, but Hamlet invented it. The world has become sad because a puppet was once melancholy," I said, "Why do you change 'sad' to 'melancholy'?" He replied that he wanted a full sound at the close of his sentence.

But Wilde might have found a better reason. "World" and "puppet" refer to objects as they are different or contrasted; "sad" and "melancholy" refer to them as they are nearly the same. But there is a difference between "sad" and "melancholy," a modulation, which corresponds to the difference between "world" and "puppet." The world is sad, simply and actually sad. But the puppet, the player, is melancholy—sad in the Elizabethan, theatrical way, that of the whimsical, self-conscious malcontent. From the imitation has proceeded the reality. There is a parallel expressed in the nearness of the words "sad" and "melancholy" and at the same time a contrast and an oblique, causal relation expressed in their difference.

To close the cycle of our discussion, we need now only refer again to the clear difference between the aspects under which things are thought of when they are thought of in completely oblique or nonparallel relation to each other. Here belongs the example from Fowler quoted at the outset:

> They dug their *own* clay, often in *front* of their *own front* doors.

To use the same word in referring to nearly the same or parallel aspects of parallel things is to produce either emphasis or monotony—as Keats would have done if he had repeated "chill." But to use the same word in referring to objects in oblique relation is to produce a marked effect of impropriety, of wrong words. In such cases the need for different words, or for phrasal recasting, is urgent.

> Their clay they dug for themselves, often before their own front doors.

Here again, however, there is need less of exact propriety in difference than of difference implicitly expressed. This is particularly clear in the prepositional strings which Fowler quotes under "Repetition of Words and Sounds" and "Jingles."

> The observation *of* the facts *of* the geological succession *of* the forms *of* life.

The resources of the language are not adequate to express such a series of relationships with accurate explicit difference. One must resort either to complete recasting or to compression and *implicit* variation. It is less offensive to write:

> The observation of geological succession *in* the forms of life.

"In" may be less accurate than "of" at this juncture, but it serves to suggest the difference between the relationship to which it refers and the relationships referred to on either side of it. The same is true even of the syllabic jingles which Fowler quotes—*ly* adverbs or *ity* abstract nouns used in oblique or dependent relation.

> Their invalid*ity* was caused by a technical*ity*.

> It is probab*ly* general*ly* known.

Here some recasting is called for. Even down to these fractions of words the rule of thumb holds good: Use different words when you mean different things.

. . . as the motion of a snake's body goes through all parts at once and its volition acts as at the same instant in coils which go contrary ways.—T. E. HULME, Speculations

VERBAL STYLE

LOGICAL AND
COUNTERLOGICAL

THE WORD *verbal* as it appears in the title of this essay looks in two directions or has two antitheses. In combination with the word *style* it designates a level of meaning distinct from the substantial, and especially from the stated part of substantial meaning. At the same time, *verbal* implies that the level of stylistic meaning is something different from what is expressed by the medium of any other art, and that the discussion will avoid such metaphors as "verbal painting" and "verbal music"—or if it employs them briefly, will do so in full overtness.

The aim of the essay is not so much to discover new instances or areas of verbal style as to correlate certain areas which have been noticed separately by earlier criticism: certain prose figures or merits defined in classical rhetoric, certain logical faults of prose, especially as defined by H. W. Fowler in his *Modern English Usage*, and certain poetic figures defined both by classical rhetoric and by recent semantic criticism.

A study of verbal style (if there is such a thing as verbal style in any peculiar sense) ought to cut in between a Platonic or Crocean monism, where meaning either as inspired dialectic or as intuition-expression is simply and severely one meaning, and the various forms of practical affective rhetoric, Aristotelian or modern, where stylistic meaning bears to substantial meaning a relation of *how* to *what* or of *means* to *end*.[1] The term *verbal style*, if it is to have any clear use, must be supposed to refer to some verbal quality which is somehow structurally united to or fused with *what* is being said by words, but is also somehow to be distinguished from *what* is being said. A study of verbal style, though it ought to deal only with meaning, ought to distinguish at least two interrelated levels of meaning, a substantial level and another more like a shadow or echo or gesture.

The distinction is made difficult by the fact that substantial meaning itself has various strata, some of which are readily confused with the level of strictly verbal style. Most examples of periphrase and paraphrase—often perhaps thought of as differing only in style from a certain plain statement—differ of course in far more than style as the latter may be strictly conceived. In Chapter XII of *Peri Bathous* Pope gives the example of plain expression "Shut the door" and its translation in pseudopoetic language: "The wooden guardian of our privacy Quick on its axle turn." In a certain essential and practical sense the meaning here does remain the same, and so the example could be used to illustrate an Aristotelian conception of rhetoric: meaning plus style, what plus how. On the other hand, the change of meaning is certainly more than verbal. It is metaphoric and ideational; more things are being said and intimated about the door. Hence the example could be used too to illustrate a Crocean monistic conception of meaning. A change of "style" has changed the substantial meaning. Wherever metaphor and associated "figures of thought" are concerned, the meaning, though it may be only intimated, is ideational and substantial. But the study of verbal style is concerned with something different. By a kind of diagram, crude and cake-like, drawn with a piece of red and a piece of white chalk, one might indicate the total structure of verbal meaning as I conceive it: a solid red stratum of stated meaning, shading into an even thicker middle ground of mixed red and white, the levels of all the complex kinds of epithetic, metaphoric, and intimated meaning which one may conceive as in some broad sense stylistic, and on top a thin solid line of white, the level of purely verbal style.

The easiest way to illustrate the strictly verbal level of style may be with certain directly presentational or iconic properties of language: the onomatopoeia of *plop, hiss,* or *murmur;* or what is called sound-symbolism or sound-metaphor by Wellek and Warren in their recent *Theory of Literature* (ch. XIII), the symbolic quality of clear, light front vowels, or heavy back vowels, or liquid consonants (as in the famous refrain of Poe's *Raven*); or the other tenuous ways in which words can be like what they mean, the shape or size of words like *mammoth, tiny, wee,* or *due* when it expresses an unemphatic causal relation. What logicians call *autological* terms (*polysyllable, expression, word*) are a special class of perfect instances, in their own way complete icons. There is no reason why one should not explore these types of mimetic meaning and call them verbal style.

What I have in mind, however, is yet different. It is the level of relational meanings—those which reside in or grow out of structures or movements and have hence an even thinner and more sheerly verbal character of iconicity. At the line where real verbal discourse grows out of logic (or fades into it), there we find perhaps the purest examples of stylistic meaning. The following series of constructions is designed to squeeze a relational stylistic meaning into a tight compass and hence to show it in its leanest and most simply definable form. Or what may be shown is the vanishing point of this kind of meaning and its intrinsically verbal character, the fact that despite its abstractness it grows only out of the soil of words.

Syllogism	Change 1	Change 2	Change 3
All A is B	All a is b	All A is B	All A is b
All C is A	All c is a	No C is A	All C is a
All C is B	All c is b	No C is B	All c is B

The original syllogism undergoes first a change which is not a change at all, or is merely a graphic change, not related to the meaning. The logic is the same. This change bears the same relation to verbal style as, let us say, a change in type fonts on a printed page. Then, secondly, the syllogism undergoes a change which is indeed logical and radical, as deep as possible. The syllogism is now so different as to violate a rule of the first figure. It is no syllogism at all. A theorist of purely stylistic meaning, who was searching for something in between these two changes, one too superficial, one too radical, might then construct change 3. And here we have the very character of relational stylistic meaning, and the question of its existence, exposed as relentlessly as possible. It is perhaps impossible to say whether change 3 is a stylistic change or a great deal more than a stylistic change. Is the syllogism valid? Does it contain three terms, or six terms? Much depends on what we are willing to concede. If there are only three terms, then certainly the shifting from capitals to lower case does not advertise this fact. A kind of stylistic quarrel with meaning has been set up. This is a thing which becomes vastly more feasible as soon as we substitute real words for the empty symbols of logic.

> All material substances have weight,
> Atmospheric air is a material substance;
> Therefore atmospheric air has weight.[2]

Manipulate this as follows:

> All material substances have weight,
> Atmospheric air is a physical stuff;
> Therefore the gas which envelops the earth is ponderable.

One might wish to insist that several syllogisms have been telescoped together. But since there are really only three terms —that is, since no relevant differences can be found between the members of the three twin pairs, not only does the logic remain valid but it remains the same logic as that of the original syllogism. Certainly some element of meaning has been changed, but it can be soundly argued that this is a stylistic change. What makes such a situation possible is the fact that, whereas the empty symbols of the pure syllogism had only one dimension of meaning, that conferred by the very structure of the syllogism, the verbal terms used in our monstrosity have two dimensions: (1) that conferred by the structure, a meaningful pull which tries to hold these terms in line and keep them logical; and (2) the suggestive semantic weight of each of these terms, which in this case yields sufficiently to the logic to make general sense, but at the same time pulls away in various disparate directions. There is, in short, a tension between kinds of meaning—a tension in this case not rich and paradoxical (according to the formula for poetry) but chaotic and disastrous. It is bad style. It is an example of what H. W. Fowler calls *Elegant Variation.*

The syllogistic structure reveals in the fullest and most formal sense the principle of inexpressiveness which underlies the various confused antitheses and parallels quoted by Fowler under the head of *Elegant Variation.* The same principle, in the obverse, underlies, as we shall note further, the opposite fault of false parallel or *Repetition* which Fowler analyzes into such minute instances as the prepositional string and the unhappy jingle of obliquely related like syllables.

II

The logical virtues of style are found most clearly in logical structures of discourse—those which expound, arrange, argue, align, distinguish, or refute (though these are usually far from pure structures). They are the virtues of any good prose writer, more obviously of a Macaulay, a Johnson, a Cicero, an Isocrates. The logical virtues of twentieth century prose style are scarcely noticeable as such, or are noticeable mainly when absent. They are the norm. They are in principle, however, the same virtues which attract attention as virtuosity in the style of Johnson or in the rhetorical styles of antiquity. What is today mostly respected as a principle of minimum decency in the implicit logic of structures asserted itself more ingeniously and emphatically in the repertoire of figures described by Aristotle or Quintilian.

At this stage in the exposition one might like to introduce a table showing the Fowlerian faults of modern prose in relation to the emphatic logical virtues of the classical. The alignment might be something like this: Opposite *Elegant Variation* or false distinction, *antithesis* or reinforced true distinction. Opposite the *prepositional string* or false structural parallel, *parisosis*, the generic figure of true structural parallel. Opposite the *jingle* or false like-ending, *homoeoteleuton*, the pointedly logical like-ending.

And one might then conveniently draw a heavy vertical line, representing a cardinal joint in the anatomy of verbal style, dividing the logical from an opposite range of stylistic meanings, the poetic, or as one might say, the *counterlogical*—those which we are next to consider. This line would represent a division between the basic movement of logical prose discourse and that of nonlogical or poetic discourse; that is, between argument and narrative or drama[3] and between the abstract predications of literal statement and the concrete, ambiguous predications of metaphor.

In poetic movements the logical virtues of verbal style do appear—since language never becomes purely illogical. The most dramatic poem is locally a tissue of parallels and contrasts. Yet running counter to these in a curiously co-operative way a different kind of stylistic virtue may more often and more characteristically be discerned than in prose movements—a virtue that may perhaps be related to the logical virtues of style as harmony is to melody, though I should not like to push this point far. The logical fault of style named *Repetition* by H. W. Fowler consists in the use of the same word when the word should be different, when it becomes in effect a homophone: "Sir William White has now received the crowning distinction of the Presidency of the Royal *Association;* his *association* with the Navy may be said to date almost from his birth." This is an example of "the sort of carelessness that, in common courtesy to his readers, a writer should remove before printing." Yet it is a curious fact that in a poetic movement a stylistic phenomenon much like this may be taken for a virtue.

One might complete a skeleton table of the stylistic figures somewhat as follows—filling out a column of the counterlogical.

Opposite the prose fault of slipshod verbal *Repetition,* one
would put *pun,* the poetic figure of significant phonetic repetition. And allied to pun or shading away from it, certain classic
and neoclassic figures: the *turn on the word, agnomination,* and
alliteration. And opposite the logical figures and faults already
mentioned (*parisosis–prepositional string, homoeoteleuton–
jingle*), the counterlogical figures *meter* and *rhyme.* So far as
I am aware no technical names have been provided for counterlogical *faults* of style. They are not so clearly definable, though
various forms of tameness, flatness, or even "cacophony" in
verse might actually come under this head.

| | Logical | | Counterlogical |
Figures	Faults	Faults	Figures[4]
antithesis	elegant variation		
parisosis	prepositional string		meter
homoeoteleuton	jingles		rhyme
	repetition		pun
	"		turn
	"		agnomination
	"		alliteration

What may appear strange to a reader is that meter should
be included among the counterlogical figures. I place it here
because the equalities of meter (a character of phonetic structure) do not march with but cut across the parallels of sense.
Shakespeare's line "Of hand, of foot, of lip, of eye, of brow"
(*Sonnet* CVI) and Milton's "And swims or sinks, or wades, or
creeps, or flies" (*Paradise Lost,* II, 950) are pronounced exceptions to the rule, brief sprints of logicality against the adjacent and prevailing movements. But meter is in fact something of an anomaly in the present discussion. It is not so
closely related to specific meanings as the other counterlogical
figures, but is more basic to the poetic pattern than any of the
others, and is best considered, I believe, as a phonetic frame of
reference which in large measure enables the extremer forms
of the others. For present purposes the pun may be looked on
as the fully developed counterlogical figure.

III

The reasons for the virtue of the pun are discovered most readily in metaphor. Puns and related figures in poetry differ from the illogical repetition in prose by having a kind of metaphoric logic. That is, a pun is something like the surface of a metaphor—in the phrase of Auden, an "auditory metaphor." It is the completion of a certain—not irrational—but at least extrarational direction in a metaphor. A pun is to metaphor as logical stylistic parallel is to literal statement. A substantial meaning underlies it.

> How neatly do we give one onely name
> To parent's issue and the *sunne's* bright starre!
> A *sonne* is light and fruit; a fruitful flame
> Chasing the father's dimnesse. . . .

A resemblance or analogy in value between *sun* and *son* is the metaphoric meaning—supported or reflected by the homophonic relation of the words. Like the classical figures of logic, the counterlogical figures attract attention. We are in the realm of virtuosity. The pun contributes nothing to the truth or propriety of the metaphor involved, but it does concentrate the symbols upon whatever propriety there may be. Puns and related figures are strong semblances of propriety.

In some forms of pun, the telescoped or elliptical, where the ambiguous sound occurs only once, the parallel to Fowlerian repetition disappears, as in Donne's version of the same pun ("at my death, thy Sonne Shall shine") or in the zeugma or syllepsis favored by Pope ("He first the snuff-box *opened*, then the case"). Puns may also be pushed apart, the distance between their halves widened, by partial phonetic variation and greater obliquity of sense—that is, they may thin out into a more adaptable and prevalent verbal "music," or rhyme. French poets, especially in the sixteenth century, and English poets from time to time, Chaucer in a few "identical" rhymes, the Augustan wit in a "Gentle Echo on Woman," or Lowell in his *Fable for Critics*, have written the full punning rhyme.

> My plot, like an icicle's slender and slippery,
> Every moment more slender, and likely to slip awry.

These may be treated like any other puns, though the sense relation may not be especially nice. A certain direction toward pun is inherent in the normal rhyme situation, even the simplest. "Oranges and lemons, Say the bells of St. Clement's." Here the weight is all on the phonetic side—for indeed the theme is the sound of bells. The bells say what sounds like their name. "Brickbats and tiles, Say the bells of St. Giles." The range from these to more sophisticated quasi-metaphoric rhymes is variously shaded. In the satires of Pope, as I have argued in another essay, are to be found some of the smartest jokes on the proper name and some of the nicest ironic juxtapositions.

But the metaphor can be quieter.

> As if his highest plot
> To plant the bergamot.

Planting the bergamot is *like* a plot in the sense that in this context it would take the place of a plot. (There is doubtless an extra oblique correspondence in the fact that the bergamot would be planted in a garden plot.) An entire poem by Wallace Stevens, *The Ordinary Women,* is centered on the curious resemblance between *guitars* and *catarrhs.* A reader unacquainted with this poem might take these words as a kind of challenge to a *bout rimé* and, for exercise in realizing the character of rhyme, speculate: What kind of poem could be centered on these words?

Again—if for the sake of fixity and simplicity, what is a streamy continuum of effects may be centered in a definition—there is the figure known to seventeenth century rhetoric as *agnomination,* the same as that called *sound-pattern* by Wellek and Warren in their *Theory of Literature* (p. 163). Agnomination is a kind of play or echo of a sound or set of sounds.[5] Among other striking examples in Milton's *Paradise Lost,* there is that in the first book where he is talking about the worship of the heathen gods. He mentions *abominations,* an *opprobrious* hill, and Chemos the *óbscene dread of Moab's sons,* and at the same time the geographical places where the gods were worshiped, *Rabba, Argob, Basan.*

> From Aroer to *Nebo*, and the wild
> Of southmost *Abarim;* in *Hesebon*
> And Horonaim, Seon's realm, beyond
> The flowery dale of *Sibma* clad with vines.

Other emphatic *b*'s and *p*'s appear throughout the passage, *besmeared, blood, timbrels, worshipped.* There is a kind of extenuated pun, a fleeting shadow of pun, an extension of the ideas of obscenity and abomination through the echo of sounds. Since the similar sounds—the partial homophones—reflect not the two sides of a metaphoric resemblance, but the parts of an oblique association, of contiguity in space and time, the counterlogicality of such a figure is even clearer than it is in the fully asserted pun of Herbert's sonnet on *The Sonne.* The figure of agnomination has a marked—if strangely transvalued—likeness to one of the subheads of the Fowlerian prose fault of Repetition: "Assonance, Rhyme, etc." Among other examples Fowler gives the following: "by committing *embezzlement*—an action too *imbecile* in the circumstances to deserve censure." Precisely such a resemblance between words would be a capital opportunity for Milton. In the third book of *Paradise Lost,* in the Limbo of Vanity:

> *Cleombrotus,* and many *more* too long,
> *Embryos* and idiots, *eremites* and friars.[6]

An analysis of agnomination into its frayed-out ends might suggest that most cases of alliteration have the same kind of counterlogical meaning, a refined form of phonetic harmony—the harmony of the sense being proportionately slender and abstract. In Shakespeare's "*Ruin* hath taught me thus to *ruminate*" we may say the alliteration expresses the aptness of ruin to produce ruminations, or at least that it increases the plausibility of the relation and cements it in a verbal pattern, as in the advertising jingle, "If hair's your pride, use Herpicide," the tie between pride in hair and Herpicide is precisely the assumption which it is the function of the sounds to promote.

The last type of figure to be mentioned here—one which is especially instructive because it is a kind of border line where logical and counterlogical qualities of style are almost indistinguishable—occurs when a given *word* or *root* is repeated (or seems to be repeated) in various connections or with various modifications. With this figure we pass from the phoneme to the morpheme, from the mere sound to the sound with a definable sense attached. This figure is called by Latin rhetoricians (the author of the *Ad Herennium* and Geoffrey of Vinsauf, for instance) *traductio,* by Puttenham the *tranlacer,* and by John Dryden the *turn* "both on the words and on the thought."[7] In the fourth book of *Paradise Lost* there is the speech of Satan to the two angels who discover him in the garden and do not recognize him (1. 827):

> *Know* ye not then? said Satan, filled with scorn,
> *Know* ye not me? Ye *knew* me once no mate
> For you, there sitting where ye durst not soar;
> Not to *know* me argues yourselves *unknown,*
> The lowest of your throng; or if ye *know,*
> Why ask ye . . . ?

The reiteration of the word *know*—a dramatic and ironic emphasis—is the opposite of both Elegant Variation and slipshod verbal Repetition and is hence a logical virtue of style. But the modulation of the root—*know, knew, to know, unknown*—introduces another aspect of meaning which, though in this instance it is no doubt under logical restraint, is capable of greater liberty. In the speech of Beelzebub at the infernal consult of the second book we find (1. 320):

> *Banded* against his throne, but to remain
> In strictest *bondage.*

Here is a real turn on modern meanings of *band* or *bond.** This is a pronounced step in the direction of homophony. In Herbert's poem *The Pulley* God pours out of a glass all His blessings on man but stops when He perceives that

> alone of all His treasure,
> *Rest* in the bottom lay.

---

* The word from which *bondage* is actually derived, OE *bond,* "householder," lies well out of sight.

God decides not to give that, lest man should *"rest* in Nature."
He says:

> Yet let him keep the *rest,*
> But keep them in repining *restlessnesse.*

Rest (what reposes) and *rest* (what remains), of different
etymologies yet surely not disparate senses, are modulated in
a restless zigzag through the poem. A clear element of pun is
caught in the structure of an elaborate turn.

The sometimes tenuous difference between logical and counterlogical values of style may be illustrated in another way by
certain groups of words which share what Bloomfield in his
Language calls "root-forming morphemes."[8] Thus:

> flash, flare, flame, flicker, flimmer
> bash, clash, crash, dash, gash, gnash, mash, slash, splash

The members of such a group have their connection with one
another almost independently of context. The connection is
a sheer fact of vocabulary. If a poet uses words of this sort as
rhyme words, the rhyme is not so flatly logical as when Chaucer rhymes simple morphemes, "worthy*nesse,*" "wilder*nesse,*"
"kynde*nesse.*" Yet the possibilities for a rhyme like *bash-mash*
are certainly not so interesting as for the fully counterlogical
rhyme—*plot-bergamot, guitar-catarrh.* Skelton confesses that
his rhyme is "ragged, Tattered and jagged." We are on middle
ground—between logic and counterlogic—with the "root-forming morphemes." That is to say, we are not dealing with clean
and complete morphemes. Neither initial *fl-* nor final *-ash* is
taken as a definable unit of meaning. Each needs the fusion
of another sound, completing the syllable, to suggest a likeness
of meaning. This is like parallels of logical expression emerging
half drawn from the raw stuff of primary experience.[9]

Bloomfield concludes his account of the root-forming morphemes as follows: "The analysis . . . is bound to be uncertain
and incomplete, because a phonetic similarity, such as, say, the
b- in *box, beat, bang,* represents a linguistic form only when it
is accompanied by a semantic similarity, and for this last, which

belongs to the practical world, we have no standard of measurement" (1933, p. 246). That is to say, we can never be sure when a writer (especially a poet) will maneuver two or more words into such a relation that a shared sound will take on a morphemic suggestion. An agent, an instrument, an action, and an effect, while related most obviously in an oblique or causal series, assume at least the parallel character of all being parts of a certain coherent situation. *Blare, dare,* and *scare* are three words which Richards suggests as having a nearly morphemic relation. *Boy beat box—Bang!* is an easy agnominative invention. Coleridge, thinking apparently of "turns," speaks of "conceits of words which are analogous to sudden fleeting affinities of mind."[10] "Momentary morphemes," one might be tempted to call the sounds which occur in various degrees of agnomination.

Internal rhymes like Swinburne's "sad bad glad mad" and Vachel Lindsay's "Hark to the pace-horn, chase-horn, race-horn! . . . Ho for the tear-horn, scare-horn, dare-horn" strive mightily, through parallel and compounding, toward the condition of morphemic root-forming. Yet the words in these examples are not true members of morphemic families. What one might conceive as a danger to rhyme from the morphemic families is diminished by the fact that the root-forming morpheme is more often initial *(b-, fl-, sl-, sk-)* than final *(-ash, -ump).* It is a relief to reflect that the clearly definable "root-forming" families of words do not actually function in poetry often as structures, that is, as members in explicit echo of one another. Poetry tends to the more inventive "turn" and agnomination. Richards in his *Philosophy of Rhetoric* has pointed out that the root-forming morphemic families do their work mostly as unheard melodies or silent witnesses—as the word *flare,* in an appropriate context, might get the benefit of *flame* or *flash* (though these were absent) or, to extend the principle but slightly, the word *blare* might conjure the shade of *dare* or *scare.* At this point the forms of counterlogical verbal meaning (pun, rhyme, agnomination, alliteration, and turn) evaporate into the general atmospheric suggestiveness of poetic language —the aura of meanings which words cannot help having round

them—which, however, they have not through any natural resemblance to things, but through resemblance to other words.

IV

Having insisted on the meaningfulness of counterlogical
verbal style, let me return to an earlier point and stress in sum-
mation precisely the highly verbal character of this style. Puns
have been assimilated into recent criticism so often with
phrases like "fruitful ambiguity" or "paradoxical tension" that
it is easy not to realize just what a curious thing a pun in poetry
is. If the *sun* is an appropriate symbol of a *son,* then that is
true in France as well as in England. But in France Herbert's
poem could not be written, because they have not *sun* and *son*
but *fils* and *soleil.* Similarly, if the rain is something like human
tears, that is true in England as well as in France. But certain
poems could be written in French and not in English, because
we have *weep* and *rain,* they have *pleurer* and *pleuvoir.* ("Il
pleure dans mon cœur Comme il pleut sur la ville.") Why, we
might ask ourselves, should puns have this power? Is there any
depth of respectability or worth in such meanings? Why
couldn't a poet arrange his own puns—which the structure of
his sentences would point up and which by a headnote he
could establish as a preliminary convention with his reader?
The French poet would say: "In this poem when I use the
sound *fils* I mean not only *fils* but *soleil.*"

Such arbitrary or pseudo puns would of course fall flat. And
first, psychologically, because it is only through an actual, not
an imagined, pun that either author or reader has the experience of the spontaneous and simultaneous double conception
and expression—Freud's momentary dip below the level of consciousness, Pound's "complex" presented "in an instant of time."
Puns have to be stored up or prepared in the history of a
language, before they can be discharged by the wit of the poet.
Secondly, or in corresponding linguistic terms, there has to be
some fact behind a pun, even if it is only the fact that in a
given language a certain homonymic relation exists, or has been

tolerated. A pun taps linguistic affinities. If language is a system of conventional norms, then a degree of contingency upon human convention is to be expected in any type of verbal discourse. In the concrete and iconic kind of verbal discourse which we call poetry, it is difficult to say how deeply this contingency will penetrate.

Language is a convention, but a spontaneous and gradual convention which would seem to take place according to certain laws of analogy and propriety in the relation of sound to meaning. It is a fact well known to philologists, for instance, that homophones "have mutually disturbing effects." If they are often used in such similar circumstances that the homophony can interfere with communication, one of a pair sometimes crowds the other out—as the English verb *let* (to permit) has done to the verb *let* (to hinder). More concrete homophones like *sun-son* seem to survive because their contexts usually distinguish them. But even here we have the familiar phenomenon of the indecent or tabu word which survives and flourishes like a sturdy weed—while its homophone (of a perfectly innocent meaning) dies out in polite circles.[11] I wonder if it may not even be possible to say that the long survival of such basic and homely homonymies as *son-sun, rest-rest* testifies to the fact that there is nothing repugnant in the ideas thus linked (though clearly distinguishable), or even that there is some harmony in the linkage. "It is possible," says the philologist, "that *light* as applied to colors . . . and *light* 'not heavy,' are sometimes felt, by a kind of synesthesia, to be merely different meanings of the same word. . . . This feeling has probably made it easier for the two homonyms to exist side by side."[12] When their sounds fell together in the seventeenth century, did *queen* banish *quean* in the interest of clarity or in that of propriety? At any rate, language to some extent takes care of itself. And different languages are rich in different poetic situations. The occurrence of *light-light, sun-son,* or *pleurer-pleuvoir*[13] in a language makes a poetic situation. (So too, for ironic purposes, does archaic *quean-queen.*) So too does the occurrence of a string of geographical names repeating a certain phoneme, though for these we may suppose the language has had less concern. We may, if we like, call these simply Milton's good luck. How witty is our language, boasts Herbert. "How neatly do we give one onely name to parent's issue and the sunne's bright starre!" And in a similar mood of linguistic celebration a different enough writer reflects: "All these sounds, the crowing of cocks, the baying of dogs, and the hum of insects at noon, are the evidence of nature's health or *sound* state. Such is the never failing beauty and accuracy of language."[14] The prose writer who commits the Fowlerian fault of Repetition ("Not having seen their sons in many suns, they spent the rest of the day with them, resting") runs afoul of the accidental and illogical element in homophonies. The poet, assisted in his boldness by a running counterlogical pattern of meter, with his rhymes, puns, turns, and agnominations realizes the lurking and oblique elements of homophonic harmony.

V

In his *Proficience and Advancement of Learning* Francis Bacon said that science buckles and bows the mind to the nature of things, poetry submits the shows of things to the desires of the mind. A more recent theory about language—that of "symbolic form"—says that instead of language being molded on reality, as traditionally thought, reality is molded on language. Words *are* things. The Crocean monism is transferred from the realm of spirit to the externalization of that realm, and a more thoroughgoing monism is thus achieved. The theory of style which I have been describing is based on the traditionally dualistic concept that language is referential, that objects are different from words. Like other monisms, that of symbolic form would scarcely seem to encourage discussion of verbal style as a level of meaning distinct from the more substantial. One advantage of a specific theory of verbal style is that it helps to show in what special sense the poetic, as distinct from other dimensions of discourse, *is* a mold of meaning. A theory of verbal style—like an analytic theory of metaphor—shows some qualities of language which strongly support the notion of symbolic form, but at the same time such a theory saves us from the extremism and practical embarrassments of that notion.

It seems worth reiterating that both the logical and the counterlogical qualities of style are iconic. In an abstract and relational way they *present* the things which language is otherwise occupied in designating. Poetic symbols—largely through their iconicity at various levels—call attention to themselves as symbols and in themselves invite evaluation. What may seem stranger is that the verbal symbol in calling attention to itself must also call attention to the difference between itself and the reality which it resembles and symbolizes. As one of the fathers of "symbolic form" has expressed it: "even the most primitive verbal utterance requires a transmutation of a certain cognitive or emotive experience into sound, i.e., a medium that is foreign to the experience, and even quite disparate."[15] In most discourse we look right through this disparity. There is one-way transparent intellectual reference. But poetry by thickening the medium increases the disparity between itself and its referents. Iconicity enforces disparity.[16] The symbol has more substance than a noniconic symbol and hence is more clearly realized as a thing separate from its referents and as one of the productions of our own spirit. Seeing a work of art, says Ortega y Gasset, is seeing the window pane with the garden pasted behind it, or the world inverted into the belvedere of our own concepts. And all this has one further important corollary, the enhancement of the symbol as metaphor. For metaphor proceeds from likeness and disparity. (I refer not to the metaphors which a poem contains, but to the total metaphoric relation between a good poem and the reality or the many circles of reality to which it refers.) As a stone sculpture of a human head in a sense *means* a human head but in another sense *is* a carved mass of stone and a metaphor of a head (one would rather have one's head carved in stone than in cheese), so a poem in its various levels and relations of meaning has a kind of rounded being or substance and a metaphoric relation to reality. The iconic structures of logical and counterlogical style, especially the latter, are the texture and polish of the verbal structure.

4

. . . κατ᾽ εἴδη δύνασθαι τέμνειν, κατ᾽ ἄρθρα.
—Phaedrus, 215

THE DOMAIN OF CRITICISM

THE ROLE which I have undertaken in this essay is that of defending the domain of poetry and poetics from the encircling (if friendly) arm of the general aesthetician. It is a role which I confess is congenial to my habits of thinking about poetry, yet I should like to protest at the outset that this is so not through any routine attitude of pluralism or nominalism. It is not one of my assumptions, and it will not even be one of my conclusions, that poetry has nothing in common with other arts, any more than it is one of my assumptions that one kind of poetry has nothing in common with another, or one poem with another. In short, the terms *poem* and *poetics* are for me univocal terms, and so, in a more difficult sense, are *beauty* and *aesthetics*. I do not see how to draw the line between nominalisms. The person who for nominalistic reasons denies the relevance of aesthetics to poetry will scarcely stop short of denying the relevance of poetics to this poem or that one. Such a person, it should be clear, is in no position to defend the domain of poetics or literary criticism. Neither our analysis nor our synthesis of the kinds of human experience can afford to proceed on a priori lines. When is it desirable to distinguish among the objects denoted by a conventional term and thus forming a traditional unity? When is it desirable to defend a traditional unity? When desirable to create a new unity from terms and concepts traditionally distinct? The answer to these questions will be determined partly by the needs of particular philosophic programs, but partly, and more importantly, by the demands of reality itself—as it has been either justly or unjustly described in the conventional systems of terms and concepts. Dialectic, Plato tells us, is cutting nature at the joints. It is because the world of our experience does have joints that we may undertake to discuss the claims of aesthetics upon literary criticism.

We wish to ask whether poems should be criticized by criteria which are so specific as to apply simply to poems themselves, or whether they may be criticized by criteria which are generic enough to include other arts. The question might be broadened to read: Are specific situations ever illuminated by our turning to principles which are more abstract than the situations themselves? The answer must be, I believe, that they always are. Such is the character of theorizing, a character not invalidated even by the high degree of relevant individuality found in works of art.

The unity and wholeness of a poem, for example, are concepts which the literary critic will do well to pursue not only in Aristotle's *Poetics* but in his *Physics* and *Metaphysics*—and in the *Enneads* of Plotinus and the *Introduction* to the philosophy of fine art by Hegel. What literary critics today recognize as the impracticality of the poem has at least been made more available to them through the "disinterest" defined by Kant, the "distance" or "detachment" spoken of by later aestheticians. The highly respected individuality of the poem owes its obvious debt to the Kantian aesthetic judgment "without concept" and the corresponding intuition-expression of Croce. In such instances as these—and they are cardinal instances—the literary theorist must be grateful to the metaphysician and the aesthetician.

Could another relationship even be suggested by another selection? A person interested in such a project might begin by reciting the facts that Aristotle composed not a general *Aesthetics* but a *Poetics* and that the Platonic concept of the beautiful was not closely connected with the emotional disturbances induced by poetry. The same skeptical person might go on to note especially certain features of the classical doctrine as it was inherited and developed by the Middle Ages. It seems likely that Thomas Aquinas (himself the author of a few rather fine poems) thought implicitly of poems as among the things which merit the name "beautiful"—those which please on being apprehended (*quae visa placent*). On the other hand, when he actually spoke of poetry, it was in certain connections, linguistic, logical, and theological, which may seem to many today rather curious. Commenting upon the *Posterior Analytics* of Aristotle, Aquinas distinguishes five grades of logical discourse, from syllogistic certitude, through dialectic and rhetorical kinds of probability, to sophistic, the lowest of all. Next to sophistic is poetry—a form of verbal statement which offers us no better than a plausible estimate of the truth.[1] Whatever the relation which poetry may succeed in establishing with beauty, it would seem that Aquinas prefers to begin by viewing it as one mode, and a tricky mode, of the art of using words. In the scholastic Middle Ages, as Maritain and others have recently explained, the bond among the several arts was not immediately a bond of beauty or of pleasure but one precisely of art, *ars* or *techne*—a knowledge of how to make something.[2] Aligned on the axis of making, the arts of music, poetry, or painting had less in common with a sunset or even with the virgins of Crotona than with other arts and crafts, carpentry and architecture, grammar, logic, and rhetoric. And the last three, along with poetry, had their own special affinity as intellectual arts. The beauties of the several arts were realized analogically through the principle of right making, that is, through the full being of each, each one's being what it should be. On this metaphysic, beauty is not a special problem. As we have been told by the sculptor Eric Gill, Beauty looks after herself. The distinction between a cathedral and a well built shed, between a hymn and a well written business letter is one of hierarchies in the order of being. Whether or not this principle is sufficient to account for the marked difference of intensity which you and I are expected to discern between sculpture or music and the ordinary run of experience, I do not feel called upon at this moment to decide. My point is only that the destructively minded person whom I have mentioned above, the secessionist who wished to detach poetics from the realm of the modern aesthetician, might find comfort in that classico-scholastic alignment of arts—poetry, grammar, logic, rhetoric—especially as new light has been thrown upon this by techniques of rhetorical analysis in our own day—and especially of course too as one notices certain accomplishments of modern general aesthetics.

The concept of aesthetics emerged victoriously through the ferment of Renaissance theories about music, painting, sculpture, and poetry. There was a time, as late as the sixteenth century, when painters and sculptors had to protest that despite the manual character of their art (and the dust on the persons of the sculptors) they too were the protégés of gentlemen and as good as the poets. Later on all that was cleared up. In the second half of the seventeenth century the term "Beaux Arts" became current, and soon after appeared Baumgarten's new science of aesthetics (dealing with clear but confused, that is with sensuous ideas). It was during this period that the Horatian phrase *ut pictura poesis,* casual in its classic context and dormant through centuries, lived a new life in the verse of Du Fresnoy and in the minds of painters, poets, and academicians. A painting of a historical subject like the *Fall of Manna* could be criticized by the Aristotelian standards of drama, the beginning, middle, and end of the action, the unity, the *peripeteia.*[3] English poets painted landscapes after "savage Rosa" or "learned Poussin"—with often a smear of opaque verbal paint that betrays too clearly the eye on the canvas. The frontispiece of Winckelmann's *Gedanken über die Nachamung* shows the painter of the sacrifice of Iphigenia with his eye scrupulously upon the text of Euripides—*ommatōn peplon protheis.* This was the time too when song and opera assumed an ideal character as approximating the union of the arts. Somewhat later architecture was "frozen music," and vowels had correspondences with colors. A *Laokoon* and a *New Laokoon* and in our day the essays of Professor René Wellek and other comparativists have outlined the three centuries of insistent parallel between the arts and the furious mélange of media which ushered in the present era of general aesthetics.

I do not mean that aestheticians today are not alert to one of the peculiar liabilities of their pursuit—that of confusing aesthetic media and capacities. The very opposite would seem to be true. The *Aesthetic Judgment* of the late Professor D. W. Prall, for example, is a book which a literary scholar may well remember for its trenchant statement of the truth that prose discourse is phonetically "thin and poor," that it is not really a musical medium (pp. 289–95). Professor S. C. Pepper's *The Basis of Criticism in the Arts* is a book noteworthy for several reasons but not least for its nice discrimination of the several arts in regard to their "physical continuants": the painted canvas or wrought stone to which we return in a gallery, the sheet of musical notes rendered by one pianist tonight, by another next year, the page of words read and reread by many readers. Such panoramic surveys as Professor Greene's *The Arts and the Art of Criticism* and Professor Munro's *The Arts and Their Interrelations* are formally devoted to the manifold description of aesthetic fields. Professor Greene speaks eloquently of the diverse forms which may be imposed upon diverse materials, and of the diverse contents which may thereby be expressed. "Each medium . . . has its peculiar limitations which can be transcended, if at all, only by a *tour de force,* and which can never be completely negated. A modern steel bridge or skyscraper cannot be built merely out of stone, wood, or brick, and polyphonic and harmonic music cannot be produced on a one stringed instrument or by one voice" (pp. 163–64; cp. pp. 41–42). At this level of discussion it is often the aesthetician who has a superior sense of where he is when he approaches a literary work of art. Literary students themselves (no doubt unhappily influenced by vague and popular currents of aesthetic attitude) most often embrace the metaphoric heresies, leaning too heavily upon the Gothic, the baroque, or the rococo to explain the literature of a period, staking too much on the concept of sensory realization, or vaguely invoking the idea of "music."

On the other hand, I believe that Professor Greene or another contemporary aesthetician would agree with me that one of the greatest difficulties in the way of achieving a general theoretical aesthetic is that such a philosophy must inevitably rise in the mind of a person preoccupied with aesthetic experience of a certain kind or kinds, the imagistic traces of which are likely to prove inconvenient when the theory has to accommodate other experiences less concretely known. It is perhaps not too much to say that most modern aestheticians have arrived at their philosophy chiefly through an absorption with the visual and auditory arts. One does not think of general aesthetics as growing out of a distinctively literary preoccupation. At this point let me introduce a fairly extended example from a recent book, *Art and the Social Order,* by D. W. Gotshalk. Professor Gotshalk's aesthetic is a four-point relational system, in which material and form, expression and function, have reciprocal instrumental values, each has its own terminal value, and each is a focus through which the whole work is apprehended. In an impressive chapter on "The Materials of the Work of Art" we read of marble, tone, and pigment, in their relation to sensation, intuition, feeling, imagination, and intellect: "the thick nervous lines, the compartments of pure color, the flat simplified shapes" which support the chief formal principle of Matisse's *Woman in the Red Caraco*—the "limestones, sandstones, and oölitic stones" which are best for abstract sculpture—"the heavy, soaring stone and colored glass of medieval cathedrals" which "contribute powerfully to the expression of solemnity, awe, and mystical intent of their interiors." More simply, in a terminal sense, we have "the gorgeous purples of a Tintoretto, the iridescent blues and greens of a Monet . . . the solid marble of an Acropolis temple, the bright wood of a freshly painted Virginia Colonial house." The same chapter begins by serving notice that it will deal only with physical media, not with antecedent physicosocial conditions and memory symbols, which are properly contained in the dimension of expression. This might seem to exclude the dimension of "material" from verbal art. But then we read in the same chapter:

The exact aesthetic stature of the material of art is realized more fully . . . only when one recalls that this material is not any old material but material of a special type. The great poet's words . . . are not the flat stereotypes of a business letter.

And again:

Nor do the materials of literature lack terminal values of their own. The language of poetry, for example, has intrinsic terminal properties as diverse as the poets. It may be the thick, sensuous language of a Keats; the homely language of a Wordsworth; the gusty, carefree language of a Whitman; or the artificial, clanging language of a Poe.

In some works of art the terminal material properties may, for various reasons, be the chief aesthetic asset. A poem recited expertly in an unintelligible foreign language may yet hold attention by the vivacious qualities of its sound. (p. 104)

These are statements which may not read so well to literary critics. We have recently been accustomed to a somewhat different theory of what it is we enjoy when we hear a poem "recited expertly in an unintelligible foreign language." And since at least as early as the time of Wordsworth we have entertained, theoretically at least, rather cold feelings for poetic diction. "The great poet's words . . . are not the flat stereotypes of a business letter." In the Foreword of his book Professor Gotshalk alludes to the *Ulysses* of James Joyce. Presumably, in his later chapter on materials he was not thinking about such a piece of inflational parody as the following in the Polyphemus chapter of *Ulysses:*

For nonperishable goods bought of Moses Herzog, of 13 Saint Kevin's parade, Wood quay ward, merchant, hereinafter called the vendor, and sold and delivered to Michael E. Geraghty, Esquire, of 29 Arbour Hill in the city of Dublin, Arran quay ward, gentleman, hereinafter called the purchaser, videlicet, five pounds avoirdupois of first choice tea at three shillings per pound avoirdupois.

One will perhaps admit that the sprawling inclusiveness of the Joycean parody style is something different from the intense poetic instances, the language of Keats or Wordsworth, which Professor Gotshalk has in mind. But the principle is broad enough. One might throw in, without looking far, "Mr. Eugenides, the Smyrna merchant Unshaven, with a pocket full of currants C. i. f. London: documents at sight," or a single Shakespearian sonnet (IV) containing the terms "legacy," "bequest," "lend," "sum," "traffic," "acceptable audit," "executor." It may be true that such arts as sculpture, painting, and music begin with materials in themselves beautiful—or at least pleasing. Professor Gotshalk's marble, diorite, or limestone are better materials for sculpture than cheese or cowdung. But verbal art notoriously includes the whole range of human experience and consequently the whole human vocabulary.[4] Philological attempts to distinguish ugly or beautiful words have been merely comic, as when the National Association of Teachers of Speech once attempted to list the ten ugliest words in the English language (*phlegmatic, crunch, cacophony, treachery,* and the like); and Wilfrid Funk made a parallel attempt to list the ten most beautiful (*dawn, lullaby, hush, luminous . . .*).[5] The example of the dunghill (or equivalent object) beautifully described is one of the oldest in literary discussion.

Literary theorists of our day have been content to say little about "beauty" or about any over-all aesthetic concept. In his most general formulation the literary theorist is likely to be content with something like "human interest." "The question of the value of poetry . . . is to be answered by saying that it springs from a basic human impulse and fulfils a basic human interest." Yet disinterestedness, we remember, is something that Kant made a character of art. While it would be wrong to say that any art has an altogether easy time achieving this state of disinterest, it seems safe to say that some arts, chamber music, abstract or nearly abstract sculpture, for example, or decorative penmanship, have in their very nature a better start than poetry. Poetry deals with Frankie and Johnnie, who were lovers, with man's first disobedience and the fruit of a forbidden tree, with Hamlet and the ghost of his father—in short, with matters of intense interest. How the poet arrives at anything like the disinterest, the detachment, the self-contained objectification of which we hear the aesthetician speak (how the poet's "rage" achieves its "order"), must be a peculiar question, the answer to which will have an odd relation to the main doctrines of general aesthetics. If poetry does achieve anything like beauty, it does not do so by starting with beautiful veins of material, agate or marble, either in the realm of things or in that of words.

If one were to push this principle just a little further, that is, if one were to insist that poetry has no material medium at all, or a medium of ideas only—externalized in verbal sounds or graphic signs but not in any way qualified or determined by these external signs—poetry would indeed be a strenuous recalcitrant to the discipline of general aesthetics. I have in mind the statement of Shelley that language "is a more direct representation of the actions and passions of our internal being . . . than color, form, or motion, and is more plastic and obedient to the control of that faculty of which it is the creation." Language, he believed, "has relation to thoughts alone; but all other materials have relations . . . which . . . interpose between conception and expression." Philosophies more recent, though certainly deriving from currents of thought in which Shelley was deeply initiate, have tended to straighten out such distinctions by saying that all reality is modeled on symbols, verbal, musical, plastic, or ritual. The fundamental doctrine in these philosophies of expression and symbolic form becomes not that symbols are only meaning, but that meanings are only symbols. On these grounds the aesthetician may not be much troubled by differences between poetry and sensory arts, but then too he will less readily be able to write a chapter on materials—rich, creamy, polished, massive, tensile, phosphorescent, saccharine, solid, flowing—as distinguished from the formal, physicosocial, and memorially symbolic dimensions of art. The literary critic too I believe will have, in his own right, far less to say. Literary critics, despite their general mistrust of poetic diction and of any strictly musical notion of verbal harmony, have manifested a chronic interest in the verbal medium.

In this the literary critics have made their most obvious overture to the general aesthetician. The intellectual character of language makes literature difficult for the aesthetician. But there are different types of verbal discourse, and one type, the poetic, seems somehow, by rhythmic, metaphoric, and punning figures, and by dramatic reflexes, to embody meanings in an exceptionally solid and intuitional form. This fact gives the aesthetician his grip upon poetry. Poetry is an amphibious organism, an ambiguous performance, with which I suspect the modern aesthetician is never quite satisfied, but in which he remains deeply interested.

One might raise the methodological issue whether we shall approach poetry as the verbal form of the aesthetic, or as the aesthetic form of what is verbal. Which is to be the genus, which the differential? By starting with the aesthetic we may assure ourselves that whatever gets into our account will be in terms of the aesthetic—if verbal compositions manage to get in at all. By starting with words, or verbal compositions, we are sure of finding in our account at least the element of words —though we may have to push or stretch them to meet the concept of the aesthetic.

Modern aesthetics has centered its doctrine judiciously between Platonic intellectualism and the opposite extreme,[6] the nineteenth century five-sense aesthetics which provided for the arts of touch, of perfumery, and of cookery—the "viscerally beautiful." The modern aesthetician, that is, while insisting on an intense degree of the sensory as an essential avenue of aesthetic experience, renders his homage to the intellectual in choosing the senses of sight and hearing as typically or par excellence the aesthetic senses. Through them (the *sensus maxime cognoscitivi*) we know the forms of space and time, and these senses are, as Professor Gotshalk says, the "distance senses," safe from the biological dangers of contact. Coming from an opposite direction, the literary theorist who is not shy of finding himself in some sense within the scope of the aesthetician will strive to show that his art of words and ideas somehow approximates the state of the visual and auditory arts —that is, attains something like their intuitively sensuous and concrete quality. But—and this is a crucial point of the argument—the duly cautious literary theorist will not say that this attainment is possible for the direct and easy reason that poetry is rhythmic and melodious, verbal music, or that it is a "speaking picture," a mosaic of vivid visual images. From such notions proceed at the level of theory the various injustices to the medium, the invalid analogies, the metaphoric fallacies, and at the level of practice the imbecilities of verbal medium, to which we have alluded in our brief historical survey. It is necessary to expose oneself to the charge of being paradoxical. For poetry approximates the intuitive sensuous condition of paint and music not by being less verbal, less characteristic of verbal expression, but actually by being more than usually verbal, by being hyperverbal. Poetry achieves concreteness, particularity, and something like sensuous shape not by irrelevance of local texture, in its meter or in its images (as in one currently sophisticated literary theory), but by extra relevance or hyperrelevance, the interrelational density of words taken in their fullest, most inclusive and symbolic character. A verbal composition, through being supercharged with significance, takes on something like the character of a stone statue or a porcelain vase. Through its meaning or meanings the poem *is*. It has an iconic solidity. Thus in a sense the poem is a paradox, through the quality of extra significance or hyperverbalism becoming anomalous among verbal expressions. The poem has, not an abstractly meant or intended meaning, but a fullness of actually presented meaning. This raises one of the most vexing problems for the critic of poetry, one which I believe he faces in a unique way. It is after all characteristic of words in their usual roles to convey intentions, and it is a feat of considerable detachment to be able to view them otherwise. Of a garden image (say a limestone snake by John B. Flanagan) we ask: What is it? Of a road sign giving the name of a town, we ask: What does it tell us? A poem is a road sign which through the complexity and fullness of its told message approximates the status of the garden image. The act of intuition which discerns this status is poetic appreciation. The analysis of the status may be a specific level of aesthetics, but since it is, in the ways which I have been laboring to describe, greatly different from what occurs in any other special branch of aesthetics or in general aesthetics, I believe it most often deserves the specific name of *poetics* or *literary criticism*. The verbal object and its analysis constitute the domain of literary criticism.

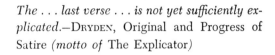

The . . . last verse . . . is not yet sufficiently ex-plicated.—DRYDEN, Original and Progress of Satire *(motto of* The Explicator*)*

EXPLICATION AS CRITICISM

MY AIM in this essay is to talk about the question whether explication of a poem is itself an act of criticism and hence of evaluation. Not whether it is necessary to understand a poem *in order* to evaluate it (The question in that form is little better than rhetorical), but whether to understand a poem is the same as to evaluate it. This indeed I conceive to be the only critical question that can be asked about explication. And this is far from a rhetorical question. The correct answer to it lies, I believe, not in a simple affirmation or denial, but in an adjustment. My effort to give an answer will move toward a "monism" of evaluation through explication, but it will insist at the same time on certain other principles.

As both the method and the philosophy of explicative criticism are strongly established in our day, it has seemed to me easiest to make my own approach to the philosophy from the direction of its difficulties. I find my own account of explication caught constantly in a pull between certain opposed pairs of

Reprinted from *English Institute Essays, 1951.* Copyright 1952 by Columbia University Press.

ideas, and these will be my main topics of discussion—namely, (1) part and whole, or the rival claims of these entities to critical consideration; (2) value and disvalue, or the difficulty of describing *dis*value in a philosophy of value which rises above the principles of pleasure and pain; (3) value and neutrality, or the difficulty of merging value with what we commonly speak of as the neutral facts. Running parallel to these three pairs and tending to involve and unite them and hence to appear in one way or another at all points of the discussion is a fourth pair, the ideas of the explicit and the implicit—or the difference between these, yet their interdependence in the meaning of the poem. In the course of an attempt to show that these four pairs of ideas are to be considered as coming inside the theory of explication, I shall have occasion to inquire if another pair, the affective and the cognitive, are to be considered in the same way.

The thesis that explication *is* criticism, or is at least immediately and intimately related to criticism, proceeds quite reasonably from any theory of poetry which sees the poem as a wholeness of meaning established through internally differentiated form, the reconciliation of diverse parts. And this will be more or less true no matter whether the kind of holism invoked be the realistic and Aristotelian, the idealistic (either neo-Platonic or romantic), or the affective, the synaesthesis of Richards—although, as I have hinted a moment ago, the course of our argument may develop certain relevant differences among these theories. The success of explication in persuading us of literary value is a kind of practical test of how well aesthetic theories of order and wholeness do apply to literary works. More precisely, a practical affinity between holism and *e*xplication arises because organization and wholeness are matters of structure and hence also of *im*plication. Organization and wholeness are at stake, for instance, if we undertake to ask what kind of coherence actually obtains between two main parts of some poem—let us say Donne's *Extasie*, where one part is mystical, the other apparently seductive. It is not clear to me, indeed, that Dryden, in providing a motto for the organ of the contemporary explicators' guild—"The last verse is not yet sufficiently explicated"—had in mind more than the explication of the explicit. But the thoroughgoing explicator will surely not conceive that he has employed his talent to the full unless he performs not only that service (as in glosses and other linguistic and historical observations) but beyond that the *explicit*ation of the implicit. For poetry is never altogether, or even mainly, "poetry of statement." The very difference between those two sides of the explicable, the explicit and the implicit, and the ways in which one may relate to the other are matters with which the explicator is bound to be deeply engaged.

II

One of the main difficulties for explicative holism is that which arises in one form or another from what we may roughly describe as the competition of parts with whole. At the metaphysical level, holistic theories of beauty have had difficulty in coping with the fact that such simple things as bright colors and sweet sounds are usually called beautiful. Our idea of beauty usually does begin with such experiences and persists naively in including them, except in the face of the most studious self-denial. As the sophist Hippias was made to remark, "Gold is a beautiful thing." One escape from the equivocation thus apparently arising for the term "beauty" is the assignment of the name *pleasant* or *agreeable* (the Kantian *Angenehm*) to such simpler experiences, the name *beauty* being reserved for the higher and more complex. A bright color or a note on a French horn will be pleasant; painting or music, beautiful. Another kind of escape, however, and one I believe to be of more interest to us as literary theorists, was that provided by the neo-Platonic and medieval aesthetic of the luminous, and to some extent by its parallel the aesthetic of numerical harmony. The latter of these, proceeding on Pythagorean and Platonic conceptions concerning relations between mathematics, music, and astronomy (the affinities of the quadrivium), arrived at a synthesis of beauty in order and unity with far less of an analogical leap. The aesthetic of the luminous was more daring and solved a bigger difficulty, saying in effect that the reason why we apply the term *beautiful* to simple bright things and to complex harmonies alike is the Platonic reason that light is an analogue of intelligible reality—light is to the eye as truth is to the mind. The radiant color of a Byzantine mosaic or of a painting of saints by Fra Angelico is an analogue of the ordered brilliance of the whole composition. The doctrine has a close relation to the equally ancient doctrine that sight, along with hearing, is a chief aesthetic sense—a sense that can understand things—not just be stimulated by them or amorphously rubbed against them. It is a doctrine which is echoed in our own inevitable habits of aesthetic praise, our metaphoric vocabulary of positive evaluation—not *dirty, drab, muddy,* or *dark,* but *clean, bright, radiant, fiery, brilliant, gorgeous.* And we are likely to feel that with these terms of approval we are doing more justice to the worth of the poem than if we were to say it is smooth or sweet.

When Plotinus devised his own expression of the theory which I have just sketched, in the sixth essay of his first *Ennead,* he did so in order to refute a notion which seemed to him implied in the Stoic theory of symmetry, that the parts of a pattern can have beauty only in virtue of their relation to the whole. And in this perhaps the relevance of the ancient problem to our own thinking can be most readily seen. For one of the most persistent implications of holism and explicationism is that the parts do have value only as interacting and making the whole. And this is an article of the philosophy which is bound to impose some hard work here and there on the explicator—even when he is working on the most highly finished poems. Perhaps the difficulty of eliciting the significance of every detail will be the greater in proportion to the largeness and greatness of the poem. Extreme holism is obviously contrary to our experience of literature. (We do not wait until the end of the play or novel to know whether the first scene or chapter is brilliant or dull—no long work in fact would ever be witnessed or read if this were so.) A poem, said Coleridge, the father of holism in English criticism, is a composition which proposes "to itself such delight from the *whole,* as is compatible with a distinct gratification from each component part."[1] The value of a whole poem, while undoubtedly reflecting something back to the parts, has to grow out of parts which are themselves valuable. *The Rape of the Lock* would not come off were not the couplets witty. We may add that good poems may have dull parts; bad poems, bright parts. How minutely this principle could be urged without arriving at a theory of Longinian "sudden flashes," of "cathartically charged images," of Arnoldian touchstones, of poetic diction, or of irrelevant local texture, I do not know. Nor what the minimal dimension of wit or local brilliance of structure may be; nor to what extent a loosely constructed whole may be redeemed by the energy of individual chapters or scenes. Yet the validity of partial value as a general principle in tension with holism seems obvious. The whole with which explication is concerned is something elastic and approximate.

III

And yet again what I have just been saying is not true in the sense that the poetic part could ever be literally like the bright color or the sweet sound of our direct experience. Poetic theory, of all the branches of aesthetics, most easily resolves the competition between part and whole which we have been describing. For poetry entertains no beautiful ideas or words as such. Its materials, unlike those of sculpture, do not have to be high-class. They include everything, "the weariness, the fever, and the fret," dung, poison, pain, deformity, and death. All, we are convinced, may be assimilated by the peculiar process of the given poem. Poetry is the art which most readily transcends the simple pleasure principle and illustrates the principle of structure and harmonious tension.

For somewhat the same reason, however, poetic theory appears to me to be that branch of aesthetic theory which has the greatest difficulty with a certain other thing. I mean *disvalue*[2] —not the absence only of value, a vacuum, and not just an inferior value, a minor pattern of order, but actual disvalue— sources of displeasure in our reading of bad poetry or pseudo-poetry, and not only locally, in blemishes or partial defects, but in total structures, poems which are wholly bad. The aesthetic of harmonious order is closely related to an ontology which sees evil in general, and hence ugliness, as a special kind of negative, an absence, or privation, where something is needed to fill out a harmony. The meaning of this doctrine is most easily realized in such examples as a man without an eye or a leg or a kidney. But even here our realization of disvalue comes about most readily through our positive sense of the inconvenient and the painful. Sheer disvalue in an ontological sense, complete, substantive chaos or disorder, is not conceivable. Anything that is anything at all has a minimal kind of order and being. Our experience of the painful, the evil, and the ugly is not actually negative:—the knife in the dark, the cunning plot, the riotous passion, the distorted countenance. If their evil lies in a deviation from the fullness and rightness of human nature, this evil is none the less powered by a violent positive activity of the human substance. Yet poetry, as we have noted, transcends and subsumes all this evil and by perspective makes it part of aesthetic value. So, we might think of poetry, the reflection of the universe and its intensification through our spirit's activity, as the art in which the ontological principle would be most easily realized—where indeed, as Keats yearned to experience, the ideal would be the real, and there would be no disvalue—only greater and lesser values, only expression and lack of expression. (A good poem, we have often heard, is simply a real poem, a genuine poem.) And how, on this theory of value, could we explicate disvalue? Would not a bad poem be simply one about which we could say little or nothing at all?

Perhaps we ought to begin by confessing that many poems which we are accustomed to call bad, or at least about which we are accustomed to profess discomfort, are not actually bad, but only less good. The element of discomfort attached to them may be a part of our snobbery—or it may come through a reflexive light cast upon the author's vanity or obtuseness. If he had not professed to write a poem, if he had not called it a poem and printed it on fine paper, the offense might be far less.

This kind of escape, however, will hardly be complete. We shall have yet to examine a matter of more critical importance; that is, the peculiar way in which two kinds of truth, that of correspondence (the accent of explicitness) and that of coherence (the accent of implication) are united in verbal discourse and depend on each other. The simplest kind of verbal assertion (let us say, hawthorn is white) if it is true has a truth both of correspondence and of coherence. The whole expression corresponds to reality; but looked at internally and verbally, this correspondence consists of a coherence between subject and predicate. They go together. Poetry is a complex kind of verbal construction in which the dimension of coherence is by various techniques of implication greatly enhanced and thus generates an extra dimension of correspondence to reality, the symbolic or analogical. But all this structure of meaning rises upon a certain element of unavoidably direct reference to outside reality and a minimal truth of such reference.

If it were otherwise, then indeed would poetry achieve the status of a pure idealism. Elements of falsity could scarcely creep into the poet's discourse. Poetry could not go wrong. Everything the poet said would simply have more or less being or character and be more or less valuable. Some such idealistic assumption or desire surely prompted Leibniz to the remark quoted with approval by Herder: "I like almost everything I read."[3] A kind of inversion of that assumption, but equally simplistic, could produce in Tolstoy the view that clarity of meaning is so much a characteristic of sincerity and of moral value that the unintelligibility of Baudelaire was almost the same thing as his immorality.[4] A more cautious neo-Platonic statement had been that of Joubert, that clarity "is so eminently one of the characteristics of truth, that often it even passes for truth itself."[5]

The response of reality to verbal expression while to some extent elastic and plastic (we can in some sense see best what we can best express) is at the same time in important ways obdurate and recalcitrant. The elasticity comes in the nexus which obtains *between* words and things, one by which words can be twisted and stretched a long way and yet maintain a coherence and validity of their own—so long as the referential relation to reality is not entirely broken. A theory of poetic wholeness and coherence need not proceed to the extreme— either idealistic or positivistic—of making the only kind of *un*-truth the unmeaningful. The kind of truth found in poetry (if either our poetry or our criticism is to survive) will have to be more than the satisfaction aroused by the contemplation of a system of symbols. Most of us are in fact practically equipped to resist this kind of total submersion of knowledge into the dimension of coherence. The routine technique of our historical studies may sometimes betray us into writing a defence of some mean work of literature just because we have come to understand the conventions according to which it was written. But we don't really think that way. We know all along that some historically understandable things are wicked or silly.

Actual disvalue in poetry arises when some abstractly true assertion or correct attitude is blurred or garbled in symbolic or stylistic incoherencies, or (more flagrantly) when some false assertion or attitude is invested with specious forms of coherence. A sentimental, that is an excessive or oversimplified, feeling about an object can be endowed, for instance, with such a pattern of coherence and suggestion of deep resonance as the metrical and rhyming scheme of a sonnet. The very fact that a poem is a sonnet may create a greater opportunity for badness than if it were a ramble in free verse. Or again, a poem can be given an illusion of depth through the introduction of apparently real but actually phantasmal or irrelevant symbols. In such cases explication reveals disvalue by explicating the absence of the truly explicable. In such cases, there is more (and less) than mere lack or meagerness of meaning. There is the positive and active carelessness and self-deception of the human will and imagination. This is disvalue and from it comes our experience of displeasure.

IV

It is a curious testimony to the inseparability of the topics which I have proposed to discuss in this essay that the difficulty concerning disvalue which we have just seen, along with such solution as I may have suggested, greatly facilitates the discussion of what I conceive to be the advantage of a fully explicative criticism—though I have to ask your patience in waiting a short space before I can show how these ideas go together. The great advantage in keeping our explicative activity as close as possible to our evaluative is that we thereby keep a clear distance from affective ways of talking about poems—ways which emphasize our minds exactly so far as they are individual agents reacting to impulses and tending to move in separate directions. The issue is not always clearly recognized; it is often disguised by a terminology of ends and means. Thus David Daiches in his *Study of Literature for Readers and Critics:*

Pattern by itself does not make literature; it must be the kind of pattern which communicates insight. A mistake made by many contemporary critics, particularly in the discussion of poetry, is to regard subtlety or complexity of arrangement as itself a criterion of literary worth. But pattern in literature is a means to an end, not an end in itself. (p. 80)

But in literature a part is never a means to another part which is the end, or to a whole which is the end—unless in the organistic sense that all parts and the whole are reciprocally ends and means, the heart, the head, and the hand. The end-means relation in literature (so far as the end is outside the means) is a relation between us the readers and the poem, by means of which the poet indeed may be aiming at us. Inside the poem there are no ends and means, only whole and parts.

The affective theory of Richards, or the affective side of his theory, was implicitly an end-means theory, about poetry as a means of working on us—except that here and there this theory got mixed up with a cognitive part-whole terminology, as in the following single sentence of his chapter on "The Language of Criticism."

This trick of judging the whole by the detail, instead of the other way about, of mistaking the means for the end, the technique for the value, is in fact much the most successful of the snares which waylay the critic.[6]

I suggest that the separation of technique from value which results from confusing means and end with part and whole was in the case of Richards a far more successful snare. It was the resolute unification of technique and value, of knowledge and value, in the system of Croce which provoked the sneering remarks about him in the early books of Richards. And Croce's idealism is indeed one plausible though extreme terminus of the cognitive tendency in criticism—a joining of reality and mind so thorough that all is united in one, the absolute reality of spirit.

The rift between technique and value accomplished by Richards' *Principles* appeared most clearly and curiously in the chapter on "Badness in Poetry." And it is here that I meant we may see disvalue (with its inherently divisive tendency) as a severe test of just how cognitive and hence how coherent a theory of poems may be. Richards distinguished two kinds of bad poems. In one the "original experience" was somehow recognized to have "had some value," but there was a serious failure to communicate the value. This was illustrated by a tiny scrap of H.D.'s imagism. In the other the reproduction of "the state of mind of the writer" was thought to be exact, but the values thus reproduced or communicated were sadly inferior. This was illustrated by a heavy-footed sonnet of Ella Wheeler Wilcox's on Love and Friendship.[7] It is to be noted in passing that this kind of division in badness produced an especially mysterious instance of "intentionalistic" interpretation. (How could he tell that H.D.'s poem proceeded from a valuable experience?)[8] But the more important thing to note is that once the merit of perfect communication (that is, expression and hence structure and meaning) was conceded to the sonnet by Ella Wheeler Wilcox, there was no way left of explaining how it was bad. Richards spoke of the "pleasure and admiration" which ensue for many readers from "the soothing effect of aligning the very active Love-Friendship groups of impulses with so settled yet rich a group as the Summer-Autumn simile brings in." "The value" of the reconciliation, he said, "depends upon the level of organization at which it takes place, upon whether the reconciled impulses are adequate or inadequate. In this case those who have adequate impulses . . . are not appeased. Only for those who make certain conventional, stereotyped maladjustments instead, does the magic work."[9] My objection to this as a critique of the poem is that instead of talking about the poem to you or to me, Richards backed off and started talking equally about the poem and about you and me—what it was going to do to our impulses if they were set in a certain way, what if not. Those remarks about our adequate or inadequate impulses were an opaque substitute for a discourse that could easily have focused an embarrassing light on the poem itself. What kind of Love was it (not Cupid, one assumed, not Venus) who had managed to *lead* us by an action composed entirely of "his own throes and torments, and desires"? Did this allegorical figure, appearing so strangely in a landscape of midsummer burned to ashes, stand for something inside us, or for something outside? What kind of love had we experienced anyway? Why *indeed* were we haunted with a sense of loss? Not only the "triteness" of the close, as Richards put it, but its fatuity was to be noted. In short, what was wrong with the poem was that neither in its main explicit statement nor in the implications of its imagistic parts (and of its overemphatic metrical pattern) did it make sense.[10] The criticism of this poem might have been much more closely unified with that of the first, even though one wished to insist that while neither poem actually conveyed anything coherent, the second was more offensive because it made an elaborate pretense of doing so.

V

We have now arrived at a point in our argument where it is convenient to introduce a final, and as it appears to me the most troublesome, difficulty that confronts a philosophy of explicative criticism—that is, a difficulty in the relation between value and neutrality. It is one which arises with peculiar force from a proposition clearly enunciated in our day—if not often perfectly illustrated—namely, that the critic's job is never to judge a poem (never, that is, to use either valuative or hortatory

terms), but only to place the poem in its historical context and
to elucidate, to compare and analyze. Thus Richards in one
of his later statements, the "Introductory" to his *Practical Criticism* (altering his earlier view):

There is, it is true, a valuation side to criticism. When we have
solved, completely, the communication problem, when we have got,
perfectly, the experience, *the mental condition* relevant to the poem,
we have still to judge it, still to decide upon its worth. But the
later question nearly always settles itself; or rather, our own inmost nature and the nature of the world in which we live decide it
for us.[11]

And Eliot in several of his essays:

Comparison and analysis . . . are the chief tools of the critic. . . .
Any book, any essay, any note in *Notes and Queries*, which produces
a fact even of the lowest order about a work of art is a better piece
of work than nine-tenths of the most pretentious critical journalism.
. . . *Fact* cannot corrupt taste.[12]

In the dogmatic or lazy mind comparison is supplied by judgment,
analysis replaced by appreciation. Judgment and appreciation are
merely tolerable avocations, no part of the critic's serious business.[13]

The critic must not coerce, and he must not make judgments of
worse or better. He must simply elucidate: the reader will form
the correct judgment for himself.[14]

Eliot was presumably not thinking about the cosmic aspects
of such statements, but the other terminus of the scale of
thought intimated in his simple defence of *Notes and Queries*
might be illustrated in this passage from Plotinus:

In the single system of Intelligence are embraced as in an envelope
other envelopes within, other systems and powers and intuitions:
it may be analysed not by a straight severance, but by progressive
explication of the implicit.[15]

That is to say, values are continuous with and embodied in
experience, in the facts and the structure of the facts. You
don't stick them in or add them on, as in a mere psychology of
values. Furthermore, since value is an indefinitely flexible and

analogical concept, coextensive with form and being, a something which is always different yet always the same—there is no excuse for intruding special terms of appreciation and evaluation into our elucidative criticism. Value is always implicit and indefinable. It looks after itself. "Beauty Looks after Herself." Criticism is the "progressive explication of the implicit."

Those seem to me to be the full entailments of the holistic and elucidative position. And how often have we not all been tempted to pursue just that policy—prune away the terms of warmth, of pleasure, of admiration (our subjective impertinences), cut close to the contour of fact in a neutral and only implicitly critical style? How often has Eliot himself perhaps not tried to do that? How often, however, have any of us succeeded?

If you look at *Catiline*—that dreary Pyrrhic victory of tragedy—you find two passages to be successful: Act II, sc. i, the dialogue of the political ladies, and the Prologue of Sylla's ghost. These two passages are genial. The soliloquy of the ghost is a characteristic Jonson success in content and versification. This is the learned, but also the creative Jonson. Without concerning himself with the character of Sulla, and in lines of invective, Jonson makes Sylla's ghost, while the words are spoken, a living and terrible force. The words fall with as determined beat as if they were the will of the morose Dictator himself. . . . What Jonson has done here is not merely a fine speech. It is the careful, precise filling in of a strong and simple outline.[16]

This passage, so bristly with several kinds of evaluative terms, was not unfairly chosen. So far have the more influential critics of our time been from practicing a style of neutral explication (and I think here not only of Eliot but especially of Leavis and Pound) that it would be nearer the truth to say that they have mainly depended on two nonexplicative powers: a confident good taste in pointing out passages and quoting them and an energetic, authoritarian bent for exhortation—that is, telling us we ought to admire these passages. I for one am prepared to defend this use of critical instruments, or at any rate to argue that the greatest influence of the critic is often exercised that way. But at the moment I am more concerned to describe and justify the kind of middle style of evaluative explication which is illustrated to some extent in the passage from Eliot just quoted.

Our critical vocabulary, I venture, may be divided roughly into three classes of terms: at one extreme the terms of most general positive and negative valuing (of which "good poem" or "excellent poem" may be taken as the center and type), at the other extreme the numerous neutral or nearly neutral terms of more or less technical description (*verse, rhyme, spondee, drama, narrative*) and along with these the whole vocabulary of referential content (*love, war, life,* and *death*), and then in between those extremes the numerous and varied terms of special valuation—*dreary, determined, careful, precise, strong, simple*—terms which of course assume their character of positive or negative valuing partly from the complex of more neutral terms among which they are set and partly from the flow of valuing started by more general and explicit value terms—*success, successful, genial, creative.*

It is true that the history of literary criticism shows a more or less constant regression of key value terms toward the level of neutrality[17]—that is, a movement of value predicates into neutral subject positions—as the growth of poetic styles and the appearance of inferior repetitions, or the maneuvers of critical dialectic itself, the assaults and counterassaults of theory, compel ever new discrimination. Croce has commented amusingly on the utility of such terms as *realistic* and *symbolic, classic* and *romantic* for either positive or negative valuing. We have heard of *true wit* and *false wit* (even *mixed wit*), of *fruitful* and *unfruitful ambiguities.* This Protean character of our valuative terminology is a function of the analogical and indefinable character of the poetic, the individual concreteness which in each different poem is strictly relevant to the requirements of the poetic formula. The *je-ne-sais-quoi* or magic of the poem, we understand, is not a mere finishing touch, a stroke or note, added here and there. It is the form itself, in which the material and neutral elements of the work of art transcend neutrality and are beautiful. The reasons for approval and disapproval given in our criticism are never quite literally universal reasons but must always be taken in the light of the example we are talking about. When Pope in his *Peri Bathous* (ch. X) gives the mock rule, "Whenever you start a Metaphor, you must be sure to *run it down,* and pursue it as far as it can go," there can be no doubt that he puts his finger on the absurdity of the passages which he quotes from Blackmore's *Job* and *Isaiah*. Yet the same standard, that of consistency in the working out of metaphor, is that according to which critics of our generation have praised metaphysical poetry and one of them has even found the measure for patronizing the sonnets of Shakespeare.

Another way of stating what this means for critical terminology is to say that the terms at the bottom of the critical scale, the merely neutral, can never add up to a demonstration of the top term, "excellent poem." That is, no definition of "excellent poem" has ever been achieved in a merely neutral, scientifically measurable predicate. Value is not translatable into neutrality. If value resides in the whole, then analysis must tend toward neutrality.

Nevertheless, our intuition of any complex whole will be improved by analysis. The effort of critical analysis and of explication is inevitably an effort to bring the two extremes of the critical scale together, the means or boosters toward this end being the intermediate terms of value—of luster or dullness, warmth or chill, speed or slowness—as such terms happen to be appropriate to our criticism, and in all the variety of ways in which they can fit the contours of the poem and interpret these in the direction of value. Such value terms may be quite subdued; they may rely little if at all on pointing by explicit and general value terms. It is perhaps under these conditions that they are most serviceable—that is, when they add to a strongly concrete and determinate coloration merely the accent of value.

It is easy to imagine instances, and to produce them from our scholarly literature, of simply neutral, philological, or otherwise historical explanation—where "explication" means glossing, that is, going outside the poem to understand its references, or where this shades into telling the content of the poem. ("This poem alludes to a society prank and tiff in the time of Queen Anne; it deals with the vanity of beaux and belles, with courtship and maidenly resistance.") It is also possible to conceive adding to such description certain simply technical notes—concerning, for instance, burlesque narrative or heroic couplets. It is further possible to conceive and produce instances where these types of neutral explication are enhanced by the addition of some general value term, like *successful, aesthetically satisfying,* or *brilliant,* but where in fact nothing has been done to bridge the gap between the neutral explicative materials and the value term or to establish the right of the former to the wedding with the latter. But then, finally, it is possible to conceive and to produce instances where explication in the neutral senses is so integrated with special and local value intimations that it rises from neutrality gradually and convincingly to the point of total judgment. It is important to observe that in such instances the process of explication tends strongly to be not merely the explication of the explicit but the *explicit*ation of the implicit or the interpretation of the structural and formal, the truth of the poem under its aspect of coherence.

The problem of explication which we have been examining is one which puts before us in a compelling way both the desirability and the difficulty of finding an escape between the two extremes of sheer affectivism and of sheer scientific neutralism. I can make that point clearer by continuing the quotation which I made above from Eliot's passage about the laziness of the critic who judges. Eliot went on to say:

> If the critic has performed his laboratory work well, his understanding will be evidence of appreciation; but his work is by the intelligence, not the emotions. . . . Where he judges or appreciates he simply . . . is missing out a link in the exposition.[18]

But on these terms it scarcely makes much difference to rational criticism which side we take—whether we say the critic should judge or say he should not. One of the latest warnings against the use of judgment in criticism has been sounded by Professor George Boas in his *Wingless Pegasus, a Handbook for Critics.* And a reviewer in the *T.L.S.* takes issue with him as follows:

This attempt would lead to the dehumanization of the whole relationship between the beholder and the work of art. Criticism has,
inevitably, as much concern with the emotions as with logic.[19]

That is, both Eliot and the *T.L.S.* reviewer (though on opposite
sides of the argument) put judgment and appreciation in the
area of emotion, separated from the area of intelligence. And
that is just what Richards did in his chapter on "Badness in
Poetry," except that instead of "logic" or "intelligence" he spoke
of "communication." And later he said, in the passage I have
quoted, that "communication" is the only thing the critic can
deal with. The extreme theory of explicative criticism cuts
apart understanding and value just as much as the avowed
theory of affects—and that is another way of saying that our
main critical problem is always how to push both understanding and value as far as possible in union, or how to make our
understanding evaluative.

At higher levels of abstraction, certain terms by which poetry
has been defined have tended to lose all specific coloration and
to become value predicates nearly if not quite synonymous with
the subject "good poetry." Yet it may be that the best of these
terms, those which define poetry as a kind of order and wholeness, are able to preserve on one side their character of the
analyzable while on the other taking on the indefinable and
unanalyzable meaning of poetry or beauty. For these are terms
which point toward the intelligible and perspicuous (toward
the implicit which may be explicated), rather than toward the
opaqueness of the merely individual, concrete, or vivid. Terms
of form and order keep to the public object and enable a critic
to make more and more relevant observations about any specific work. And translated into a statement about theory, this is
to say that formal and intellectual theory is theory par excellence. It is what is implied in the very concept of a theory—if,
that is, there is to be any correspondence between the form of
our thoughts and their content—more simply if we are to *know*
what we are talking about.

*Kritik ist so wohl für Theorie als Kunstge-
schichte das unentbehrliche Organ, und das
verbindende Mittelglied beider.*—A. W. VON
SCHLEGEL, Vorlesungen über schöne Litteratur
und Kunst, I.

HISTORY
AND CRITICISM

A PROBLEMATIC
RELATIONSHIP

THE TOPIC which I am undertaking to discuss—that of the
relation between history and literary criticism—is one which
today apparently invites the polemic style. I wish, however, to
forego that style and at the same time to refrain from the special
defense of, or attack upon, any critic or historian or any school
of critics or historians. What I have in mind is the delineation
of a certain issue which arises between literary criticism and
historical scholarship. This issue I look upon as something unavoidably problematic, part of a troublesome opposition which
runs through all our experience—between the particular and the
universal, between the contingent and what is in any sense
necessary, probable, or ideal, between what merely *was* and
what in any way *is*. We may think Aristotle's statement that
poetry is a more serious and a more philosophic thing than history[1] only a rude beginning of theory (unhappily antithetical),
but it is a beginning which can scarcely be left alone. The
problematic relation between history and criticism has always
existed. It may have been adjusted during one long epoch of
our tradition, the classical, by a certain neglect of the claims of

history. The modern advance of historical techniques and consequent sharpening of historical conscience have, however, sufficiently reasserted the problem and sufficiently increased its difficulty.

Let me offer the preliminary explanation that I am concerned to define and vindicate the role of history in criticism, and this, for one thing, by asserting a distinction between history in its several antecedent or causal relations to the writing of literature and history as meaning in works of literature. Whether antecedents themselves, if viewed in a certain light, do not become meanings, may often be difficult to say. But in so far as the distinction between the two may be maintained, it is highly relevant to this discussion. To offer one instance: the fact, so amply documented by Alexander Beljame, that English writers in the age of Addison and Swift were dependent on political rather than on courtly patronage helped to produce the further fact that these writers dissipated a good deal of their energy in pamphlet and newspaper controversy, partisan assaults and panegyrics. Here I should say that practical motivation, though closely related to literary expression, may be readily enough distinguished from the quality of that expression. On the other hand, consider the not quite parallel truth that the dependence of authors on patrons in that age and even more in the preceding age of Dryden created opportunities for a special kind of servility—in prefaces and dedications—and that this servility in turn, if sufficiently jolted, could precipitate a special kind of irony and hence give a special character to controversy and satire—Dryden's debate with Sir Robert Howard about rhyme or Pope's *Epistle to Augustus*. Here we have a social relation which becomes part of the very mind and expression of authors in their work. In such cases, and they are many, historical causes enter in a pronounced way into the very meaning of literary works.

In such cases it is clear that history precedes and enables the understanding and hence the criticism of literary works. And in a broader sense something like this is always so, for words, the medium of literature, have to be understood, and understanding is derived at least in part from historical documents.

But let me for the moment reverse that emphasis. Or let me supply its complement in making a second and equally important preliminary point—namely, that understanding is derived not only from historical documents but also from our own living and thinking of the present. No amount of deference paid to history can escape the fact that every explanation of a word is in the end an appeal to things, or the companion fact that old documents are mediated in the direction of things by new documents. "For myself," says a distinguished Shakespearian editor, "I have learnt more about Shakespeare's Henry from Wavell's *Life of Allenby* than from all the critics put together."[2] To understand the heroism of Henry or the irony of Pope and Dryden we have to draw upon historical information and linguistic glosses. But we have to draw equally upon the modern world and our own experience. We find the meaning of heroism and of irony ultimately in the objects of our own experience and in our own minds.

II

What I have called the issue, or what may perhaps better be called the tension, between literary criticism and historical scholarship, is something which may be most difficult to define in one of our most flourishing modern disciplines, the history of ideas. The history of anything general—of institutions, arts, or philosophies—is always an attempt to reduce the general to the particular. "History of Ideas" means ideas taken as events which have occurred in time—waxing and waning—not as references to a world of experience, more or less correct. Nevertheless, I believe that history of ideas, so far as it enters into the meaning of literary works, often has a special affinity for criticism—the reason for this lying not in the emphasis of the discipline on history, but in its emphasis on ideas. The modern school has worked hard toward a kind of atomism, a discrimination and definition of unit ideas, conceived like slogans or catchwords. But ideas as such tend to have implications or to be connected in philosophies, and to that extent, even when their referential character is small, they may have coherence

and hence present a kind of interest and even truth. And
literary works which are explainable by the history of ideas are
likely to participate in some of the same values. It would be
difficult, for example, to expound Pope's *Essay on Man* in the
light of Professor Lovejoy's essays on Nature, deism, and classicism without imputing to the poem itself some qualities either
of coherence or of incoherence. And this kind of imputation
is closely related to the act of evaluation or criticism.

But again there are limitations to this role for the history of
ideas—and of these let me now speak somewhat more emphatically. They arise from the other emphasis of the discipline, that on history: on the fact that in a certain age and by
certain persons an idea or system of ideas was actually entertained. Within the era of modern scholarship we have heard
a great deal about research leading to understanding, and
understanding in turn leading to correct evaluation. But we
shall have to invoke more than the strictly historical sense to
see how this is true. For example: Professor Merritt Hughes,
in an able essay contributed to the *Journal of the History of
Ideas*,[3] has come to the defence of a well known passage in
Spenser's *Faerie Queene*—that where Guyon and the Palmer
respond to the attractions of Acrasia's Bower with the tactics of
a police raid on a "clip" joint. For Spenser and his readers, explains Professor Hughes, "Acrasia stood for something more
complex than mere physical lust—for something quite as complex indeed as . . . [a] disease of the whole sensual nature."
This seems to me the correct view. Yet not simply in that it
tells us something about either Puritanism or Renaissance
mythology, about a view of Circe and Gryll in so far as this
happened to prevail in the minds of Spenser and certain of his
contemporaries. If our sympathy for Spenser's "Puritan" imagination is increased by this kind of knowledge, surely this can
happen only in virtue of the fact that the knowledge has per-
formed a service of focusing and insight for our own imagination. I have not yet seen it demonstrated that Puritanism as a
philosophy is not preferable to that which underlies the art of
the pin-up. To take an opposite example—one in which his-

torical knowledge can scarcely claim to affect evaluation: my distaste for the ending of *The Two Gentlemen of Verona,* in which Valentine not only forgives the philandering of his Protean friend but generously offers to make over all his interest in a sweetheart, has not been diminished by reading about the classical ideal of friendship in the highly informative book *One Soul in Bodies Twain.* And to take another: in a well known play by Robert Greene an aristocratic lover named Lacy treats a country maid named Margaret with such cavalier brutality that she is about to retire from the world into a nunnery when, at the last moment, he returns, with the explanation that what he did was only à test; he is met with open arms, and the ending reverts to romance. When an article appears explaining this denouement in the light of some "received" and normative feudal view of hierarchical relations between aristocracy and peasantry, I shall be interested in the history. I find it difficult to believe that my evaluation of the drama will be radically revised. (And I do not mean that such a view or any other is incapable of successful literary treatment. Chaucer's tale of the Patient Griselda will in this instance provide the contrast between historical reporting and illuminated dramatization.)

Our value judgments of past literature can certainly not be decided by the simply historical side of empirical findings about what groups of persons, larger or smaller, for longer or shorter periods in the past, have thought or felt about this or that—anthropomorphism or anthropophagy. This is Kinsey Report technique. It is the opposite of value judgment. And if it is more "scientific" than the criticism of poetry, this should warn us against attempting to apply to criticism what can be only a parody of "scientific" method. Let me quote here the eloquent words of Benedetto Croce concerning the historical study of ideas in the *Divina Commedia* of Dante:

It is therefore necessary to treat the poetry of Dante, not according to Dante, but according to the truth, in the same way, for that matter, as we treat Plato and Aristotle, not according to their own philosophy, but according to what is the new[4] truth of philosophy, and Homer, not according to the little-known poetic theories of his contemporaries, but according to the eternal[4] principles of poetry. If we wished to do otherwise, and to think Aristotle with the thought of Aristotle, and Dante with the thought of Dante, we should find ourselves desperately engaged in an impossible effort to distort our own mind.

It is possible that more than a few readers will incline to reject the metaphysics which may be implicit in the argument at this point. If that is so, I suggest that what I am saying is at the very least an inescapable fact of psychology. We are bound to have a point of view in literary criticism, and that point of view, though it may have been shaped by a tradition, is bound to be our own. Points of view cannot be slipped in and out of our minds like lantern slides. Our judgments of the past cannot be discontinuous with our own experience or insulated from it. To evaluate the past we have to penetrate it with our own intelligence.

III

What several hundred thousand literate persons thought in the course of a century is history of ideas. What one man said or meant in a line of a poem is history of a person. I am using the term "history of a person" in a broad, but I think legitimate, way, to refer not only to biography proper but to much that is usually placed under the head of bibliography and the techniques of textual study. Let me insist that my purpose in this part of the argument is to present a distinction. I have once before been guilty of saying in print that the critic as critic is not interested in questions of authenticity. At the same time I pleaded that he is innocent of the desire to reduce literary history to an anonymous sludge of collaboration between authors and printers' devils. The distinction which I have in mind, as it is one which we are seldom if ever called upon to translate into a practical choice, may perhaps be best illustrated in a hypothetical example. The folio text of Shakespeare's *Henry V* reads in one celebrated passage: "a Table of greene fields." In 1726 Theobald supplied his brilliant aesthetic guess: "a babbled of green fields." More recent and more scientific conjecture, based on a knowledge of Shakespeare's handwriting and of Elizabethan playhouse and printing practice, has tended to support Theobald. For the sake of my distinction, however, I ask you to suppose the opposite. Suppose scientific study actually to have argued, on the same type of evidence, what is at least conceivable, that Shakespeare wrote "a talked of green fields." Suppose this to be a fairly certain conclusion. There is no critic, so far as I know, certainly no school of critics, who would resist the restoration of Shakespeare's word. At the same time, few historians or textual students, I believe, would argue that this restoration was itself an act of criticism or evaluation —proving that "talked" in this context is better than "babbled." One could scarcely do so, unless on the principle that every word which Shakespeare wrote is bound to be better than any word which Theobald wrote. We tend to admit, I guess, that an author could improve his own poem ("Would he had blotted a thousand!"), as by exercise or diet he might improve his own body, or by reading, his own mind. And nobody else could do this for his body or his mind. Analogy may suggest that the same is true for his poem, and in practice, this is perhaps most often so, a genetic and psychological probability. But it is not a critical principle. The critic is a person who would be prepared to argue that Theobald had done better than Shakespeare. He is a person who is not much surprised when scholarship discovers that Sir Walter Scott's informant Mrs. Brown of Falkland used a very free hand in the reproduction of ballads and seems to have been at least as skillful as if she had lived three hundred years earlier.

One of the most eminent modern textual scholars, W. W. Greg, once delivered a lecture entitled, "The Function of Bibliography in Literary Criticism Illustrated in a Study of the Text of 'King Lear.'" "A knowledge of the true text," he asserted, "is the basis of all criticism; and textual criticism is thus the root from which all literary science grows." In the light of the distinction which I have just labored to make, I suggest that this is entirely too simple a view of the matter. What we have is more like several roots—or at least two, text and critical evaluation—growing together and intertwined. The textual argument about the authority of the Quarto and Folio versions of *Lear* relies frequently upon the superior sense to be found in Folio variants. That is to say, criticism (albeit of an elementary sort) is in this case (as in most others) antecedent to knowing the true text and an instrument for knowing it. The same principle, applied in a wider theater, argues that there can be no literary history independent of criticism—that such is indeed unimaginable—because even the selection of works for inclusion in a history is an act which implies evaluation.

IV

It would be only a slight oversimplification to say that we have now indicated four aspects of history under which all problems about the contribution of history to criticism may be sorted. That is, we have made a preliminary distinction between (1) history as antecedent or cause of literature and (2) history as meaning of literary works, or, as we might now put it in brief, history as lexicography. We have next entertained, somewhat more deliberately, a distinction between (3) the special modern branch of lexicography, with its broad value implications, called history of ideas, and (4) history as part of literary works in a more restricted sense, that is, history as text of literary works. Various more complicated problems tend to be translatable into terms which we have considered under these heads.

Textual study aims to determine what the author said—what words he used, in the most simply definable sense. "At bottom," says Greg, "all problems of transmission are concerned with material factors, in the shape of pieces of paper or parchment covered with certain written or printed signs." A deeper way of invoking the author may be thought to occur when we inquire into the character or meaning of his words after they are safely determined—for example, into the full connotation of the words *nature* or *blood* for Shakespeare, or the significance of fools, of bastardy, or of kingship. Such inquiries may assume a distinctly personal or biographical cast—as, for example, when we inquire into the meaning of blindness in Milton's *Sonnet on*

His Blindness. At the same time, all such inquiries, so far as they relate to anything publicly accessible in the literary work itself, may also be subsumed under the general head of history as lexicography or sometimes more precisely under that of history of ideas—and it is under these heads that the critic will be interested to employ them. Milton's career as a public servant does not escape being part of the history of ideas.[5]

By a certain complication of lexicographical study we arrive at another frequently honored kind of historical effort, that which consists in the search for the author's sources. Here the most special kind of caution required of the critic relates to the fact that history as meaning of a literary work is likely to fall off sharply into history as antecedent. One would hope that critics and historians could agree that there is a difference between a quotation or an allusion, something which has its full literary value only when it is recognized as such, and a simple borrowing, something which when recognized helps only to explain how a work came about. The allusion to Hecuba and the fustian style of the player's speech in *Hamlet* enjoy a different status from that of the vestigial earlier *Hamlet* which scholars have been interested to uncover. The earlier *Hamlet* may help to account for a certain incompleteness and mystery in Shakespeare's play. But the existence of such a *Hamlet* is not part of the meaning of Shakespeare's play and, furthermore, can scarcely disqualify any part of that meaning from critical consideration.

To notice yet another kind of historical effort: it is possible to investigate what we may call the degree of an author's deliberacy—his responsibility for and evaluation of his own performance. This investigation may be linked with source study (in a way which we have just now suggested), but more characteristically it is a special branch of the history of ideas, that of aesthetic or critical history. And this is a branch which has uniquely reflexive and deceptive relations to the literary work. Here we ought especially to be on guard for the difference between ideas as influences and ideas as references having truth and coherence. It is worth while to notice that the structural and more objectively durable characteristics of the literary work are here what come most often into question, those which, one might say, are least capable of suffering alteration upon being placed under one light of intention rather than another. "Whether Shakespeare knew the unities, and rejected them by design, or deviated from them by happy ignorance," said Samuel Johnson, "it is . . . impossible to decide, and useless to enquire." It has been the tendency of such inquiries, so far as they have had critical aims, to recoil upon themselves. There was, for instance, that phase in the study of "Shakespeare improved" when it was more or less normal to throw up the hands in dismay at the vandalism of Davenant, Nahum Tate, or Garrick. They did not understand Shakespeare's aims. They were guilty of treating him unhistorically. An answer to that view was to be expected—when students whose sympathies were strongly enough Augustan had got to work with their historical dialectic—and the answer has appeared. It is now more or less normal, I believe, to deliver an econonium upon a scholar in this field if he has sufficient sympathy with the improvers of Shakespeare—if "He knows what they were trying to do, and why." I quote from a review in the *Times Literary Supplement* during 1945.[6] Critical scholarship along these lines can look very much like a reciprocal cannonade between champions entrenched in adjacent literary periods.

V

Differences of opinion about the relation of criticism to an author's mind arise mainly because of the ordinary function of words as expressions of intention. We may have some difficulty with the style of a friend's hastily scribbled message that he will meet us in the cocktail lounge at a given hour, but the message succeeds if we divine his intention. If there can be such a thing, however, as resistance or refractoriness either in the world with which the literary artist deals or in his medium of words, and if compositions in words are to be considered susceptible of criticism either as compositions or as expressions, then it would seem that our way of criticizing them will have to be more complicated. I take poetry and the practical message to be polar extremes in the respect which we are discussing. In between, one would put, for instance, history—a document the meaning of which we assume we ought to discover and accept, an authority (except as to some extent we test its reliability by the analogy of our own experience). And somewhat closer to poetry one would put philosophy and science, not quite such great authorities, for as they pretend to discuss universals, we discover their meaning only to criticize it—and scientists, even philosophers, become outmoded. Science and philosophy one might say occupy a position of extreme exposure to the criticism which proceeds from our own experience. It is not, however, a position of maximum exposure. That distinction is reserved for poetry—a type of discourse which has traditionally submitted to criticism not only of its contentual meaning (in all the referential and emotive senses) but of its meaning at those other levels which we call its form and its style. Poetry in short suffers criticism of its organization and of its language, and this in a way that may penetrate deeply into its peculiar substance. A fault of style in a scientist is not a scientific fault—but in a poet it is a poetic fault. And this is only another way of saying that poems are taken by the critic not as abstract or intentional, but in what might be called solid, or artifactual, dimensions. The verbal object will be viewed by a critic in a kind of stereoscopic perspective which makes it look somewhat like a physical object. The poet himself is taken as artist, not as intender, but as accomplisher.

VI

Certain arts which enjoy a more fully concrete physical medium than literature often afford us the best opportunity to distinguish a critical from a noncritical interest—and, what may be surprising, to observe that the noncritical is preferred. Let me return to the simplest relation between the artist and his work, that of authenticity. We have the recently and widely advertised instance of the Dutch painter Van Meegeren, who painted six canvases nearly enough in the style of Vermeer to be able to sell them for about $3,000,000, and who by a curious turn of fate was driven to confess his forgeries—a thing that turned out to be far from easy. The confession was officially accepted, more than two years later, only after the demonstrative painting by Van Meegeren of a seventh Vermeer under court supervision and, what was of far more weight, the most rigorous radiographic, spectrographic, and microchemical testing of the forgeries by a large corps of Dutch, Belgian, British, and American technicians. Mere critics and connoisseurs—and historians—were divided in the face of Van Meegeren's achievement. His paintings had been internationally acclaimed, especially the first and most lovingly conceived, *The Disciples at Emmaüs,* the master stroke of a Chattertonian plot against the art critics. This had been called *the* masterpiece of Vermeer. One of the most reliable reporters on this episode in art history, Dr. P. B. Coremans, Director of the Central Laboratory of Belgian Museums, and a member of the Commission appointed by the Dutch Court to examine the paintings, speaks of the *Disciples* as a "beautiful painting," "a magnificent painting." "It would have been advisable, however, in the interests of prudence," says Dr. Coremans, "to have submitted this painting to a laboratory examination, prior to concluding the purchase."[7]

The truth would seem to be that a large part of our concern for the fine arts, and for literature no less, our collecting, our virtuosity, our connoisseurship, our iconography, our bibliography, is noncritical, that is to say, nonaesthetic, or not directed to the work of art as such. We have seen the premium placed not only on the first edition and the holograph, but upon the lock of hair, the teapot, and the writing desk. The study of Shakespeare's imagery, wrote a scholar whose name has specially attached itself to that imagery, throws light not only on the meaning of the play but, "most important of all—on the way Shakespeare himself saw it."[8]

We shall have to say, apparently, that this kind of interest has its own reasons, the most important of these being, in the case of literature, the fact that works of literary art are only structures of verbal meaning—structures which, when separated from their authors, have, to speak metaphysically, no substantial existence. Certain obviously practical reasons—relating to identification and classification—might be named by the historian and even by the critic in defence of their respect for the names of authors. But the final reason for our interest in authors is, I believe, one which is both deeper and less practical, one which we may simply have to call the need of the human mind for reference to a substantial entity—to a person, rather than to words or thoughts. We must always suppose *a* speaker for the poem, a dramatis persona. It is a fairly normal movement of the imagination to establish *the* speaker of the poem as the terminus of our devotion.

Even a person of rigorously critical inclination might almost accept the statement of Coleridge: "Assuredly that criticism of Shakespeare will alone be genial which is reverential. The Englishman, who without reverence, a proud and affectionate reverence, can utter the name of William Shakespeare, stands disqualified for the office of critic." The person of rigorously critical inclination (have I said?) might almost accept that statement. He might almost, but the fact remains—and it has been the purpose of my essay to describe the relation of this fact to history and to biography—the fact remains that he could not accept it. If Coleridge himself pursued his criticism of Shakespeare with unlimited reverence, that no doubt is one of the reasons why there are moments in his criticism which are somewhat less than critical. And if on the other hand there were limits to his reverence for Wordsworth, that was scarcely an impediment to the penetration of his Wordsworthian criticism. When distinguished from criticism and carried in its appropriate direction—as it can well be—the personal interest in literature is no doubt indefeasible. Yet it is a thesis worth many times repeating that the personal interest is not the critical. The history of literary study shows the difference between the two to have been often rather obscurely understood. The personal interest in literature has always been, and will always be, in need of a difficult adjustment with the claims of the critical. "Bardolatry" is a name which may all too well be applied to the excess of the personal and to its corruption of the critical.

There foamed rebellious *Logic,* gagged and bound,
There, stripped, fair *Rhetoric* languished on the ground.
                              —*The Dunciad, Book* IV

                    . . . the Argument
Held me a while misdoubting his Intent,
That he would ruin (for I saw him strong)
The Sacred truths to Fable and Old Song.
                    —ANDREW MARVELL, *On Paradise Lost*

POETRY AND
CHRISTIAN THINKING

THE TERM "poetry" when joined, as it is in the title of this essay, with the term "thinking" is almost sure to mean in effect thinking about poetry, or poetics. This is the more true today because literary critics have for some years been so vigorously concerned to reconsider their activity and to define and vindicate it as a modern liberal art. The title of a recent survey aptly designates the last fifty years in America as *An Age of Criticism*. Such an age is bound to give a new theoretical tilt to certain ancient questions concerning the relation of poetry and religion.

There is certainly a broad sense in which Christian thinking ought to be sympathetic to recent literary criticism—a sense arising simply from the fact that recent criticism *is* criticism; that is, an activity aimed at understanding a kind of value, and a kind which, if not identical with moral and religious values, is very close to these and may even be thought of as a likely ally. Religious thinkers should be sympathetic to criticism because it is a branch of philosophy; it is an effort to get at certain truths about signs, knowledge, and reality. If these remarks

seem at all platitudinous, let me add that I have taken the
trouble to make them because it seems to me possible for the
thought and scholarship of religious persons (especially in
America today) to be too far sold in the cultivation of certain merely historical, informational, and neutral techniques.
This may have been for a time a necessary phase of competition with secular science and secular education. But there is no
reason why Christians should be the last (or even be slow) to
transcend the limitations of such knowledge, to outgrow pe-
dantic misconceptions and participate in literary philosophy.

II

Let me now proceed to sketch certain parallels and certain
contrasts between recent literary theory and some aspects of
the Christian tradition in thinking.

One of the most distinctive features of recent criticism has
been its realization of the inherently ambiguous or polysemous
nature of verbal discourse, and especially of poetic discourse.
But this is something pre-Cartesian and prescientific in spirit,
and if it does not immediately derive from, is at least compatible with, an approach to verbal exegesis which persisted
from remote antiquity to the Renaissance and has played a not
inconspicuous part in the reading of Christian revelation. The
recent school has carried refinements of exegesis and respect
for both puns and syntactic uncertainties to a degree which I
think was never matched in earlier ages. And it is true that
Aristotle in his logical works and in his *Rhetoric* looks on ambiguity as a defect of clarity, a mean trick for soothsayers rather
than for honest pleaders. But then Aristotle was a scientist.
Even in his day and before it there were the etymological and
allegorical interpreters of meaning and the Stoic philosophers
of the Logos, and somewhat later both Hellenistic grammarians
and Roman orators who had a vested interest in the fullness of
verbal power.[1] The doctrine of the creative Logos among the
Church Fathers might be invoked to illustrate the same theme,
and the assertion of various levels of verbal meaning by both

Church Fathers and medieval theologians and poets—Dante in his *Letter to Can Grande* or Aquinas in the well known Tenth Article of the First Question of the *Summa Theologiae: Utrum Sacra Scriptura sub una littera habeat plures sensus*.[2] In the comparison which I am suggesting between modern critical polysemous reading and the Patristic and Stoic view of words, only one important reservation has to be made—but it is one which is important enough to need making. I mean that whereas the modern interpretation of poetry is fully concrete —reading the poet's words not within his limits as intender but in the fullness of his responsibility as public performer in a complex and treacherous medium—on the other hand the exegesis of Scripture, if I understand its rationale, has been implicitly intentional; because, indeed, it has dealt with inspirations. There may be several meanings—but they all have to be sharp and definable enough to be imputable to an inspired intention. It is this difference, I believe, which lies behind some of the confusion appearing today between historical and critical methods of literary scholarship. Because of its ancestry in scriptural exegesis (the critics from the sixteenth through the nineteenth century having been so often either Catholic or Protestant clerical scholars)—literary scholarship, I suggest, has come rather slowly to realize that it has to deal not with revealed messages[3] but with the achievement of expression in words taken as a fully concrete, aesthetic medium. A close partner of this distinction appears in a distinction which may be drawn between kinds of symbolism. Whereas biblical exegesis has pursued a symbolism not only of words but of things, and has found a more or less determinate symbolic significance in certain species of things and in individuals—the significance of life or resurrection in the sun, for instance, or that of death and regeneration in water[4]—on the contrary recent literary criticism has pursued a symbolism of words, or if of things, of things only as refracted through words, and the limits of such a pursuit are set only by verbal contexts. The sun may be ordinarily a symbol of life, but in an equatorial desert or ocean it may be a symbol of death and of alienation.

All in a hot and copper sky,
The bloody sun, at noon,
Right up above the mast did stand,
No bigger than the moon.

III

The multiple meaning of words when realized through appropriate contexts is the technical side of a quality in poetry which we may call something like "complexity"—provided, however, that we mean by that not the negative complexity of disorder or mere obscurity or mere multiplicity, but a positive and structural complexity, the varied fabric of organic unity. Recent literary criticism has much to say about this kind of order and unity. If you don't like recent critics, you call them "rhetoricians," or "formalists," or even "neoscholastics," these terms implying that recent critics neglect the content of poetry and its urgent social and moral relations to real life. Whatever the correctness of that implication (and I believe this slight) it is through this formalism—an interest, that is, in poetic order and hence in poetic reality—that recent critics participate in a kind of Aristotelianism and even scholasticism—or let us say, more liberally, in the ideas about order, harmony, and unity which we may read in neo-Platonic sources of late antiquity, Pagan or Christian, in the medieval scholasticism of Aquinas, in early modern aesthetic speculation such as that of Leibniz or Baumgarten, in the theories of later German transcendental philosophers and English romantic poets, and most recently in the neoscholasticism of Maritain, Gilby, and others. I allude to Maritain's stress on the radiance of a concrete, if ontologically secret or mysterious, kind of form, and to Father Gilby's on the substantive completeness of the poetic experience—though the latter may be rather heavily shaded toward subjectivism. It appears to me, by the way, that James Joyce in that freely romantic rendering of Thomist aesthetic to be found in his notebooks and in *A Portrait of the Artist* has misapplied the Thomist specific *quidditas,* but that while doing this he has placed the correct accent on radiance or *claritas*—the radiant epiphany of the whole and structurally intelligible *individual* thing. It was in this direction of course that Hopkins had been working with his interest in certain Scotist technicalities which favor the individually formal inscapes of things.

But to go back to the notion of form entertained by recent literary critics: We must note an important difference between this and the metaphysical tradition. It is a difference that corresponds to the two main and perennially opposed axes of literary theory, the cognitive and the affective, the axis of order or being against chaos or nothing and, always somewhat oblique to that, the axis of pleasure against pain. The view of Allen Tate, that poetry is a unique total or substantive kind of knowledge, a verbal tension between denotation and connotation, the early view of J. C. Ransom, that poetry is logical structure filled out with irrelevant texture, and the view of Yvor Winters, that poetry is correspondence between logical structure and qualitative surface, are remarkable in the contemporary scene for their bias toward the metaphysical. Far more congenial and influential has been the psychological view of I. A. Richards, that poetry is harmony of impulses, and along with this the middle view of T. S. Eliot, that poetry is verbal formula or objective correlative of emotions. These views, especially that of Richards, prefaced as it is by an attack on the "phantom aesthetic state," constitute a reaction against the concept of "detachment" or "distance" or Kantian "disinterest," so dear to the modern general aesthetician, and hence also against such earlier metaphysical concepts as the *pulchrum . . . cujus ipsa apprehensio placet* of Aquinas.

At the same time (to turn the direction of our argument once again) it must be noted that Eliot repeatedly asserts the detachment of poetry from life, or as he puts it, the separation of the man as poet from the man as suffering human being. In a parallel way, the emphasis upon impulses that are only "incipient" or "imaginal" and upon the equilibrium of these makes a clause in the system of Richards which corresponds to the detachment or disinterest of other systems and performs the same function of setting off aesthetic from other values. The

Richardsian criticism, by dwelling upon patterns and harmony of responses, has, in fact, accomplished something very much like a reconciliation of earlier and cruder theories of pain and pleasure with metaphysical theories of order and being. It is true that the being which is now set up as the center of poetic interest is conscious or internal man himself, rather than man or any part of his environment as externally reportable or imitable. But this is not altogether revolutionary—for the Aristotelian theory of poetic imitation referred, after all, to the internal actions of men, their characters and passions, and the scholastic *pulchrum*, through ideas of connaturality and proportion between object and sense, had a strong bias toward the subject, as the neoscholastic interpreters have been reminding us—though just how strong may be doubtful. To fill out the historical picture, one should add that recent literary versions of harmony and form owe an obvious debt to romantic and Crocean expressionism.

IV

But how, in fact, is either the Thomist *apprehensio* or the Kantian "disinterest" to be applied to the study of beauty in general or to the study of poetry? An irrelevant matter of possession, that is the power to control or to consume and destroy, seems likely to haunt our thinking here. To see a landscape painting, we need only be allowed to approach it as it hangs in someone else's gallery; we can see an apple in a store window; to taste an apple we have to possess and consume it. But this distinction, as Santayana has argued, hardly seems to interpret "disinterest" in a way relevant to aesthetic theory. Every experience of value is a form of knowing and at least a minor fruition of desire. The apple tasted is desired; the picture seen is desired. Even God, God as supreme good and supreme beauty, is desired, and He is attained only in being *known*, in the Beatific Vision. One must apparently be content to say that the Thomist and Kantian doctrines have their most manageable meaning in the fact that certain sensory experiences, those of sight and hearing, are more pervaded with the force of intelligence than others: they have pattern and form, are shaded by recollection, and induce contemplation—whereas the experience of the so-called lower senses is more restless from moment to moment, and notably incomplete. But there is another and more special sense in which the doctrine of aesthetic detachment may be taken—and this, I believe, is the more usual modern sense—one which applies to works of art only in so far as they are references to something beyond themselves. It is this sense which is chiefly if not entirely operative in Stephen Dedalus' distinction between kinetic feeling (that excited by didactic and pornographic art) and static emotion (the truly dramatic and aesthetic). The painting looks like a landscape, but we rest in the looks and need not be moved to go outdoors. The tragedy is about murder, but we rest short of wishing to save the victim or punish the criminal. In short, the aesthetic symbol absorbs the interest of its referents into itself and contains it in an impractical stasis. Recent poetic theory continually implies this doctrine—in part acquired from aestheticians and in part worked out by litterateurs for themselves. Perhaps this special doctrine of disinterest can be an avenue into a fuller (if in a way reversed) comprehension of the other—an analogy which opens the imagination to see that even the beauty of natural objects and of "abstract" art is, in virtue of its intelligibility and formality, charged with symbolism. At any rate, poetic theory, while starting with a renunciation of disinterest, concludes by a return to at least one sort of disinterest. Or, we might say, poetic theory is willing to make an overture toward the metaphysics of the beautiful —and who indeed has any right to insist that it do more—for where has it ever been established that poetry is a department of the beautiful? The theme of "beauty" is one peculiarly associated with a certain romantic strain of poetry: "beauty is truth, truth beauty"; "Euclid alone has looked on beauty bare." And we are likely enough to speak of a "beautiful" line or a "beautiful" sonnet. But our sense of the normal meaning of words is far less likely to prompt us to speak of a "beautiful" tragedy, a "beautiful" comedy, or a "beautiful" novel. The

Thomist aesthetician will note that Aquinas himself, echoing an ancient idea, treats poetry as a first cousin of sophistical rhetoric.

V

Poetry, then, as seen in the focus of recent criticism is a fusion of interest and form. As such (the religious or moral thinker may wish to remark) poetry may have certain rather blurred relations with the departments of our more practically normative thinking. Formal complexity or unity through parts implies difference or heterogeneity of parts. That is to say, it implies contrast. And contrast, when it involves human interests, involves conflict. Plato observed as much about poetry —and with disapproval.

> Does not the . . . rebellious principle . . . furnish a great variety of materials for imitation? Whereas the wise and calm temperament, being always nearly equable, is not easy to imitate or to appreciate when imitated, especially at a public festival. (*Republic* X, 862)

Recent theory (reviving spontaneously an idea known once to German romantic critics) counters the Platonic complaint with an emphasis on the reconciliation or ironic preservation of warring interests and of the opposite views of the world from which they arise. Poetry is *discordia concors;* it is observed to be inclusive, rather than exclusive or simplistic; it presents the fullness and complication of personality in action. Its psychology and ethics are the counterpart of the rhetorical polysemism of which we have spoken. Cleanth Brooks has supported this thesis by convincing analyses of widely various English poems —Donne's *Canonization,* Gray's *Elegy,* Tennyson's *Tears, Idle Tears,* or even so innocent-looking a poem as Wordsworth's "A slumber did my spirit seal." It would appear to me that recent criticism has made out a strong case indeed for some kind of paradoxical tension as an intrinsic character, or mainspring, of most if not all poetry.

It is difficult to say how far this view tends to make poetry not only indifferent to our normative, doctrinal, and practical

views of the world (as indeed do other versions of poetic disinterest) but even more positively antagonistic. Yet right belief
and right action, a moralist like Yvor Winters may plausibly
argue, are only subverted by ironies and hesitations, Laforguian
double visions. The demands of a public and socially practical
faith may seem scarcely to be reflected by Eliot in his essay on
Pascal "facing unflinchingly the demon of doubt which is inseparable from the spirit of belief," or by R. P. Warren in his
essay on "Pure and Impure Poetry," as he draws his contrast
between ironic "self-criticism" and the parody of values which
he finds in a "hand-me-down faith," in "hand-me-down ideals."
A certain transvaluation is intimated. This irony is not a transitional stage in an aesthetic to ethical *Either/Or*, but is more
like a dual terminus of value. The conflict assumes perhaps a
more intricate and reflexive form than the usual one between
Camelot and Carbonek, but it may be nonetheless ultimate.
Piety is doubtless not easier than either poetry or paradox, but
the triumph of piety, we may have to say, is a kind of simplification which does not increase the scope of paradoxical experience.

VI

During the seventeenth century science first succeeded in
raising active suspicions about poetry, in weakening its didactic
prestige, and making it fall back rather heavily on its reputation
as entertainer and beautifier. But by the nineteenth century
science had carried its simultaneous attack against religion so
far that a curious turn of events occurred: poetry—no other than
poetry—was rediscovered as a cultural force and was recruited
in the cause of religion. In the now well known formula,
poetry was more and more to take the place of both religion
and philosophy. At the same time, in a parallel response to the
challenge of science, the earlier defense of poetry along the line
of its autonomous power to give pleasure was continued and
culminated in the doctrine of Art for Art's Sake and expressionism. Although literary criticism of the twentieth century has
been divided between the two modes of justification, the quasi-
religious has in recent years, with the aid of psychological,

anthropological, mythological, and ritual idioms, made considerable advances. The defense of religion is nowadays frequently couched in terms which appeal to the power of poetry, and the defense of poetic imagination, in terms which implicate a defense of religion. Despite the discriminatory efforts of some writers—Eliot's insistence that nothing is a substitute for anything else, Brooks' clear avowal that "literature is not a surrogate for religion,"[5] and Blackmur's that "critics are not fathers of a new church,"[6] the vocabulary and main assumptions of recent criticism have been developing in a way that makes it now difficult to speak well of poetry without participating in a joint defense of poetry and religion, or at least without a considerable involvement in theology.

Today the person who has a serious interest in both religion and poetry, but does not identify the two, may well address himself to considering what the relations between the two may be. Does it not appear, for instance, that many basic religious documents *can* be read quite successfully as poems—as dramas, allegories, parables, lyrics—whereas scientific documents can scarcely be read that way? In the last century Cardinal Newman reconciled the poetic character of the Christian Scriptures with their doctrinal or revelatory character by equating the poetic with the personal or subjective. This was good romantic and evangelical theory—such as Newman had grown up with. If we like, we may call it "expressionism"—and here we may find ourselves on more or less satisfactory ground. But in doing this we ought to note that we have scarcely taken into account one further fact, namely, that Christian exegetes and theologians have traditionally claimed symbol and analogy as avenues of insight into the supernatural. In the light of *that* fact, how close does poetry appear to be to either natural or revealed theology? If there is poetry in the Scriptures, is there poetry too in the *Summa Theologiae* of Aquinas? And if there is poetry either in the Scriptures or in Aquinas, what relation does the poetry bear to the revelation or to the metaphysics? We are familiar with the conception found variously stated or implied in Aquinas, and recently expounded by Father Gilby,[7] that poetic symbol and metaphor are lower or subphilosophical types of analogy. But exactly what that means, or how far it will take us, may not be clear.

Let me draw to a conclusion by indicating two extremes which it would appear to me have to be avoided by a person who wishes to be seriously concerned with both religion and poetry. One of these is the view of poetry as a disjunct kind of knowledge, a precious technique—at best or at worst, in its most strenuous exercise, an instrument of propaganda, but one which is always external to and never affects the truth or falsity, dignity or meanness, of the message propagated. This is a view which, I believe, needs only to be stated to be revealed as insufficient. As the British Dominican Father Gerald Vann has recently put it, "Good writing is part of truth. If you take a true proposition and state it in a sentimental way, in a sectarian way, in a vulgar way, you damage the truth of it."[8] In the long run it is not enough for even the moralist that art be kept merely pure—for there is such a thing as art which is pure and at the same time sickly, maudlin, mawkish, tawdry, or fraudulent (or pure and morbid, as with E. A. Poe), and such an art is a dubious auxiliary of any other value. How shall we interpret that jungle of journalistic, patriotic, religiose, belletristic, commercial, and scientific reminiscences and parodies which are the very form of expressiveness in certain chapters of Joyce's *Ulysses*, our modern Odyssey of dismemberment and distraction? How otherwise than as a most eloquent celebration of what Joyce conceives to be the dissolution of our culture, a dual dissolution of language and thinking? We have heard the same theme, more quietly and personally intense, in the religious poetry of our time. "Words strain . . . Decay with imprecision."

> With shabby equipment always deteriorating
> In the general mess of imprecision of feeling,
> Undisciplined squads of emotion.

At an earlier date the romantic poet in the Preface to his *Lyrical Ballads* spoke of "frantic novels . . . deluges of idle and extravagant stories," a "degrading thirst after outrageous stimulation," and as a consequence of all that the reduction of the contemporary mind "to a state of almost savage torpor." At an even earlier date the same abuses were the galling inspiration of the ethical poet and satirist. Alexander Pope's Fourth *Dunciad* begins with a portrait of Logic, Rhetoric, Tragedy, and Comedy in servitude or death throes, goes on to chronicle the fantastic distortions of verbal learning for which he thought his age distinguished, and soars in conclusion to a sublimely negative triumph, an inverted image of the very Logos.

> Lo! thy dread Empire, CHAOS! is restored;
> Light dies before thy *un*creating *word*.

Such warning voices—ancestral as well as contemporary— might seem to propose a sufficient program of constructive activity for the teacher of verbal powers, the critic of poetry, the molder of taste. They might seem to, and they would do so—except for the second extreme notion of which I spoke a moment ago, the notion which today is uttered from under the mantle which fell from the shoulders of Matthew Arnold and before that from greater German theorists of the high romantic period. It is only a little, if at all, unfair to this message to say that today what it amounts to is the intimation that we need more and better help from poetry in the practice of our "private rituals," that we need a new faith in myth—or even a new myth, something which Yeats and Melville have apparently fallen just short of giving us. This is a message which represents a highly experimental state of mind—one which, having translated religion, government, and private ethics into myth, would reverse the translation with another myth—regain the heights with a balloon that is known to have a hole in it. They want a new myth when the main thing alleged against the old myth is that it *was* a myth. There was a time, a primitive and golden age, celebrated by earlier defenders of poetry, by Horace and Sir Philip Sidney, when poetry had great influence—the days of Amphion and Orpheus, of blind Thamyris and blind Maeonides —and, one should not forget to add, of Teiresias and Phineus—

"prophets." For if poetry then had influence, that was in part because poetry was more than poetry or was at least thought to be more. It was history and prophecy. And myth was more than myth. It was believed. Today, when professors of poetry know too well what poetry is—a way of ordering our impulses, or of self-expression, or of private ritual—there must be small use in appealing to poetry to do the things it did best in the pre-Homeric age—unless in some cynical indulgence of brain-truster scorn for the mass mentality.

What then is an adequately serious view of poetry? I submit that this has always been, and remains, difficult if not impossible to define with any rigor. What is the formula by which we shall recognize the metaphoric capacities of language and the moral importance of valid linguistic expression without surrendering our conception of truth as a thing beyond language, without yielding to the lead of the idealistic symbolists, the ritualists, and the myth-makers? I confess that I do not clearly see the answer. I have not found the book in which the answer is permanently and canonically formulated. But I insist that this question is a real and important one—and not only for more dogmatic Christians and less dogmatic Christians, but for all persons who are interested to inquire into the norms by which they live.

NOTES AND REFERENCES

THE INTENTIONAL FALLACY

[1] *Dictionary of World Literature*, Joseph T. Shipley, ed. (New York, 1942), 326–29.

[2] J. E. Spingarn, "The New Criticism," in *Criticism in America* (New York, 1924), 24–25.

[3] Ananda K. Coomaraswamy, "Intention," in *American Bookman*, I (1944), 41–48.

[4] It is true that Croce himself in his *Ariosto, Shakespeare and Corneille* (London, 1920), chap. VII, "The Practical Personality and the Poetical Personality," and in his *Defence of Poetry* (Oxford, 1933), 24, and elsewhere, early and late, has delivered telling attacks on emotive geneticism, but the main drive of the *Aesthetic* is surely toward a kind of cognitive intentionalism.

[5] See Hughes Mearns, *Creative Youth* (Garden City, 1925), esp. 10, 27–29. The technique of inspiring poems has apparently been outdone more recently by the study of inspiration in successful poets and other artists. See, for instance, Rosamond E. M. Harding, *An Anatomy of Inspiration* (Cambridge, 1940); Julius Portnoy, *A Psychology of Art Creation* (Philadelphia, 1942); Rudolf Arnheim and others, *Poets at Work* (New York, 1947); Phyllis Bartlett, *Poems in Process* (New York, 1951); Brewster Ghiselin (ed.), *The Creative Process: A Symposium* (Berkeley and Los Angeles, 1952).

[6] Curt Ducasse, *The Philosophy of Art* (New York, 1929), 116.

[7] And the history of words *after* a poem is written may contribute meanings which if relevant to the original pattern should not be ruled out by a scruple about intention.

[8] Chaps. VIII, "The Pattern," and XVI, "The Known and Familiar Landscape," will be found of most help to the student of the poem.

[9] Charles M. Coffin, *John Donne and the New Philosophy* (New York, 1927), 97–98.

THE AFFECTIVE FALLACY

[1] Richards has recently reiterated these views in the context of a more complicated account of language that seems to look in the direction of Charles Morris. See his "Emotive Language Still," in *Yale Review*, XXXIX (1949), 108–18.

[2] "If feeling be regarded as conscious, it is unquestionable that it involves in some measure an intellectual process." F. Paulhan, *The Laws of Feeling* (London, 1930), 153.

³ Strictly, a theory not of poetry but of morals, as, to take a curious modern instance, Lucie Guillet's *La Poéticothérapie, Efficacités du Fluide Poétique* (Paris, 1946) is a theory not of poetry but of healing. Aristotle's catharsis is a true theory of poetry, that is, part of a definition of poetry.

⁴ *As I Remember Him,* quoted by J. Donald Adams, "Speaking of Books," in New York *Times Book Review,* April 20, 1947, p. 2. Mr. Adams' weekly department has been a happy hunting ground for such specimens.

⁵ *New Yorker,* XIX (December 11, 1943), 28.

⁶ "The final averages showed that the combined finger movements for the Byron experiments were eighteen metres longer than they were for Keats." R. C. Givler, *The Psycho-Physiological Effect of the Elements of Speech in Relation to Poetry* (Princeton, 1915), 62.

⁷ "Ueber den Film," in *Die Forderung des Tages* (Berlin, 1930), 387.

⁸ The term, as Winters indicates, is borrowed from Kenneth Burke's *Counter-Statement.*

⁹ *New Yorker,* XXIII (May 31, 1947), 33.

¹⁰ Cp. Paulhan, *The Laws of Feeling,* 105, 110.

¹¹ "The anthropologist," says Bronislaw Malinowski, "has the myth-maker at his elbow." *Myth in Primitive Psychology* (New York, 1926), 17.

THE CHICAGO CRITICS

¹ The big difference between Crane and Professor Lowes, whose MLA presidential address of 1933 in favor of criticism Crane cited, was that Crane believed a large part of literary historical studies not only noncritical but not even ancillary to criticism. *English Journal,* XXIV (1935), 645, 660.

² R. S. Crane and others, *Critics and Criticism Ancient and Modern* (Chicago, 1952).

³ See, for instance, pp. 185, 465–67, 473–78, 490, 504, 523, 537, 539.

⁴ Cp. p. 646, Crane on *Tom Jones.*

⁵ "Now in a sense these propositions are not about literature at all. Their subjects when the propositions are stated in a primary form, are not works or the properties of works but persons—writers or readers as the case may be." Crane, "History versus Criticism," 648.

⁶ Cp. Olson, p. 558.

⁷ Cp. R. S. Crane, "Semantics and the Teaching of Prose Literature," in *College English,* IV (1942), 12–19.

⁸ The italics are mine. Crane's sketch of "English Neoclassical Criticism" might be quoted to much the same effect (for example, p. 384).

⁹ See, for instance, Crane, p. 22, 646.

¹⁰ "The distinction between arguments directed against the expression and arguments directed against the thoughts is absurd." McKeon, p. 209.

¹¹ But see McKeon, p. 212: "Discourse not only supplies the matter from which the tragedy is constructed . . . but also the form . . .; the poem itself, moreover, may be viewed in its unity as a single speech." The interest shown by J. C. Scaliger in the verbal "matter" of poetry is discussed by another member of the Chicago team, Professor Bernard Weinberg, "Scaliger versus

Aristotle on Poetics," in *Modern Philology*, XXXIX (1942), 337-60. Weinberg, pp. 341-43, makes quite clear the *Platonic* orientation of Scaliger's view of words as matter. Words as mere matter are words considered simply "as sounds." Book II of Scaliger's *Poetics* deals with words just as they enter into feet, meter, rhythms—as if these things could be dissociated from sense. Cleanth Brooks, who has often been accused of being a mere "formalist," becomes in the Chicago terminology a "materialistic monist" (p. 93).

[12] Hoyt Trowbridge, review in *Comparative Literature*, III (1951), 361.

[13] Crane spoke very clearly about geneticism in his essay in *English Journal*, XXIV (1935), 657-59. I conjecture that, so far as there is any difference between us on this point, it lies in the fact that Crane does not recognize "intention" as having a strongly genetic aspect. "Intention" has, I believe, been one of the chief tools of the historical school of literary study which provoked Crane's essay of 1935.

THE CONCRETE UNIVERSAL

[1] Charles W. Morris, "Esthetics and the Theory of Signs," in *Journal of Unified Science*, VIII (1939), 131-50.

[2] *Metaphysics*, VII (Z), 1 (1028). Cp. Mortimer J. Adler, *The Problem of Species* (New York, 1940), 24-25. And see below, p. 136.

[3] "The arts are not to be slighted on the ground that they create by imitation of natural objects; for, to begin with, these natural objects are themselves imitations; then, we must recognize that they give no bare reproduction of the thing seen but go back to the ideas from which Nature itself derives." *Enneads*, V, viii, 1, *Plotinus—The Fifth Ennead*, Stephen MacKenna, tr. (London, 1926), 74.

[4] *Kant's Critique of Judgment*, J. H. Bernard, tr. (London, 1931), 88-89.

[5] *The Introduction to Hegel's Philosophy of Fine Art*, Bernard Bosanquet, tr. (London, 1886), 67. Cp. Walter T. Stace, *The Meaning of Beauty* (London, 1929), 41.

[6] *The Introduction to Hegel's Philosophy of Fine Art*, 16. Cp. pp. 72-78, 133-37.

[7] It is true that Croce has protested: "Ce qu'on démontre comme inconciliable avec le principe de la pure intuition, ce n'est pas l'universalité, mais la valeur intellectualiste et transcendante donnée dans l'art à l'universalité, sous la forme de l'allegorie ou du symbole." "Le Caractère de Totalité de l'Expression Artistique," in *Bréviaire d'Esthétique*, Georges Bourgin, tr. (Paris, 1923), 170. But the main drift of Croce's aesthetic, in being against conceptualization, is radically against the universal.

[8] Henri Bergson, *Laughter, An Essay on the Meaning of the Comic* (New York, 1928), 161-62.

[9] Roger Fry in his Introduction to Reynolds' *Third Discourse* argues that the species presented in painting are not those of the natural, but those of the social world, as king, knight, beggar. *Discourses*, Roger Fry, ed. (London, 1905), 46. And a modern critic of sculpture, R. H. Wilenski, offers what is perhaps the last retreat of the doctrine of universals in visual art: not man,

flower, or animal but the forms of life analogous in (that is, common to) man, flower, and animal are abstracted and presented pure in sculptural art. R. H. Wilenski, *The Meaning of Modern Sculpture* (London, 1939), 159–60.

[10] *The New Criticism* (Norfolk, 1941), 315. Maritain, coming from a different direction, arrives at somewhat the same poser. "If it pleases a futurist to paint a lady with only one eye, or a quarter of an eye, nobody denies him such a right: all one is entitled to require—and here is the whole problem—is that the quarter eye is all the lady needs *in the given case.*" *Art and Scholasticism* (New York, 1937), 28. Here indeed is the whole problem. Aristotle said, "Not to know that a hind has no horns is a less serious matter than to paint it inartistically." *Poetics*, XXV, 5.

[11] *Discoveries*, Maurice Castelain, ed. (Paris, 1906), 139. Jonson translates from Heinsius.

[12] *Ariosto, Shakespeare and Corneille* (London, 1920), 146–47.

POETRY AND MORALS

[1] Victor Hamm, "Literature and Morality," in *Thought*, XV (1940), 278, 280.

[2] *The Defense of Poesy*, A. S. Cook, ed. (Boston, 1890), 11. In other passages Sidney is more inclined to make a Platonic distinction between poetic and moral power. "Poesy may not only be abused, but . . . being abused, by the reason of his sweet charming force, it can do more than any other array of words" (p. 38).

[3] Jerome Kobel, "Literature and Morality: A Prefatory Essay," in *The Franciscan Educational Conference*, XXII (1940), 267. The italics are mine.

[4] "It would seem," says Adler, "that the excellence of a work of art is due only to a technical mastery of materials by the artist and is unaffected by the direction of his moral character toward good or evil." *Art and Prudence* (New York, 1937), 443. But on the next page: "In the case of the fine arts, the situation is complicated by . . . the fact that for most of the fine arts, poetry and music certainly, the object of imitation is human action, the moral life."

[5] "Dans toute forme ou toute espece d'art il y a comme un principe ou un germe secret d'immoralité." Ferdinand Brunetière, *L'Art et la Morale* (Paris, 1898), 15.

[6] *Ariosto, Shakespeare and Corneille* (London, 1920), 241. Antony and Cleopatra, says Dryden, were "famous patterns of unlawful love; and their end accordingly was unfortunate." *Preface to All for Love, Essays of John Dryden*, W. P. Ker, ed. (Oxford, 1926), I, 191.

[7] S. L. Bethell, *Shakespeare and the Popular Dramatic Tradition* (Westminster, 1944), 128–31.

[8] "Though I might use the privilege of a poet, to introduce her into Alexandria, yet I had not enough considered, that the compassion she moved to herself and children was destructive to that which I reserved for Antony and Cleopatra." Dryden, *Preface to All for Love*, I, 192.

[9] "Shakespeare nowhere approves suicide outside the Roman plays, but in them he seems to accept it, along with the pantheon, as data." Bethell, *Shakespeare and the Popular Dramatic Tradition*, 129.

[10] Roy W. Battenhouse, "Theology and Literary Criticism," in *Journal of Bible and Religion*, XIII (1945), 21.

[11] Battenhouse, 20.

ROMANTIC NATURE IMAGERY

[1] This paragraph alludes especially to Joseph Warren Beach, *The Concept of Nature in Nineteenth-Century English Poetry* (New York, 1936), chaps. II-VIII; Newton P. Stallknecht, *Strange Seas of Thought* (Durham, 1945), chaps. II-III; Carl H. Grabo, *A Newton among Poets* (Chapel Hill, 1930), chaps. VI-VII, and *Prometheus Unbound: An Interpretation* (Chapel Hill, 1935), 142–43, 151; Frederick A. Pottle, *The Idiom of Poetry* (Ithaca, 1941), chap. I. For a survey of recent writing on the English romantic theory of imagination, see Thomas M. Raysor (ed.), *The English Romantic Poets, A Review of Research* (New York, 1950).

[2] The sonnet "To the River Lodon" (1777) by Bowles' Oxford senior, Thomas Warton, shows sensibility with even less structural support.

[3] Coleridge's sonnet first appears in its entirety and as a separate poem in the pamphlet collection which he published privately in 1796; the sonnet reappears in the 1797 *Poems* of Coleridge under the half-title "Sonnets attempted in the manner of the Rev. W. L. Bowles."

[4] "It is among the chief excellencies of Bowles that his imagery appears almost always prompted by surrounding scenery." Coleridge to Southey, December 17, 1794 (*Letters*, I, 115).

[5] Perhaps too sweeping. See, for instance, Alfred H. Barr, Jr. (ed.), *Fantastic Art, Dada, Surrealism* (New York, 1947), 83, "Head–Landscape" in the tradition of Arcimboldo.

SYMBOL AND METAPHOR

[1] Martin Foss, *Symbol and Metaphor in Human Experience* (Princeton, 1949).

[2] Cp. Stanley Hyman, "Myth, Ritual, and Nonsense," in *Kenyon Review*, XI (1949), 455–75. Nonsense for Hyman is the euhemeristic view.

[3] John Peale Bishop, "Obscurity, Observations and Aphorisms," in *Western Review*, XII (1948), 72.

[4] Owen Barfield, *Poetic Diction, A Study in Meaning* (London, 1928), 64.

[5] Ernst Cassirer, *Language and Myth*, Susanne Langer, tr. (New York, 1946), 85.

THE SUBSTANTIVE LEVEL

[1] "Over and over again," says a writer in the London *Times Literary Supplement*, whose anonymity may well stand for the universality of his opinion, "the exact word is the beautiful word" (April 18, 1942, p. 178).

[2] The problem is not merely Aristotelian but perennial. See the recent brilliant statement by Mortimer J. Adler, "The Hierarchy of Essences," in *Review of Metaphysics*, VI (September, 1952), 3–30.

3 *Metaphysics*, VII (Z), 1; cp. VII, 4, "Nothing . . . which is not a species of a genus will have an essence."

4 Thomas Munro, *The Arts and their Interrelations* (New York, 1949), 195, concerning the "system" of Urries y Azara.

5 *Life*, XXVIII (January 2, 1950), 62.

6 John Ray, *Wisdom of God in the Creation* (London, 1797), 149.

7 *Rambler*, no. 60. Cp. my *Philosophic Words* (New Haven, 1948), 76, 94–104, for the general relation between Lockean epistemology and abstraction in prose style.

8 Wesley's adaptation of "The Elixir" appeared first in his anonymous *Collection of Psalms and Hymns*, 1738.

9 Georges Louis Leclerc, Comte de Buffon, *Address Delivered before the French Academy*, 1753.

10 Damon Runyon, *Take It Easy* (New York, 1938), 145–70, "Cemetery Bait."

11 Cp. James Joyce in the same vein, *Stephen Hero* (New York, 1944), 78. In the field of visual art, the school of formalists has participated in the anti-romantic desire for precision. "Whether it be a church or only a tooth-pick he must know what it *is*." Eric Gill, *Beauty Looks after Herself* (New York, 1933), 226. Cp. Gill's *Autobiography* (London, 1940), 15, on lettering as a "precise art." The view may be prefigured in Arnold's complaint against Horace for saying "down where . . . Tullus and Ancus are," when Homer says "the Elysian plain." *On Translating Homer, Third Lecture* (New York, 1883), 207.

12 *Oxford English Dictionary*, "denotation" 5; "connotation" 2b.

RHYME AND REASON

1 The most formal statement seems to be that of Goethe's friend J. S. Schütze, *Versuch einer Theorie des Reimes nach Inhalt und Form* (Magdeburg, 1802). I have been unable to consult this work and owe my knowledge of it to a summary in Dr. Henry Lanz's *Physical Basis of Rime* (Stanford University, 1931), 162–66.

2 *Pro Milone*, II, 5; *Institutio Oratoria*, IX, iii, 73 ff. Cp. Aristotle, *Rhetoric*, III, 9.

3 "Althoughe hetherto Euphues I have shrined thee in my heart for a trustie friende, I will shunne thee heerafter as a trothless foe." *Euphues* (*Works*, R. Warwick Bond, ed., Oxford, 1902, I, 233); cp. I, 123.

4 The parallels of Hebrew poetry are, of course, the outstanding exceptions to the generality which I propose, but in this connection I believe it ought to be observed that the lines and half lines of Hebrew poetry are not equal with the metrical exactitude of classical and modern European verse. The number of accents is the same, the number of syllables indeterminate, and the parallel of sense plays an important role in strengthening the equality and pattern of the verse.

[5] Cp. the morning *laudate* of Adam and Eve—recited in "holy rapture" and "various style." *Paradise Lost*, V, 146–47, 192–99. This passage affords an instructive comparison with the King James version of Psalm cxlvii, 2–4, 8–10, where the Hebrew parallel of sense and rhythm is largely preserved.

[6] *Complaint of Venus.*

[7] I base my statements in this part of the essay on a general impression which has been borne out in a line-by-line analysis of four passages from each author: Chaucer (*Works*, F. N. Robinson, ed., Boston, 1933), *Legend of Good Women*, Prologue F, lines 1–148; *Canterbury Prologue*, lines 1–148; *Knight's Tale*, first 148 lines, 1355–1502; *Nun's Priest's Tale*, first 148 lines, 2821–2968; Pope (*Complete Poetical Works*, H. W. Boynton, ed., Boston, 1903), *Essay on Criticism*, I, lines 1–148; *Rape of the Lock*, I, lines 1–148; *Epistle to Dr. Arbuthnot*, lines 1–148; *Dunciad*, Book IV, lines 1–148.

[8] For three exquisite examples of chiasmus from three other poets, see the rhymes of "dust" and "lust" in Andrew Marvell's "Coy Mistress," "thrush" and "bush" in Christina Rossetti's "Spring Quiet," and the double chiastic rhyme of "leaping" and "sleeping," "laid" and "fade" in A. E. Housman's "With rue my heart is laden."

[9] Professor Tillotson, looking in the right direction, has recorded his impression that Pope prefers "a verb for at least one of the rime-words in a couplet" and that "a verb at the end of the first line is often followed by its object in the next line." *On the Poetry of Pope* (Oxford, 1938), 124.

[10] *Physical Basis of Rime*, 293.

[11] Cp. G. W. F. Hegel, *The Philosophy of Fine Art*, F. P. B. Osmaston, tr. (London, 1920), IV, 7–10, 84, 90–91, part III, subsection III, chap. III.

[12] Lanz, *Physical Basis of Rime*, 121, 342.

RHETORIC AND POEMS

[1] Samuel Wesley, *Epistle to a Friend* (London, 1700), 15.

[2] We have long ago been equipped by Professor Lowes with a theory of Convention and Revolt which provides for the appearance of poetic diction in every poetic generation. If then we have a theory equal to discriminating between good and bad poetic diction within a given age (I am not sure that we have), I do not see that it can apply any more to the age of Pope than to that of Wordsworth or that of Eliot.

[3] *Eleventh Discourse*, second paragraph.

[4] Smith's *Mysterie* was apparently the reigning popular rhetoric of the age, reaching a tenth edition in 1721.

[5] It was known by Ben Jonson and perhaps by Drayton, and was copied by the mid-century metrical theorist of Poole's *Parnassus*—perhaps John Dryden. George Williamson, "The Rhetorical Pattern of Neo-Classical Wit," in *Modern Philology*, XXXIII (1935), 59–60.

[6] "I learned versification wholly from Dryden's works." Joseph Spence, *Anecdotes*, S. W. Singer, ed. (London, 1820), 212.

7 The terms "ellipsis," "zeugma," and "syllepsis" have been used variously by English writers. See *O.E.D.* under "zeugma"; John Smith, *Mysterie of Rhetorique,* 1657, under "zeugma"; H. W. Fowler, *Modern English Usage,* under "ellipsis" and "technical terms: zeugma." It is sufficient for our purpose to follow Puttenham.

8 Cp. Pope, *Peri Bathous,* chap. X, on "The Paranomasia, or Pun," "where a Word, like the tongue of a jackdaw, speaks twice as much by being split."

9 Butler in his often quoted character of *A Quibbler* had predicted its decline. Dryden's enthusiasm was waning in his Dedication of the *Aeneis* and Preface to the *Fables.*

10 The figure of *Antimetavole* found in Puttenham is a combination of chiasmus and the turn.

11 *Critical Works of John Dennis,* E. N. Hooker, ed. (Baltimore, 1939), I, 297, 375–79, 430, 499–500.

12 *Preface to Britannia Triumphans,* 1704 (*Works,* I, 376–77).

13 *Reflections on an Essay upon Criticism,* 1711 (*Works,* I, 413).

14 *Remarks on the Rape of the Lock,* 1728 (*Works,* II, 347–49).

"ELEGANT" VARIATION

1 *Time,* XXXVI (December 23, 1940), 56, 28.

2 *Beowulf,* John Lesslie Hall, tr. (Boston, 1892), XXX, 43–47; XXVIII, 17–30. I have used this translation because it seems to me to do justice to the descriptive force of the variations and to the variations as such by preserving their character as singular substantive terms each standing for the whole ship and each the subject or object of a different finite verb. In the ship passage the Old English terms are: *sundwudu, wēgflotan, sǣgenga, fāmigheals, bundenstefna, cēol, sīdæþme scip, wudu wynsuman* (Klaeber, ed., Boston, 1928, lines 1906–19). John R. Clark Hall in his prose translation (London, 1940) tends to alter this character. Thus: "wave-borne timbers," "ship floating," "ship," "with foam at her twisted prow," "keel." The same may be said for the earlier form of his prose translation (London, 1911), for his metrical translation (Cambridge, 1914), and for the metrical translations of Francis B. Gummere (*The Oldest English Epic,* New York, 1929) and Charles W. Kennedy (Oxford, 1940). It is perhaps the modern mistrust of variation that makes these translators blur the effect as much as possible.

3 J. R. R. Tolkien in his Prefatory Remarks to the 1940 edition of John R. Clark Hall's prose translation points out a passage of eighteen lines (210–28) in which there are six terms for boat, three for wave, five for men, and four for sea (pp. xxxvii-xl).

4 Sherwood Anderson, *Winesburg, Ohio* (Modern Library ed.), 283.

5 Washington *Post,* June 26, 1935.

6 I leave out of account certain forms of two-thing variation which for one reason or another may be justifiable. There may be, for example, such a thing as pronominal two-thing variation, as in this from Shakespeare: "The goats

ran from the mountains, and the herds *Were* strangely clamorous to the frighted fields." 1 *Henry IV*, III, i, 39–40. And perhaps there is a kind of humor through variation in such a passage as Johnson's comparison of punch and conversation: "The spirit, volatile and fiery, is the *proper emblem* of vivacity and wit; the acidity of the lemon will *very aptly figure* pungency of raillery, and acrimony of censure; sugar is the *natural representative* of luscious adulation and gentle complaisance; and water is the *proper hieroglyphick* of easy prattle, innocent and tasteless." *Idler*, no. 34.

VERBAL STYLE

[1] Cp. Ogden and Richards, *The Meaning of Meaning* (New York, 1930), 227, n. 1, quoting with approval Professor Conington on "surplusage"; Richards, *Principles of Criticism,* chaps. III and XXV, the split between technical and value criticism; and Herbert Spencer's classic essay of this genre, "The Philosophy of Style."

[2] W. S. Jevons, *Elementary Lessons in Logic* (London, 1934), 153.

[3] Kenneth Burke in his *Lexicon Rhetoricae* (*Counter-Statement*, New York, 1931, p. 157) distinguishes *repetitive* form from *progressive*, and under the latter distinguishes *syllogistic* and *qualitative*. Narrative form is apparently for him included under syllogistic. I believe it important to distinguish the two.

[4] The kenning is a kind of poetic counterpart to Elegant Variation which I have discussed in my essay "When Is Variation 'Elegant'?" I exclude it from consideration here, as its meaning is far from purely verbal.

[5] "*Agnomination* is a pleasant sound of words, or a small change of names; or it is a present touch of the same letter, syllable, or word with a different meaning." John Smith, *The Mysterie of Rhetorique Unvail'd* (London, 1657), 105. Agnomination as treated by Smith and other rhetoricians is much like paronomasia (pun): "Ab aratore orator. Be sure of his sword, before you trust him of his word." Cp. *O.E.D.*, "agnomination" 3, alliteration.

[6] This example differs from the "obscene dread of Moab's sons" in that the main like-sounding words, though oblique or accidental in their semantic relation, are brought into *parallel alignment* by the structure. Where pairing of ideas is emphatic, a degree of antithesis or paradox is likely to underlie phonetic likeness: "Imperial glamour with an impish glint."

[7] Dedication of *Examen Poeticum,* 1693 (*Essays*, W. P. Ker, ed., Oxford, 1900, II, 10).

[8] The term "phonestheme" has lately been applied to elements such as these. Cp. Dwight L. Bolinger, "Rime, Assonance, and Morpheme Analysis," in *Word*, VI (1950), 130, n. 34.

[9] Cp. Dwight L. Bolinger, "On Defining the Morpheme," in *Word*, IV (1948), 22: "There are hints of meaning with vague resemblances of form at inferior levels, such as the *n* of *un, in, non, nude, numb, nix, no,* or the vowel of *goof, boob, google* . . .; but constituent analysis should stop before it reaches this stage."

10 *Anima Poetae* (Boston, 1895), 91.

11 Cp. Leonard Bloomfield, *Language* (New York, 1933), 396–98; R. J. Menner, "The Conflict of Homonyms in English," in *Language*, XII (1936), 229–44; R. J. Menner, "Multiple Meaning and Change of Meaning in English," in *Language*, XXI (1945), 59–76.

12 Menner, "The Conflict of Homonyms in English," 242.

13 It is my impression that the French language, because of the great number of its silent letters and its general plasticity (consider, for example, *sang, sens, sent, cent, sans, s'en*) is more friendly than English to puns which could receive only a minimum defense along these lines. To mention a single striking instance, Clément Marot's *Petite Epistre au Roy*, 1532, makes thirteen "rimes équivoquées" on the root *rithm–*: for example, *en rithme-enrime, ma rithmaille-marry maille, rithmassé-Henry Macé, rithmette-ris mette.*

14 Thoreau, *A Week on the Concord and Merrimack Rivers* (Modern Library ed.), 320. "Mouth, south," speculates Stephen Daedelus. "Is the mouth south some way? Or the south a mouth? Must be some." *Ulysses*, Cave of Winds chapter (Modern Library ed.), 136.

15 Ernst Cassirer, *Language and Myth*, Susanne Langer, tr. (New York, 1946), 87.

16 "Imitation is the mesothesis of Likeness and Difference. The difference is as essential to it as the likeness; for without the difference, it would be Copy or Fac-simile." Coleridge, *Table Talk*, July 3, 1833 (*Works*, New York, 1884, VI, 468).

THE DOMAIN OF CRITICISM

1 Cp. Walter J. Ong, "The Province of Rhetoric and Poetic," in *Modern Schoolman*, XIX (1942), 25, quoting Aquinas, *In I. Analytica Posteriora*, lect. 1.

2 Cp. Jacques Maritain, *Art and Scholasticism*, J. F. Scanlan, tr. (New York, 1942), 20–22. Maritain, pp. 33–34, goes on to give the fine arts their own special relation to the transcendental quality of beauty. "Certain arts tend to make a work of *beauty* and thereby differ essentially from all the rest." In this respect his account differs from the generalizations which I offer.

3 See Rensselaer W. Lee, "*Ut Pictura Poesis:* The Humanistic Theory of Painting," in *Art Bulletin*, XXII (1940), esp. 255–60.

4 Cp. Gotshalk, 45–49.

5 *Saturday Review of Literature*, XXIX (September 21, 1946), 16.

6 Exceptions to this generality include the encyclopedic *Arts and Their Interrelations* by Professor Munro. See esp. pp. 136–39, "Lower-sense arts."

EXPLICATION AS CRITICISM

1 *Biographia Literaria*, chap. XIV (J. Shawcross, ed., Oxford, 1907, II, 10).

2 The term "disvalue" is not, so far as I know, in frequent use. I choose it in preference to "ugliness" as being more generic and less familiar—and hence less concretely committed in certain awkward directions.

[3] Herder, *Briefe zu Beförderung der Humanität,* 1795 (*Werke,* B. Suphan, ed., XVII, 338).

[4] Chap. X of Tolstoy's *What Is Art?* never quite makes that equation but drives hard toward it. In another essay, his Introduction to the works of Maupassant, Tolstoy faces the facts better when he finds Maupassant highly intelligible but is willing to call him at the same time immoral.

[5] Matthew Arnold, "Joubert," in *Essays in Criticism, First Series* (London, 1902), 282.

[6] *Principles of Literary Criticism* (New York, 1934), 24.

[7]
                    The Pool
            Are you alive?
            I touch you.
            You quiver like a sea-fish.
            I cover you with my net.
            What are you—banded one?

After the fierce midsummer all ablaze
        Has burned itself to ashes and expires
        In the intensity of its own fires,
Then come the mellow, mild, St. Martin days
Crowned with the calm of peace, but sad with haze.
        So after Love has led us, till he tires
        Of his own throes and torments, and desires,
Comes large-eyed Friendship: with a restful gaze
He beckons us to follow, and across
        Cool, verdant vales we wander free from care.
        Is it a touch of frost lies in the air?
Why are we haunted with a sense of loss?
        We do not wish the pain back, or the heat;
        And yet, and yet, these days are incomplete.

[8] Unless by something like "stock responses" to a vocabulary of vitality, sensation, and outdoor nature.

[9] P. 202.

[10] A single sentence of Richards' critique was technical and cognitive. "The heavy regular rhythm, the dead stamp of the rimes, the obviousness of the descriptions ('mellow, mild, St. Martin'; 'cool, verdant vales') their alliteration, the triteness of the close, all these accentuate the impression of conclusiveness" (p. 201).

[11] *Practical Criticism* (New York, 1935), 11.

[12] "The Function of Criticism," in *Selected Essays* (New York, 1932), 2.

[13] "Studies in Contemporary Criticism," in *The Egoist,* V (1918), 113.

[14] "The Perfect Critic," in *The Sacred Wood* (London, 1920), 10.

[15] *Ennead,* VI, vii, 14 (E. R. Dodds, *Select Passages Illustrating Neoplatonism,* London, 1923, p. 46).

[16] "Ben Jonson," in *Selected Essays,* 130.

[17] J. W. Bray's neglected book, *A History of Critical Terms* (Boston, 1898), is a good anthology of English critical terms in their contexts, with a suggestive Introduction.

18 "Studies in Contemporary Criticism," 113.

19 London *Times Literary Supplement,* April 20, 1951, p. 242.

HISTORY AND CRITICISM

1 Aristotle seems to have meant something like "natural history." Cp. Seymour Pitcher, "Aristotle: On Poetic Art, A Translation," in *Journal of General Education,* VII (1952), 61, 76. But if the scientific bent of modern "history" is remembered, the Aristotelian antithesis remains sufficiently relevant to the present context.

2 J. Dover Wilson (ed.), *King Henry V* (Cambridge, 1947), lvii.

3 "Spenser's Acrasia and the Circe of the Renaissance," in *Journal of the History of Ideas,* IV (1943), 381–99.

4 My own emphasis falls upon the second of these words.

5 I beg leave to say very little about a certain other kind of history, what may be called the history of the detached fact—whether Cortez or Balboa gazed at the Pacific, whether Charles of Sweden was killed by a cannon ball or a musket ball. The relatively casual relation of this kind of history to history as lexicography will scarcely be questioned.

6 April 28, 1945, p. 200, review of Gerald E. Bentley, *Shakespeare and Jonson, Their Reputations in the Seventeenth Century Compared* (Chicago, 1945).

7 P. B. Coremans, *Van Meegeren's Faked Vermeers and De Hooghs, A Scientific Examination* (Amsterdam, 1949), 26, 34, 35. It is not essential to my argument that the evaluation of Dr. Coremans be the correct one, and the negative view of certain other critics, notably M. M. Van Dantzig (*Johannes Vermeer, De "Emmausgangers" en de Critici,* Leyden, 1947), be mistaken. In either case, the emphasis on authenticity prevails. The impression which I myself receive from the reproductions is that the *Disciples at Emmaüs* is remarkably unlike Vermeer in certain ways and remarkably like certain erotic and mystical drawings of Van Meegeren, but that it may be nevertheless a fine picture.

8 Caroline Spurgeon, *Shakespeare's Imagery and What It Tells Us* (New York, 1935), 335.

POETRY AND CHRISTIANITY

1 Cp. H. M. McLuhan, "Edgar Poe's Tradition," in *Sewanee Review,* LII (1944), 24–33.

2 Of verbal ambiguity in general, a British Neo-Thomist, Father Thomas Gilby, in his *Phoenix and Turtle* (London, 1950), observes: "There is no statement however simple that cannot . . . be taken in many different senses. That is to be expected if a common theme runs through all the variations. . . . Ambiguity has to be taken in our stride if we are to arrive anywhere at all" (pp. 23–24).

[3] The emphasis of certain French Catholic writers of the last generation, that of Bremond on inspiration, trance, or ecstasy, that of Peguy on the sacred rightness of first inspiration, was not a help toward clarifying this issue—though this emphasis did have the merit of tending to defend poetry against the aggressions of science.

[4] Jean Daniélou, "The Problem of Symbolism," in *Thought*, XXV (1950), 426–427.

[5] "The Formalist Critics," in *Kenyon Review*, XIII (1951), 72.

[6] "A Burden for Critics," in *Lectures in Criticism* (*Bollingen Series* XVI, New York, 1949), 201.

[7] *Barbara Celarent* (London, 1949), 88–91. Walter J. Ong, "Art and Mystery: A Revaluation," in *Speculum*, XXII (1947), 324, quotes Aquinas, *In Sententias Petri Lombardi Commentaria,* proleg., q. 1, a. 5, ad 3: "The science of poetry is about things which because of their deficiency of truth cannot be laid hold of by the reason. Hence the reason has to be drawn off to the side by means of certain comparisons. But then, theology is about things which lie beyond reason. Thus the symbolic method is common to both sciences, since neither is accommodated to the human reason." Cp. *Summa Theologiae,* I, i, 9, ad 1: "Poetry makes use of metaphors to produce a representation, for it is natural to man to be pleased with representations. But sacred doctrine makes use of metaphors as both necessary and useful."

[8] "Catholic Journalism," in *Commonweal,* LIII (1951), 491.

INDEX